GCSE

Business Studies

Complete Revision and Practice

Contents

Section One — Business Basics

Section Two — Marketing

Section Three — Production

Section Four — People

Section Five — Finance

Contents

Section Six — Growth of Firms

Section Seven — External Influences

Section Eight — Business and Change

Assessment Tips

Practice Assessment

Published by CGP

Editors:
Helena Hayes
Andy Park
Dave Ryan

Contributors:
Colin Harber Stuart
David Kittson
David Morris
Adrian Murray
Keith Williamson
Michael Southorn
Katherine Stewart
Lynda Turner
Andrew Wright

With thanks to Emma Warhurst and Victoria Skelton for the proofreading.

ISBN: 978 1 84762 414 7

Website: www.cgpbooks.co.uk
Clipart source: CorelDRAW® and VECTOR
Printed by Elanders Ltd, Newcastle upon Tyne.

Based on the classic CGP style created by Richard Parsons.

Why Businesses Exist

Businesses exist to provide goods or services to customers. Most businesses are started when somebody decides that they can make goods or provide a service that they can sell to people who are willing to pay.

Most Businesses Have the **Same** Main **Objective**...

An objective is anything that someone wants to achieve. (For example, your objective in using this book is to get a better GCSE grade.) For a business, one objective is more important than any other...

1) The most important objective is to make a profit in order to survive.
   If a business does not make a profit it will go bankrupt and have to close down.

Businesses will usually have other objectives too. For example...

2) Some will try to be the biggest in their market.
3) Others will try to provide the highest quality product possible.
4) Some might aim to maximise sales or wealth creation.
5) Others might be more concerned with stability — maintaining their market share or a reasonable income.
6) Some will focus on expanding the business.
7) Other possible objectives include being independent, satisfying customers, or trying to limit the environmental damage caused.

Usually firms will only pursue these other objectives if it will help make a profit in the longer term — although firms with genuinely public-spirited owners might give up some profit for other objectives.

...But **Some** Businesses Have **Different Priorities**

1) For some businesses, profit is not their main objective.
2) This is either because they are a 'not-for-profit' organisation (e.g. a charity) or they are in the public sector (which means they're owned by the government).
3) Not-for-profit organisations and public-sector businesses need to earn enough income to cover their costs. Any surplus is then put back into the business.
4) Some profit-seeking businesses exist to achieve social objectives, such as providing help for the homeless, or farmers in poorer countries. They're called social enterprises or 'more than profit' organisations. This is because their main aim is to use the profit that they make for the benefit of society.

People Start Up Businesses for **Various Reasons**

Different people start up businesses for different reasons:

1) Financial reasons — e.g. to make a huge fortune, or just a steady income for themselves.
2) Personal reasons — e.g. the independence of being their own boss, difficulties finding a job elsewhere, or a desire to see their ideas for a product put into practice.
3) To help others — by starting a charity, for example.

There's more about this on page 85.

Most businesses need to make a profit to survive...

Well that's an easy enough page to start with. Make sure you know why businesses exist and why people start them up. You should also know what the main objectives of the different types of businesses are. Cover up the page, scribble down everything you can remember, and then check that you didn't forget anything.

Enterprise

Enterprise can mean either a business or organisation, or the personal qualities that mean you can see and take advantage of new business opportunities.

Entrepreneurs Take Advantage of **Business Opportunities**

1) Enterprise involves identifying new business opportunities, and then taking advantage of them. There's always a risk of failure, but the reward for a successful enterprise activity is profit.
2) Enterprise can involve starting up a new business, or helping an existing one to expand by coming up with new ideas.
3) A good business idea is for a product/service that no other business is already providing but which customers will be willing to pay for — i.e. there's a gap in the market.
4) A market niche (or niche market) is a similar idea. A market niche is a small part of the overall market, and is made up of customers with a particular need. Big companies often don't bother trying to make products for niche markets, so they're great opportunities for small companies.

An entrepreneur is someone who takes on the risks of enterprise activity.

Enterprise Means **Taking Risks**

Enterprises always involve balancing risks against possible rewards.

1) An entrepreneur needs to gather together all the resources needed to start or expand a business. The key resource is money, which is needed to buy equipment and pay workers.
2) Very often an entrepreneur will use their own money, but they'll probably need to raise more from banks or other investors as well.
3) An entrepreneur will hope that the business will make enough profit to pay back any money that's been borrowed. If not, the business will fail and the entrepreneur will lose all the money that's been invested in the company.
4) A good entrepreneur will take a calculated risk — they'll do research, plan the business carefully to make sure it has a good chance of success, and weigh up the consequences of failure. If the risk is worth taking, the entrepreneur will go ahead with the new business venture.

Entrepreneurs Need Particular **Qualities**

A successful entrepreneur is likely to have most of the following qualities:

- **the ability to think ahead** — to identify opportunities for the future
- **initiative** — to seek out or seize business opportunities
- **drive and determination** — to turn ideas into practice
- **decisiveness** — so they don't shy away from making tough decisions
- **networking skills** — to identify people who can provide money or other resources
- **leadership skills and powers of persuasion** — to motivate other people to support their ideas
- **a willingness to take calculated risks** — and to profit from their enterprise activities
- **an ability to plan carefully** — to minimise the risk of failure
- **an ability to learn from mistakes** — and to see mistakes as "part of learning to succeed"

A good entrepreneur will weigh up the risks against the rewards...

Bit of a funny page this one, all about concepts and personal qualities rather than facts. Cover up the page and see if you can remember all the qualities that an entrepreneur should ideally have. Scribble down what is meant by a calculated risk too — have another look at the page if you're unsure.

Business Ownership Structures

There are four types of business structure you need to learn.
Make sure you know what they are and all about the differences between them.

1 Sole Traders — the Easiest Businesses to Start

Most small businesses are sole traders. You don't need to do anything except start trading.
Examples include plumbers, hairdressers, newsagents and fishmongers.

ADVANTAGES

1) They're dead easy to set up. Get an idea and you're in business.
2) You get to be your own boss.
3) You alone decide what happens to any profit.

DISADVANTAGES

1) You have to work long hours. You don't get many holidays either.
2) You have unlimited liability. If the business goes bust owing £10 million, you may have to sell everything you own to pay your debts.
3) Sole traders are unincorporated. The business is not legally separate from its owner. So if someone dies from eating a dodgy dover sole, they sue the fishmonger personally — not the business.

2 Partnerships Are Like Two or More Sole Traders

Partnerships are not that common — but you get them a lot in jobs like accountancy, solicitors and doctors.

Partners have an equal say in making decisions and an equal share of the profits — unless they have an agreement called a deed of partnership that says different.

ADVANTAGES

1) More owners means more ideas, and more people to share the work.
2) More owners means more capital (money) can be put into the business.

DISADVANTAGES

1) Each partner is legally responsible for what all the other partners do.
2) Like sole traders, most partnerships are unincorporated and have unlimited liability. However, some partnerships can have limited liability — see next page for more about "limited liability".
3) More owners means more disagreements. You're not the only boss. If the partners disagree about which direction the business should go in and how much time to put in, it can get unpleasant.

Howdy partner — let's start a business...

Unlimited liability is really important. Examiners love testing you on it. Memorise the advantages and disadvantages of sole traders and partnerships, then cover up the page and write them all down.

Business Ownership Structures

These two types of business structure are more expensive to set up but carry less financial risk for the owners.

Limited Companies Have **Five Differences**

There are two types of limited company — private and public. But both kinds have these five important differences compared to sole traders and partnerships.

1) The business is incorporated — it has a separate legal identity from the owner.
2) It has limited liability so the owners only risk losing the money they invest in the business — no matter how big its debts are.
3) It must have a Memorandum of Association. This tells the world who the business is and where it is based.
4) It must also have an Article of Association. This sets out how the business will be run.
5) It is owned by shareholders. The more shares you own, the more control you get.

③ **Private** Limited Companies — Ownership Is **Restricted**

Private means that shares can only be sold if all the shareholders agree. The shareholders are often all members of the same family. Private limited companies have Ltd. after their name.

PRIVATE LIMITED COMPANIES — ADVANTAGES

1) The big advantage over sole traders and partnerships is limited liability — you can't lose more than you invest.
2) Being incorporated, the company can continue trading after a shareholder dies — unlike partnerships.

PRIVATE LIMITED COMPANIES — DISADVANTAGES

1) They're more expensive to set up than partnerships because of all the legal paperwork you have to do.
2) Unlike sole traders or partnerships, the company is legally obliged to publish its accounts every year.

④ **Public** Limited Companies — **Anyone** Can Buy Shares

'Public' means that shares in the company are traded on a stock exchange, and so can be bought and sold by anyone. Public Limited Companies have 'plc' after their name.

Firms generally become PLCs when they want to expand.

PUBLIC LIMITED COMPANIES — ADVANTAGES

1) Much more capital can be raised by a PLC than by any other kind of business.
2) That helps the company to expand and diversify.

PUBLIC LIMITED COMPANIES — DISADVANTAGES

1) Each shareholder has very little say in how the company is run — unless they own an awful lot of shares.
2) It's easy for someone to buy enough shares to take over the company — if they can convince shareholders to sell.
3) A PLC can have a large number of shareholders — and there needs to be a general agreement on company objectives. This makes it difficult for a PLC to sacrifice profit to other objectives, like helping the environment.

Limited liability takes a weight off your mind...

Learn what limited liability is and how buying and selling shares is different in Ltds and PLCs. This is a favourite topic for examiners — so make it one of yours too. Well, you don't have to like it — just learn it.

Franchises & Other Ownership Structures

Franchises are very popular these days, so they're a favourite topic with the examiners...

A **Franchise** Is the Right to Sell Another Firm's Products

1) Some companies give other firms the right to sell their products or use their trademarks. For example, most car manufacturers sell their cars through dealer franchises. These franchises trade under their own name but advertise that they sell a particular manufacturer's products.
2) Branded franchises take this one stage further. The franchisee buys the right to trade under the name of the other firm (the franchisor), and pays the franchisor either a flat fee or a percentage of the profits. As far as the public are concerned, it appears that they are buying from the franchisor, not a different firm.
3) Most of the big firms in the fast-food industry sell their products through branded-franchise outlets. The franchisee usually buys everything needed to run the business from the franchisor — including the ingredients needed to make the finished product.

Franchises Have Benefits and Problems

1) The franchisee gets quite a few benefits from running a franchise business, such as:
    - They are buying the rights to sell an established product. There is less risk of a franchise failing than a totally new business, so banks are more willing to lend money to people who want to buy a franchise.
    - Things like marketing and promotion are often done by the franchisor.
    - Training in how to run the franchise, plus help with things like staff management and accounting are often provided by the franchisor.
2) The main problems for the franchisee are that the business can only sell the products of the franchise — and they have to run the business according to the franchisor's rules, so the owner's freedom is limited.
3) The main benefit to the franchisor is that they are able to increase their market share without increasing the size of their own firm — this can make franchising a very profitable way to expand (see page 92).
4) A problem for the franchisor is that they may have little control over how the franchisee sells their products. If their franchisees don't have good standards, the franchisor's brand could get a bad reputation.

Co-operatives Are Owned by Their Workers

1) Co-operatives work a bit like limited-liability partnerships. Producer co-operatives are owned and controlled by their workforce. Retail co-operatives are owned and controlled by their customers (though usually a board of directors makes the day-to-day business decisions — see page 9).
2) The main benefit is that there should be no conflict between the main stakeholders — they are the same people (see p9 for more about stakeholders). A problem is that the only big, easily available sources of finance are the owners' capital and retained profits — this makes it harder for the co-operative to expand.

Public Corporations — Owned and Funded by Government

1) A good example is the BBC. Unlike a PLC it does not have a board of directors chosen by shareholders — it has a board of trustees who are appointed by its owner — the government.
2) The main source of funds is a government grant, paid for by the licence fee. However, the BBC is also encouraged to generate its own funds by selling goods and services for a profit.
3) Public corporations do not have to make a profit — instead they follow objectives set by the government. This can make it easier to satisfy all its stakeholders.

Co-operative firms are nice to their customers...

Make sure you know what a franchise is and its benefits and problems. Learn the stuff, then cover it up and scribble down a mini-essay. Then repeat for co-operatives and public corporations.

Warm-Up and Worked Exam Questions

Warm-up Questions

1) What is the most important objective for most businesses?
2) Give two benefits of being a sole trader.
3) What is a co-operative?
4) Name the two types of limited company.
5) What is a franchisee?

Worked Exam Question

It's really important to get the key business terms clear in your mind before going on to the rest of the section. Have a look at these worked exam questions, then have a go at the questions on the next page.

1 Read **Source A** and then answer the questions that follow.

Source A

Edwina started up her business several years ago. It is a successful business, although it has taken on a lot of debt. Initially, she ran the company as a sole trader. She later decided to change the legal status of the firm, and so she set up Anyfirm Ltd. She is currently deciding whether to change her company to a public limited company (plc).

a) Explain what is meant by the term "limited liability".

Limited liability means the owners of the business are not personally liable for the debts of the business. ✔ [1 mark] *The owners only risk losing the money they have invested in the business.* ✔ [1 mark]

There are 2 marks available for this question, so you should aim to give at least two pieces of information in your explanation.

(2 marks)

b) A sole trader is unincorporated. Explain what this means.

This means that the business does not have a legal identity of its own. ✔ [1 mark]
The owner is personally responsible for everything the business does. ✔ [1 mark]

(2 marks)

c) Discuss the advantages and disadvantages for Edwina of converting Anyfirm Ltd to a public limited company.

Public limited companies can raise capital more easily, ✔ [1 mark] *which may allow it to expand, diversify or reduce its debt.* ✔ [1 mark] *However, shares in PLCs are traded openly on the stock exchange.* ✔ [1 mark] *This means anyone can become a shareholder, and Edwina will probably lose some control over the company.* ✔ [1 mark]

(4 marks)

Exam Questions

1 Anna Conda runs a branded franchise selling industrial cleaning products to public-sector organisations.

a) What is meant by the term "public-sector organisation"?

....

....

(2 marks)

b) What is a branded franchise?

....

....

(2 marks)

c) Explain the advantages and disadvantages for Anna of operating her business as a branded franchise.

....

....

....

(4 marks)

2 David is a successful entrepreneur who runs a company selling toothbrushes.

a) Identify and explain **two** qualities that are needed by an entrepreneur.

1. ....

....

....

2. ....

....

....

(4 marks)

b) David believes that business success is all about planning and then taking calculated risks.

Explain what is meant by a calculated risk, and why planning is important when assessing whether a risk is worth taking.

....

....

(Continue your answer on a separate piece of paper) *(5 marks)*

Legal and Taxation Issues

Entrepreneurs have certain legal responsibilities when they start a new business.
They need to know all about these responsibilities, and so do you.

A New Business has to Choose its **Legal Structure...**

When you start a new business, you need to decide whether to have limited or unlimited liability (see p.3-4).

1) Smaller businesses (sole traders and partnerships) tend to have unlimited liability, while larger businesses have limited liability (they'll be "Ltds" or "PLCs").
2) The other thing to decide is the amount of control you want over how the business is run. Sole traders and private limited companies (Ltds) tend to give an entrepreneur more control than partnerships or PLCs.

...and its **Name**

Businesses need to have a name — for two basic reasons...

1) LEGAL — a limited liability business is incorporated (it has a separate legal identity), and the government needs to know the name of the business so it can contact it.
2) MARKETING — the name of the business can tell potential customers something about the business and what it does.

Actually, businesses can have several names:

- *the legal name of the business (e.g. The Arcadia Group Limited) — used for contracts and legal stuff.*
- *trading names (e.g. Topman or Miss Selfridge) — to help customers identify what the business does (useful when a business owns a large number of smaller companies).*

A Business Needs to **Keep Careful Records**

1) All businesses must keep records of the money coming into and going out of the business.
2) This is to show potential investors that the business is being properly run, and helps prevent fraud (e.g. an owner keeping all the money but then saying they can't pay suppliers).
3) Another reason is that the business needs to make sure they are paying the right amount of tax to the government. The main taxes businesses pay are:

Value Added Tax (VAT) — depends on the difference between the price the business charges for its products and the amount they cost to make. So businesses need accurate records of what's been paid to suppliers and received from customers.

Income Tax and National Insurance — these depend on how much employees are paid, so the business needs accurate records of how much it pays its workers.

Employers have to deduct income tax and National Insurance from their employees' pay and give it to the government.

Employers also make an extra National Insurance payment for each person they employ.

Corporation Tax — depends on how much profit the business makes. Businesses have to produce a profit and loss account each year (see p72).

The records of limited liability companies have to be audited (checked) each year to make sure that records of income and spending are accurate and meet legal requirements. The checks are done by an auditor.

Keeping careful records doesn't have to be too taxing...

It's really important that firms keep clear financial records — it makes it easy to see what money is coming in and out of the firm. Make sure you know the names of the four main taxes — scribble down a description of each.

Stakeholders

Everyone with an interest in seeing a company do well is called a stakeholder.
There are two types: internal stakeholders and external stakeholders.

Internal Stakeholders are *Inside* the Firm

1) The owners are the most important stakeholders. They make a profit if the business is successful and decide what happens to the business. In a limited company the owners are the shareholders.
2) Shareholders delegate responsibility for deciding the general direction — the strategy — of the business to the board of directors. The directors are interested in making sure the company is successful so the shareholders make a profit.
3) Employees are interested in their job security and promotion prospects — they also want to earn a decent wage and have pleasant working conditions. Both directors and employees may become unemployed if the company does badly.

External Stakeholders are *Outside* the Firm

1) Customers want high quality products at low prices.
2) Suppliers are who the firm buys raw materials from. The firm provides them with their income. They may face cash-flow problems if they do not get paid quickly enough. They will also lose work if the firm has to close.
3) The local community where the business is based will suffer if the firm causes noise and pollution. They may gain if the firm provides good jobs and sponsors local activities. Firms may also provide facilities which the local community can use.
4) The government will receive taxes when the firm makes a profit.

Most Important are the *Shareholders*

1) No business can ignore its customers. If it can't sell its products it will go bankrupt.
2) And if a business doesn't keep its workers happy it may become unproductive.
3) But a company may not mind being unpopular in the local community — if it sells most of its products somewhere else.
4) The one group no business can ignore for long is its shareholders. If they are unhappy they can sack the directors or sell the business to someone else.

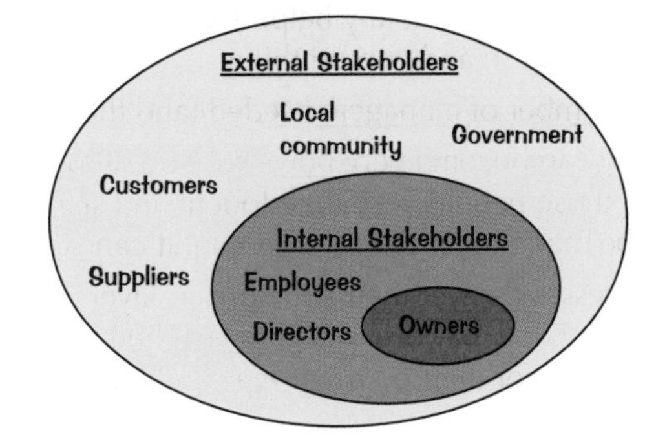

You can please some of the people some of the time...

The key point is that shareholders usually get their way — after all, it's their business. Learn the stakeholders diagram — cover the page, scribble it down and then explain why it has three sections.

Hierarchies and Centralisation

The amount of authority each person in an organisation has is determined by their place in the hierarchy...

Businesses are Organised into **Hierarchies**

1) A hierarchy is a series of levels within the business, where each level has responsibility and authority over the levels below.
2) Generally, the number of people at each level decreases as you move up the hierarchy.
3) At each level, a certain amount of responsibility is delegated to people in the level below.

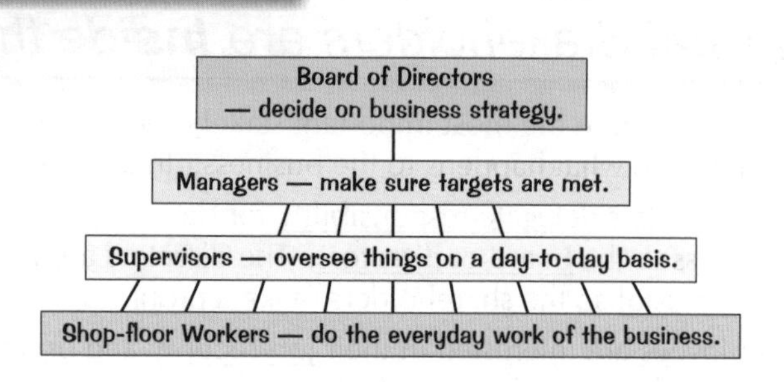
Board of Directors — decide on business strategy.
Managers — make sure targets are met.
Supervisors — oversee things on a day-to-day basis.
Shop-floor Workers — do the everyday work of the business.

Organisations can be **Centralised** or **Decentralised**

How much power and authority is delegated at each level in the hierarchy will depend on whether the bosses want a centralised or decentralised structure.

Centralised Organisations

1) All major decisions are made by one person or a few senior managers at the top of the hierarchy.
2) Advantages are that these senior managers tend to have plenty of experience, and can get an overview of the whole business. Policies will be uniform throughout the business.
3) On the downside, decisions can take a long time to filter through to employees. This means that the organisation reacts slowly to change. Also central managers may lack specialist knowledge.

Decentralised Organisations

1) The authority to make most decisions is shared out — for example, power might be delegated to regional managers or to more junior employees.
2) Advantages are that employees can use expert knowledge of their sector to make decisions, and these decisions can be made more quickly.
3) The disadvantages are that inconsistencies may develop between departments or regions. Also the decision makers might not be able to see the overall needs of the business.

See p95 for more about business structures.

The Structure of a Business Can **Change** Over Time

1) Businesses tend to become more hierarchical as they get larger (i.e. their hierarchy develops more layers).
2) A small business is often run by just the owner without any help. As the business grows and employs more staff, managers might be needed to help organise and control things.
3) The bigger the business, the greater the number of managers needed (and the greater the costs).
4) Senior managers at the top of a hierarchy can become very powerful. But depending too heavily on a few people at the top can cause problems if those people 'lose their touch' and start making poor decisions. And if all decisions ultimately need to be made by one or two people, it can slow down decision-making.
5) To overcome these problems some businesses delayer their structure — layers of management are removed (usually from the middle of the hierarchy). They may also decentralise their organisation and encourage groups of workers to take more responsibility for their own self-management.

You should now be able to speak with authority about hierarchies...

Make sure you understand the terms hierarchy, centralised and decentralised, and you know the pros and cons of being a centralised and decentralised organisation. Remember — firms often start out with a centralised structure, but are forced to decentralise as they get too big to make all the decisions at the top.

Organisational Structure

There are three main ways a business can structure its organisation. However you do it, you end up with a diagram that looks slightly like an upside-down tree. Hence the name "organisation tree".

① You Can Organise by Function...

1) You get this a lot in limited companies.
2) Each functional area does one part of the work of the business. Examples of functional areas are sales, marketing, customer service, operations, finance, human resources... and so on.
3) The main advantage is that specialists can concentrate on their particular job.
4) The main disadvantage is that the different departments may not work well together.

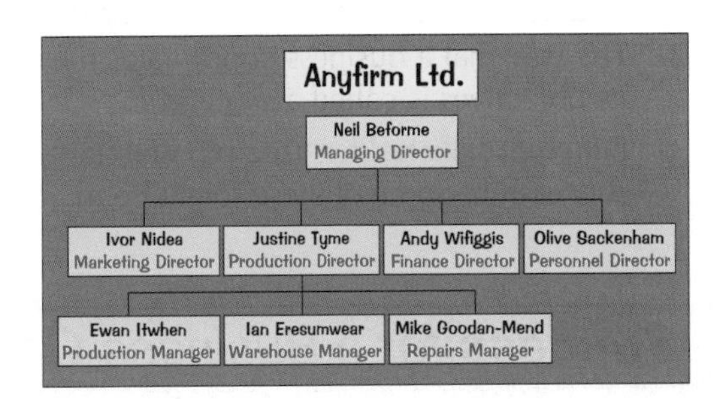

② ...You Can Organise by Product...

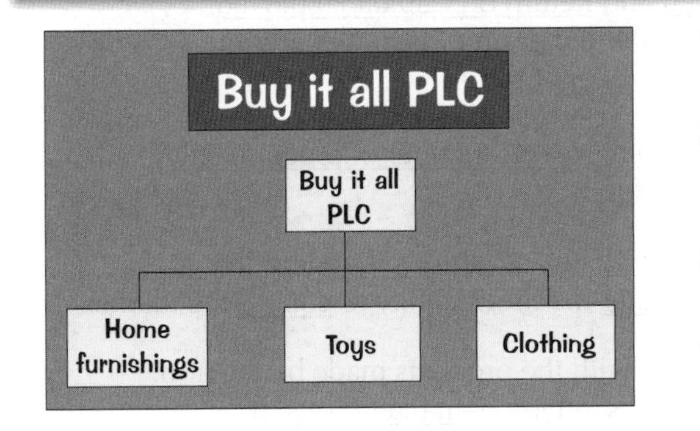

1) This is common with large manufacturers who make lots of different products.
2) A product-based structure splits the organisation into different sectors. For example, Buy-It-All PLC has three sectors — home furnishings, toys and clothing.
3) The main advantage is that managers can make decisions that are relevant to each product sector.
4) A disadvantage is that there can be a wasteful duplication of resources between sectors.

③ ...Or You Can Organise by Region

1) This is normal for a multinational business.
2) The divisions may be regional or national.
3) The main advantage is that spreading management between regions makes day-to-day control easier.
4) A disadvantage is that there can be a wasteful duplication of resources between regions.

Megabucks (Global) PLC

Megabucks (Global) PLC

Megabucks (North America) | Megabucks (Europe) | Megabucks (Asia)

Loadsamoney (UK) | Argent Grand (France) | Grosse Gelde (Deutschland)

No single structure is right for every business. Individual businesses need to decide what will suit them best.

Businesses choose a structure to suit their needs...

Basically you've got three diagrams to learn. Make sure you can draw each one from memory. Remember that individual businesses have to find a structure that works for them — it could be any of these three.

Objectives and Business Success

Business Studies examiners want you to tell them that there's more to being a successful business than just making a big profit. This page tells you about a few other ways to think about success.

A *Firm* and its *Stakeholders* may have Different *Objectives*

1) For a business to be successful it has to meet its objectives (see p1). The business will also set itself success criteria — these are the targets it will use to measure whether or not it has met its objectives.
2) The way that a business coordinates the activities of its various departments in order to try and achieve its objectives is called a strategy.
3) Different stakeholders (see p9) will have different opinions about what a business needs to do to be successful. Some of these might be in conflict with the objectives the firm sets itself.

Success for a Business Can Mean *Different Things*

Most businesses will define success using one or more of these ideas...

1) SURVIVAL is the main short-term objective of any business. Over two thirds of new businesses close within five years of starting. Unless a business survives, it can't achieve its other objectives.
2) PROFITABILITY is measured by indicators such as Profit Margin and Return on Capital Employed. These are explained in Section 5, but basically the bigger they are the more profitable the firm is. Profitable firms are an important source of wealth creation for the economy.
3) GROWTH can be measured in different ways — e.g. number of employees, number of products sold, or income from sales. Larger businesses tend to be more successful.
4) MARKET SHARE is measured by dividing the sales of the firm's products into the total sales of the market (and multiplying by 100%). The bigger the market share, the greater the firm's ability to control the market.
5) CUSTOMER SATISFACTION measures how happy consumers are with the products made by the firm. The firm can measure this by carrying out customer opinion surveys, a type of market research.
6) ETHICAL CONSIDERATIONS are about whether the company acts in a way that society believes is morally right (e.g. many consumers think that it's wrong to test cosmetics on animals).
7) ENVIRONMENTAL SUSTAINABILITY means minimising the impact of the firm's activities on the environment.

You need to know how the different stakeholders will have different ideas of success based on their interests. Here are four examples — learn them.

I am an activist in a pressure group. I think most firms are too big and powerful. They pollute the environment and treat animals badly. I know they create lots of jobs but I think we'd be better off with a lower income and a healthier planet.

I'm a shareholder. I want the firm to be as profitable as possible so I can earn a large dividend when the profit gets divided up. I don't care too much how the business achieves this, but I don't want the firm upsetting the other stakeholders too much — otherwise profitability might suffer.

I'm a consumer. I want the firm to make good quality products at a low price — but I worry that some firms are too powerful and charge too much. I am also concerned about the environment but I can't always afford to buy environmentally friendly products.

I'm in the government. I want the business to create wealth and jobs for the economy — that way the voters will think I'm doing a good job and vote for me again at the next election.

Everybody's got their own opinion...

The basic idea is that success can be measured — but different people will measure different things.
Make a list of all the different success criteria that each stakeholder on page 9 would use.
Then for each stakeholder find one or two criteria that might conflict with the interests of others.

Objectives and Business Success

Right, the last page of the section and you've come full circle back to the objectives of a business (page 1). This page looks at how a business measures how successful it's been.

Businesses Set Themselves **Success Criteria**

Success criteria are linked to objectives. It's important that success criteria are quite specific, so that a business can measure whether it's actually been successful.

Set Numerical Targets for a Period, and Afterwards Compare them to Actual Performance

E.g. a business could set itself a target of £25m sales, and profits of £5m, after one year. It could then aim to increase sales by 5% and profits by 10% for each of the next five years.

At the end of each year, the business can measure how well it has met these targets, and take action to improve its performance. And if it found the first target was easy to meet, it might decide to make the later targets harder — e.g. increase profits by 15% each year.

Conduct Impact Assessments

It's simple to set targets for things that can be described as a number (e.g. sales and profits). It's more difficult for "soft" objectives such as "behaving in an ethical way". There are a couple of alternatives...

a. A business could list some ethical activities it will do, and some unethical activities which it won't do — then it can check later whether it has kept its promises.

b. Or a business can conduct impact assessments — these are surveys (sometimes done by researchers with no connection to the business) to find out what stakeholders think of the business's behaviour. For example it could carry out an environmental impact assessment.

1) Most medium and large businesses publish an annual report describing their performance — in particular whether or not they met their financial objectives. The report would usually include details about the profit and loss account (see page 72), and balance sheet.
2) But these days lots of businesses also report on their ethical or environmental performance.

A Company's Objectives can **Change over Time**

1) New and small businesses are most likely to be concerned with survival.
2) But as a business grows, it might focus more on the needs of its wider stakeholders.
3) PLCs have to protect the interests of their shareholders — meaning they're likely to place profit as their most important objective. But PLCs often consider other stakeholders' interests too.
4) A business needs to react to the changing needs of its stakeholders. The power of different stakeholder groups may change over time. For example, employees were a very powerful stakeholder group in many large UK businesses in the 1970s. Today, consumers are much more powerful and businesses have had to react to the growing importance of ethical and environmental concerns.

Objectively, I think this section has been a success...

Well, there we are. You made it to the end of the first section — and here's a nice straightforward page to learn as a reward. You know the drill by now — cover the page, scribble down all the details and repeat until you've remembered it all. The next three pages will test what you've learnt about the basics of business...

Warm-Up and Worked Exam Questions

Warm-up Questions

1) List two internal and two external stakeholders.
2) Which of the following businesses is unlikely to have a hierarchy — a PLC, the army, a sole trader, a multinational company?
3) Who makes the decisions in a decentralised structure?
4) Describe three ways in which a business can structure its organisation.
5) Give one reason why a firm's objectives might change over time.

Worked Exam Question

Here's a typical exam question. Try covering up the answers and working through the question on your own. Then you can compare your answers with the answers in blue.

1 Affirm plc, a company that manufactures furniture, has the objective of increasing market share. In order to achieve this, it has decided to reorganise its UK business.

a) What is meant by the term "market share"?

Market share is the firm's total annual sales divided by the total annual sales for the whole market, [1 mark] expressed as a percentage. [1 mark]

(2 marks)

b) Suggest how Affirm can use success criteria to help measure whether the reorganisation has achieved its aim.

Success criteria are targets that the company can aim to achieve [1 mark] (e.g., the firm could set itself a target of increasing its market share by 10%). If its increase in market share is greater than this target, then the reorganisation will have achieved its aim. [1 mark]

(2 marks)

c) An employee suggests that Affirm should set itself an objective of improving its environmental sustainability rather than increasing market share.

Explain why the aims of different stakeholders in a firm often conflict.

Firms have many different types of stakeholders, such as shareholders, customers and employees. [1 mark] Different stakeholders will have different interests and priorities, [1 mark] and so will also often have different aims for the firm. [1 mark] For example, shareholders may think profits are most important, whereas a customer may prefer a firm to invest in its product range or customer service. [1 mark]

[There is also 1 mark available for an answer that is well structured and well written.]

(5 marks)

Exam Questions

1 Read **Source B** and then answer the questions that follow.

> **Source B**
>
> Eye-Make-It-Up Ltd. is a company which makes eyeshadows.
> It is organised as a hierarchy, with a centralised decision-making culture.
> Most directors wish to increase profits by reducing costs by 10%.
> One of the directors suggests that reducing costs is unnecessary, and that the firm can achieve its aim to increase profits by increasing prices instead.

a) What is meant by the term "hierarchy"?

....

....

(2 marks)

b) What is a "centralised organisation"?

....

....

(2 marks)

c) Explain two ways in which a cost-cutting strategy might affect the firm's employees.

....

....

....

....

(4 marks)

d) Recommend whether the board of directors should follow this cost-cutting strategy. Give reasons for your recommendation.

....

....

....

....

....

....

....

(6 marks)

Revision Summary for Section One

Okay, so that's the first section over with — now it's time to find out how much you remember.
Have a bash at these questions. If you can do them all, pat yourself on the back and feel smug.
If you can't, then go back and look at the section again and keep plugging away until you can answer them all.
Yes, I know it's a pain but life's like that — and after all, it's the only way you're going to get ready for the exam.

1) Do charities aim to make a profit?
2) Describe some of the objectives other than profit that businesses might pursue.
3) What is a social enterprise?
4) List five qualities that an entrepreneur is likely to have.
5) Which two of these are problems if you're a sole trader?
   a) long hours; b) unlimited liability; c) smelly fish.
6) What does a sole trader gain and lose if it becomes a partnership?
7) What information might be contained in a deed of partnership?
8) If you own part of a business and the business goes bankrupt, would you rather have limited or unlimited liability? Why?
9) What does a partnership gain if it becomes a private limited company?
10) What big advantages does a PLC have over a private limited company?
11) Describe two benefits of franchising for the franchisee.
12) Give two reasons why a business needs to choose a name.
13) Why might a business have several different trading names?
14) What are the main taxes collected from businesses?
15) What role do the directors carry out in an organisation?
16) Name six stakeholders and say which are internal.
17) Who are the most important stakeholders and why?
18) Define the term hierarchy.
19) Describe the differences between a centralised and a decentralised organisation.
20) Explain what is meant by delayering.
21) What are the three main ways that businesses can be structured?
22) Say which type of organisational structure would be most suitable for these companies:
   a) a transnational oil company with offices all over the world;
   b) a limited company that manufactures washing machine parts.
23) List seven types of success that a company might hope to achieve.
24) Explain why the shareholders of a business and consumers might have different opinions about how successful the business is.
25) Describe two ways a business could determine whether it's met its objectives for 'being ethical'.

Marketing — What It Is

Human beings have needs — essential things like water, food and shelter. Once our needs are satisfied, we start to want luxuries, and we're prepared to pay for them. Marketing is about coming up with a product that people need or want — then making it as easy as possible for them to buy it.

There are Four Ps in Marketing

The four Ps are the key to understanding what marketing is all about.
If a firm gets them right it will be easy to sell its product. If it gets even one of them wrong, it's in trouble.

Together the four Ps are called the marketing mix.

1. PRODUCT — the firm must come up with a product that people will want to buy. It must fulfil some of the customer's needs or wants.
2. PRICE — the price must be one that the customer thinks is good value for money. This is not the same as being cheap.
3. PROMOTION — the product must be promoted so that potential customers are aware that it exists.
4. PLACE — the product must be available for sale in a place that the customer will find convenient.

Depending on the situation, some of the Ps might be more important than others. For example, if customers really want the product, they may be prepared to pay a higher price.

Customers' needs and wants usually change over time — a business should adapt its marketing mix to meet these changing needs.

A Market can be a Place, a Product or a Group of People

The word market can mean three slightly different things:

1) A meeting place between customers and suppliers — i.e. a place where goods are traded. A village market square seems pretty different from an internet shopping website — but they're both examples of markets.
2) The type of product being bought or sold, e.g. the oil market.
3) The potential customers for a product — e.g. the age 18–25 market.

MASS MARKETS contain very large numbers of customers buying ordinary products, e.g. bread.

In a NICHE MARKET, smaller groups of customers buy more specialist products.

Markets are Segmented into Different Groups of People

It's obvious when you think about it — we're all different. Some people even like to wear flares.
There are five main ways of dividing people into different market segments.

- AGE → for example the teenage market, or "grey power" (the over-55s).
- GENDER → for example, chocolate manufacturers target some items at women (e.g. Flake) and some at men (e.g. Yorkie®).
- SOCIAL CLASS → class A (professionals) down to class E (the unemployed).
- LOCATION → try selling stottie cakes outside the Northeast, or jellied eels outside London.
- CULTURE OR RELIGION → different groups have their own unique products.

The marketing mix — a recipe for business success...

Customers are absolutely crucial to marketing. A good marketing mix makes customers want to spend money on your product. But customers' needs change — so the marketing mix also needs to change to keep up.

Analysing the Market

Businesses can't succeed without understanding their place in the market. They need to know who their customers are, what they need, and whether these needs are being met by the competition.

Businesses **Map the Market** to Find Information

Mapping the market helps a business understand its location within the market, and the market's key features. The kind of information usually shown in a market map includes...

1) How many customers are in the market — and how much they spend.
2) Which segments the customers belong to.
3) Which products are popular and unpopular.
4) Competitors selling similar products — and where they sell them.

Market maps are often in the form of a diagram, but there are different kinds. Here's one example...

SWOT Analysis Can Help a Business Come Up With Ideas

SWOT stands for Strengths, Weaknesses, Opportunities and Threats. A business uses SWOT to analyse itself and other factors in the market. It can then use the results to help decide on its marketing strategy.

1) What are the strengths of your business? These strengths will help the business move forward.
2) What are the weaknesses of your business? These may harm the business.
3) What are the opportunities in the market? These are outside your business, but may be helpful — e.g. new technologies could reduce your costs, or demand for a certain type of product might be increasing.
4) What are the threats in the market? These are factors outside your business that may be harmful. For example there may be new competitors entering the market, or new products from existing competitors.

Once you understand yourself and the rest of the market, it's much easier to come up with sensible strategies.

Here's a possible SWOT analysis for a firm in the corned beef market:

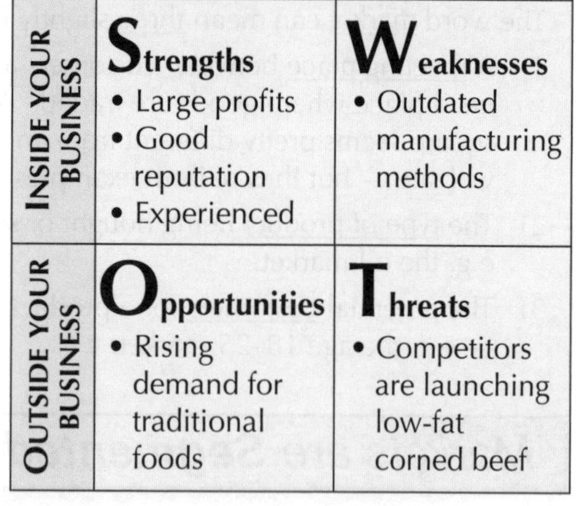

	HELPFUL	HARMFUL
INSIDE YOUR BUSINESS	**Strengths** • Large profits • Good reputation • Experienced	**Weaknesses** • Outdated manufacturing methods
OUTSIDE YOUR BUSINESS	**Opportunities** • Rising demand for traditional foods	**Threats** • Competitors are launching low-fat corned beef

Market Analysis Can be Used to Find a **Gap in the Market**

1) Sometimes a group of customers will have a need that isn't being met. This is a gap in the market.
2) A business needs to move quickly to fill the gap — before its competitors do. It needs to develop a way to meet the customers' needs.
3) This might mean developing a new product. Or it might mean selling an existing product in a new place or at a new price, or maybe just promoting it in a new way to convince customers it's just what they need.
4) A gap in the market can be a great opportunity for a business. If it gets the marketing mix right, a gap can expand to become a large market.

A bit of swotting up can help a firm think of new ideas...

SWOT analysis is good for helping firms look at the whole market, rather than just themselves — this can help them become more competitive. Cover the page and scribble down a mini essay all about SWOT analysis.

Market Research

Marketing is all about giving customers what they want. Market research involves finding out what that is. There are two types of market research — field research and desk research.

Field Research is Doing Your Own Donkey Work

1) Field research is also called primary research or original research. It involves things like questionnaires and telephone surveys.
2) It's useful for finding out new information, and getting customers' views on your products.
3) A business can't ask every potential customer for their views — they usually survey a relatively small sample of people.
4) Advantages of field research are that it provides data that's up to date, relevant and specific to your products.
5) Disadvantages are that it's expensive to collect, it's time consuming, and it needs a large sample size to be accurate. Businesses with a limited budget might compromise by using small sample groups, or carrying out field research over the telephone or internet.

Desk Research is Looking at Other People's Work

1) Desk research is also called secondary research or published research.
2) Desk research gives businesses access to a wide range of data — not just the views of their sample groups. It's useful for looking at the whole market, and analysing past trends to predict the future.
3) It involves looking at things like market research reports (such as Mintel), government publications (such as the Family Expenditure Survey or Social Trends), and articles in newspapers, magazines and on the internet.
4) Advantages are that it's cheaper than field research, and the data is easily found and instantly available. This makes it ideal for a business with a limited budget.
5) Disadvantages are that it's not always relevant to your needs, it's not specifically about your products, and it's often out of date.

Data Can be Quantitative or Qualitative

1) Suppose you want to do some market research about chocolate pizza. You can find out two kinds of information.
2) QUANTITATIVE information is anything you can measure or reduce to a number. Asking "How many chocolate pizzas will you buy each week?" will give a quantitative answer.
3) QUALITATIVE information is all about people's feelings and opinions. Asking "What do you think of chocolate pizzas?" will give a qualitative answer.
4) Qualitative data is tricky to analyse because it's hard to compare two people's opinions. Good market research will use both types of information.

Looking at other people's work — not a good idea in the exam...

Market research is important to any business, but it's crucial for new businesses — if you don't understand the market before you start out, things will go wrong pretty quickly. Businesses need to decide what they want to find out about the market — then choose the best method for collecting the data.

Market Research

Businesses can use sales data to analyse how products sell. If a product's sales are poor, the problem might be with the product itself, its price, the way it's being promoted, or the place it's being sold. Whatever the problem, it needs to be dealt with before the business makes too much of a loss.

Sales can be Split into **Two Categories**

1) Product trial — this is when customers buy a product for the first time to try it out. Businesses want customers to follow up their trial with the second type of sale...
2) Repeat purchase — customers come back after their first purchase to buy the product again and again. If a product isn't attracting repeat purchases, the marketing mix probably needs to be changed.

EXAMPLE

'Crazy Juice Ltd' wanted customers' views of damson juice. They sent a questionnaire to 2000 of their existing customers. You need to be able to interpret what the data means.

For this example you might say...

'The results show that more than a quarter of the sample group have made a trial purchase of damson juice. This shows that the company's advertising for the product is successfully attracting customers. However, very few of these customers go on to make repeat purchases. This suggests that there is a problem with the product itself. Crazy Juice Ltd need to consider changing the product, or dropping it altogether.'

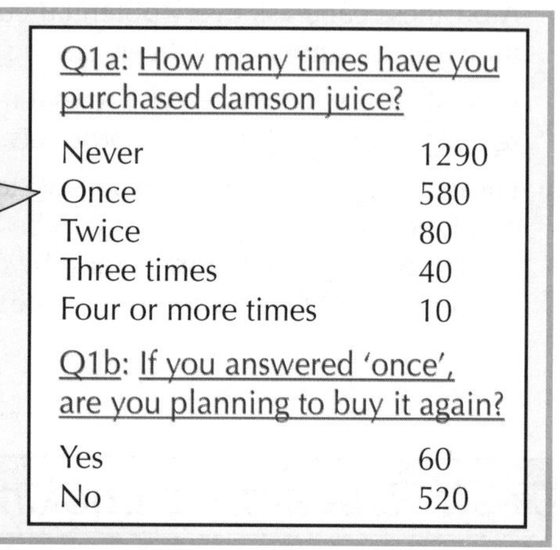

Q1a: How many times have you purchased damson juice?

Never	1290
Once	580
Twice	80
Three times	40
Four or more times	10

Q1b: If you answered 'once', are you planning to buy it again?

Yes	60
No	520

Businesses Need to Build Up **Customer Loyalty**

A loyal customer is one who makes lots of repeat purchases. Businesses want you to be a loyal customer — and they have plenty of ways to keep you coming back to their products. For example:

1) PRICE MATCHING If Brand X costs the same as Brand Y, people won't switch brands just to save money.
2) LOYALTY CARDS Earn points on your card every time you shop at HipStore. The points will save you money — but only if you keep going back to HipStore, of course.
3) PRODUCT DEVELOPMENT If you keep customers informed of updates to a product, they might want to upgrade to the improved version. This happens a lot with computer software.

Customer Preferences Can **Change** Over Time

Changes in customers' views and habits can have a big effect on their purchases. It's important for businesses to compare new and old data to spot new trends and patterns.

EXAMPLE

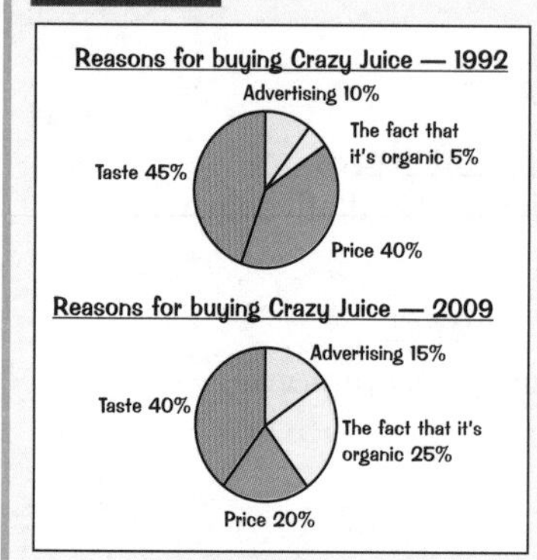

These pie charts show the results of Crazy Juice Ltd's recent research into why people buy their juice, as well as the results from similar research carried out in 1992. An analysis of the charts would include points like...

'Taste is still the most important factor,'
'The biggest increase is the fact that it's organic,'
or 'Price is less important now than in 1992.'

This analysis could lead to a new marketing mix based on the quality and environmental friendliness of the product.

Sales analysis — go on, try it. You might like it...

The point of all this is that market research can be used to understand customer habits. This is vital stuff for any business, so make sure you can explain why customer loyalty and repeat purchases matter.

The Product — Four Golden Rules

This is the first of the four Ps in the marketing mix. Getting the product right is the basis of all good marketing. Learn the four golden rules and the key terms on these next three pages and you won't go wrong.

① Be **Market-Driven** — not Product-Driven

1) Market-driven firms will use market research to find out what people want, then make it. This usually means the product is useful — like an MP3 player with a built-in radio.
2) Product-driven firms will design or invent a new product and then try to sell it. This often means they make something nobody really wants — like an MP3 player with a built-in toaster.
3) With very few exceptions, market-driven firms do best.

② Develop a **Brand Image** for the Product

Having a good brand image is the secret to marketing success.

1) Products with a strong brand image are easily recognised and liked by customers.
2) A strong brand image is usually built up over a number of years. Businesses can spend a lot of money on building a positive brand image — think Coca-Cola®, BMW and Apple® Computers.
3) The brand has to be constantly managed using the marketing mix. Products, prices, methods of promotion, and places where they're sold all have to be right to build a positive brand image.
4) Brand image can help to increase sales — both product trials and repeat purchases. If a brand is liked and easily recognised, it will often be chosen over competing products.
5) Probably the most important element of brand image is a reputation for high quality products. Customers won't be loyal if products fall to pieces after a week (unless they're really, really cool).

③ Make your Product **Different** from the Competition

Product differentiation is about making your products distinctive in the market. These differences should make customers want to buy your product instead of competing products.

1) Without product differentiation, customers will think your product is identical to others. They'll have no reason to buy it unless it's cheaper — which means less profit for you.
2) Product differentiation can be achieved in many ways — e.g. your product might be particularly reliable, or have a sexy brand image.
3) Design is also hugely important for product differentiation. The design mix has three main ingredients:

Function — the design must be fit for its purpose. A car without an engine would be a non-starter. Unique features can also help — a razor with seven blades shaves better than a razor with one. Probably.

Cost — a good design will lead to low manufacturing costs. This means higher profits.

Appearance — a good product should look attractive and distinctive. Packaging can also help a product to stand out (and protect it till it reaches the customer).

The Product — Four Golden Rules

④ Know your Product's **Life Cycle**

All products go through the same life cycle — but the sales life of some products is longer than others'. For example, the sales life of most cars is about ten years, but the sales life of many computer games is only a few months. Whatever the product, its marketing mix will need to change during its life cycle.

Below are the five stages in a product's life cycle — the graph on the next page shows how the cash flow of a business changes during this time.

1 Development

This is the first stage. Research and Development (R&D) and market research are used to develop an idea and turn it into a marketable product.

- Scientific research is vital for product development. A lot of scientific research is done in universities. It's often "pure" science — without any kind of commercial aim.
- Large businesses often then have teams of "applied" scientists — who try to use recent scientific discoveries to develop new or improved products to sell.
- One aim during product development is to find the most cost-effective materials and methods to use.

2 Launch

The product is put on sale for the first time. This is usually backed up with lots of advertising and sales promotions. Place is also an important P here — there's no point launching a product in places where nobody will be interested in buying it.

3 Growth

During this phase, sales and profitability increase, until the product becomes established.

4 Maturity

Sales are at their peak. Promotion becomes less important at this stage — businesses will continue to advertise the product, but generally less than at the launch. As a product's popularity grows, businesses will try to make the product more widely available.

Towards the end of the maturity phase, the market becomes saturated. There is no more room to expand — sales are at their peak. Firms might try to extend the life of a product by using an extension strategy, like making changes to the design or offering discounts on the price.

5 Decline

Eventually sales start to fall as rival products take over, and the product becomes obsolete.

The Product — Four Golden Rules

*A Firm's **Cash Flow** is Affected by the Life Cycle of its Products*

The cash flow of a business will change during the life cycle of one of its products.

DEVELOPMENT AND LAUNCH

The firm spends money on research and promotion, but sales of the product are usually low. The business will expect to make a loss during these stages.

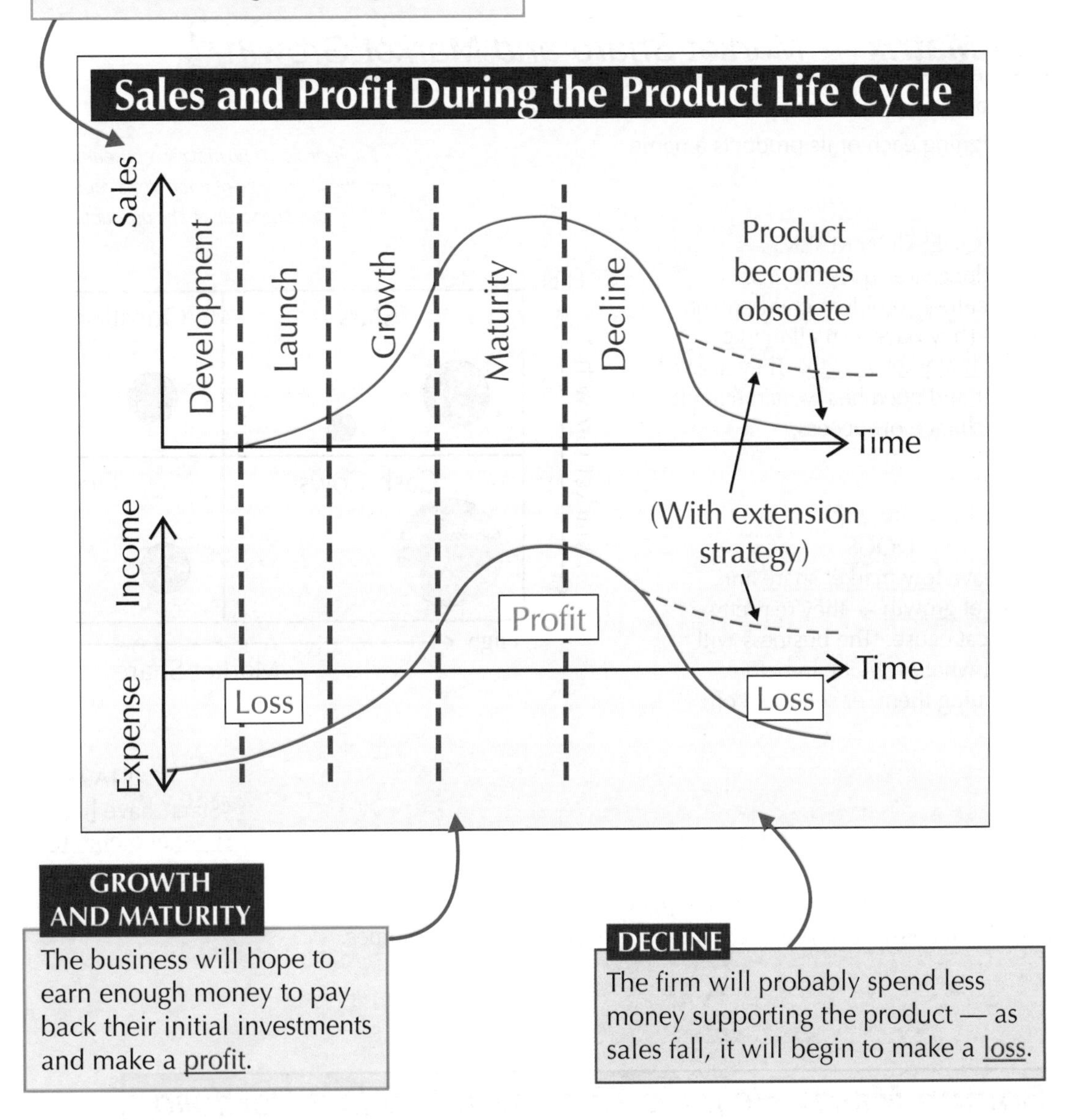
Sales and Profit During the Product Life Cycle
Sales
Development
Launch
Growth
Maturity
Decline
Product becomes obsolete
Time
(With extension strategy)
Income
Expense
Profit
Loss
Loss
Time
GROWTH AND MATURITY
The business will hope to earn enough money to pay back their initial investments and make a profit.
DECLINE
The firm will probably spend less money supporting the product — as sales fall, it will begin to make a loss.

The business might decide to use an extension strategy — if it works, the product will make profit for longer. But it means spending more money on the product — this takes away cash from other parts of the business. There has to be a balance between supporting old products and investing in new ones.

All products go through the same life cycle...

So... make a product that people want. Give it a positive image. Make it stand out from the crowd. Nurture it throughout its life cycle by mixing up its marketing. Then watch as it grows old, becomes unpopular and starts losing you money... that's the product life cycle for you. Make sure know everything from the last three pages.

Product Portfolios

A firm's product portfolio is basically a list of all the products that it sells. Companies need to make marketing decisions not just for single products, but for their whole product portfolio.

A **Product Portfolio** is a **Range** of Products

1) Businesses aim to have a balanced product portfolio. What this means is that they ideally want to be selling a variety of different products, all at different stages of the product life cycle.
2) This means that if one product fails, they should still be able to depend on the others.

Boston Matrix — Market Share and Market Growth

The Boston Matrix is a way for a firm to analyse its product portfolio.
It involves assigning each of its products a name.

Each circle in the matrix represents one product. The size of each circle represents the turnover of the product.

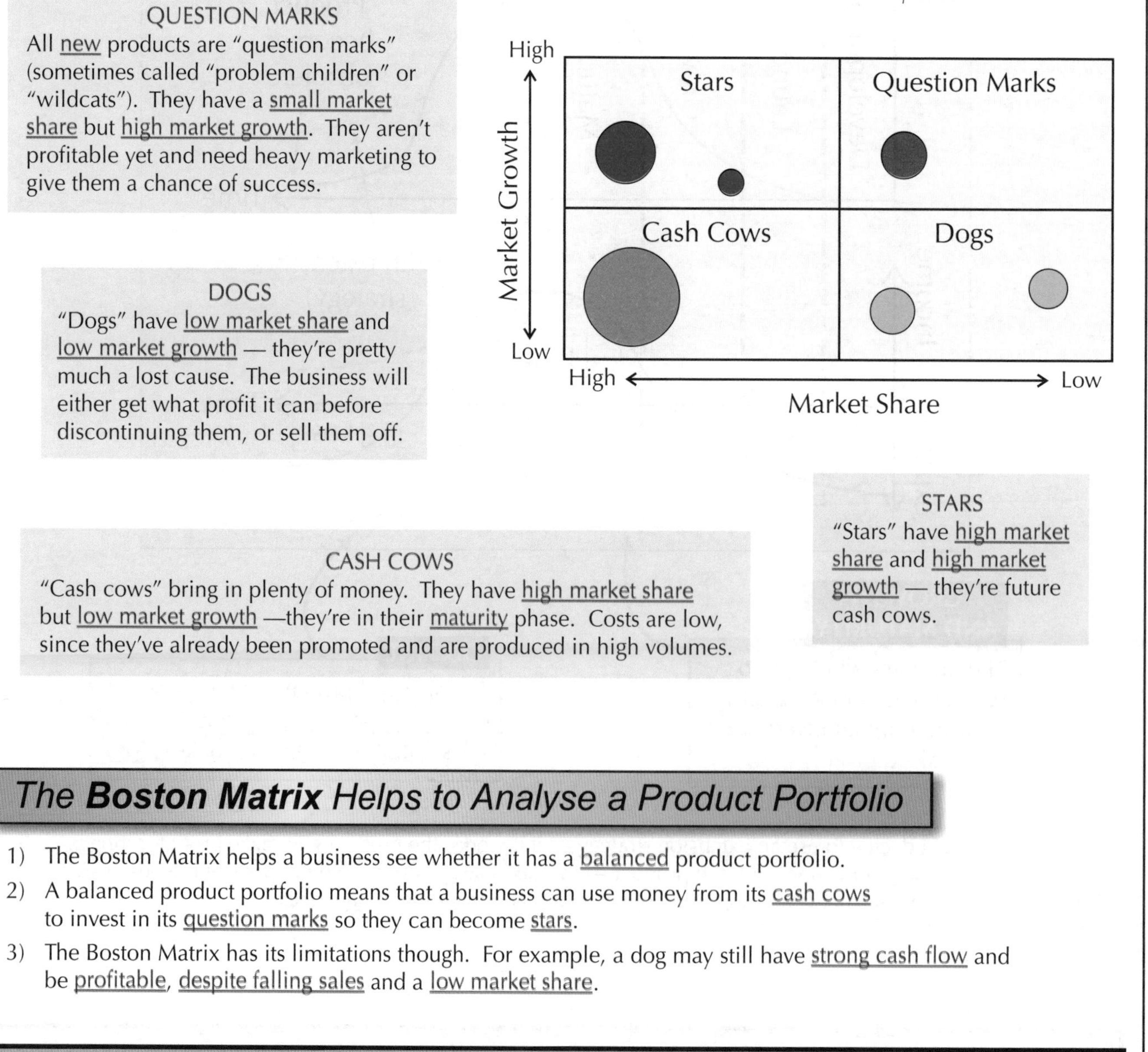

QUESTION MARKS
All new products are "question marks" (sometimes called "problem children" or "wildcats"). They have a small market share but high market growth. They aren't profitable yet and need heavy marketing to give them a chance of success.

DOGS
"Dogs" have low market share and low market growth — they're pretty much a lost cause. The business will either get what profit it can before discontinuing them, or sell them off.

STARS
"Stars" have high market share and high market growth — they're future cash cows.

CASH COWS
"Cash cows" bring in plenty of money. They have high market share but low market growth —they're in their maturity phase. Costs are low, since they've already been promoted and are produced in high volumes.

The **Boston Matrix** Helps to Analyse a Product Portfolio

1) The Boston Matrix helps a business see whether it has a balanced product portfolio.
2) A balanced product portfolio means that a business can use money from its cash cows to invest in its question marks so they can become stars.
3) The Boston Matrix has its limitations though. For example, a dog may still have strong cash flow and be profitable, despite falling sales and a low market share.

You should be able to write about this 'til the (cash) cows come home...

This page is nice and straightforward. Learn what the Boston Matrix is and what it's useful for. Cover the page, write down the four categories, then scribble down a description of each one. Check you got them right.

Warm-Up and Worked Exam Questions

Warm-up Questions

1) What four elements make up the marketing mix?
2) What is a niche market?
3) What does 'SWOT' stand for in 'SWOT analysis'?
4) Name the two fundamental types of market research.
5) What is qualitative information?
6) State the five stages in the life cycle of a product.

Worked Exam Questions

Marketing is an important part of any business. It's also an important part of lots of Business Studies exams. Have a look at these worked exam questions, and think whether you would have given the same answers.

1 *Vroom* is a car manufacturer with many models in its product portfolio.
The company wishes to prolong the sales life of one of its models, the TouraCar.

a) What is meant by the term product portfolio?

It is the range of products or services that a business sells. ✔[1 mark]

(1 mark)

b) Identify two categories in the Boston Matrix.

1. *Cash cows* ✔[1 mark]

2. *Dogs* ✔[1 mark]

The other two elements are stars and question marks

(2 marks)

c) Explain how a business can benefit from managing its product portfolio.

Ideally, a business should have products at various stages of their life cycle in its portfolio. ✔[1 mark] *High profits from 'mature' products* ✔[1 mark] *can help develop or promote more recently launched ones.* ✔[1 mark]

(3 marks)

d) What is the name of the type of strategy designed to extend the sales life of a product?

An extension strategy. ✔[1 mark]

(1 mark)

e) Explain one strategy that Vroom could use to extend the sales life of the TouraCar.
Give reasons for your answer.

They could provide additional extras at no additional price, ✔[1 mark] *e.g. alloy wheels,* ✔[1 mark] *to give improved value for money* ✔[1 mark] *and to improve product differentiation.* ✔[1 mark]

(4 marks)

Exam Questions

1 Bob is thinking of starting a business. He is considering opening a 'sports bar' aimed at young people aged 18-30 years. Before he starts the business, he has been told he should do some field research.

a) Explain what is meant by **field research**.

....

....

(2 marks)

b) State two **disadvantages** of field research.

....

....

(2 marks)

c) Explain why Bob might undertake market research.

....

....

....

....

(4 marks)

d) Bob decides to carry out a questionnaire. He stands outside his local supermarket and asks people between the ages of 18 and 30 if they would go to his sports bar at least once a week. Below is a table of his results.

Question: Would you go to the sports bar at least once a week?		
Answer	**Number of respondents**	**% of total respondents**
Yes, definitely	40	22%
Yes, probably	18	10%
Maybe	16	9%
No	106	59%
Total respondents	180	100%

Would you recommend that Bob opens the sports bar? Explain your answer.

....

....

....

....

(Continue your answer on a separate piece of paper) *(8 marks)*

Price — Demand and Supply

Customers like to buy things at bargain prices. Businesses like to sell things at high prices and make profits. The laws of supply and demand force them to settle their differences.

Demand *Rises* as Price *Falls*

1) Demand means the quantity of a product that consumers are willing and able to buy. The law of demand is that as the price increases the quantity demanded will fall — and vice versa.
2) There are two reasons. At a lower price more people can afford the product. And it becomes cheaper compared to its substitutes — that is, similar goods that people might buy instead.

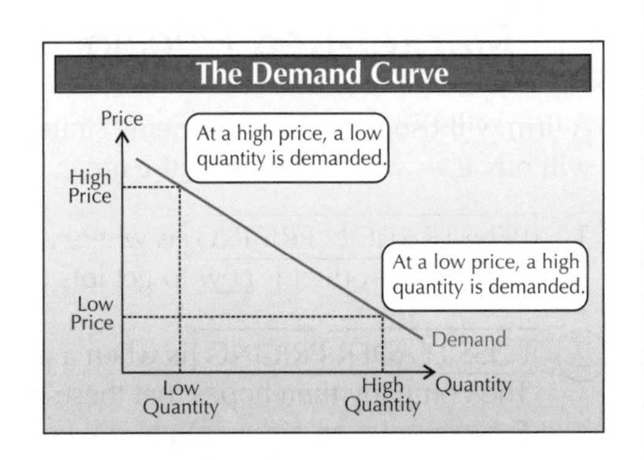

Supply *Rises* as Price *Rises*

The Supply Curve

Price
Supply
High Price
At a high price, a high quantity is supplied.
Low Price
At a low price, a low quantity is supplied.
Low Quantity
High Quantity
Quantity

1) Supply is the quantity of a product producers are willing and able to make for sale. The law of supply is that as the price increases, the quantity supplied increases — and vice versa.
2) When the price is low, very few producers will be able to make a profit — so the supply is small. At high prices even inefficient producers can make a profit — so the supply is large.

Equilibrium — where Producers and Consumers *Agree*

1) Producers want to sell at a high price and make a large profit. Consumers want to buy at a low price. The marketplace forces a clever compromise.
2) If the price is too low there'll be a shortage of supply. Some consumers will be willing to pay more, so producers increase prices.
3) If the price is too high, there'll be a surplus of supply. Producers will have to reduce prices to persuade people to buy unsold goods.
4) Eventually producers and consumers agree on the price and quantity to be exchanged. The point where they agree is called equilibrium.

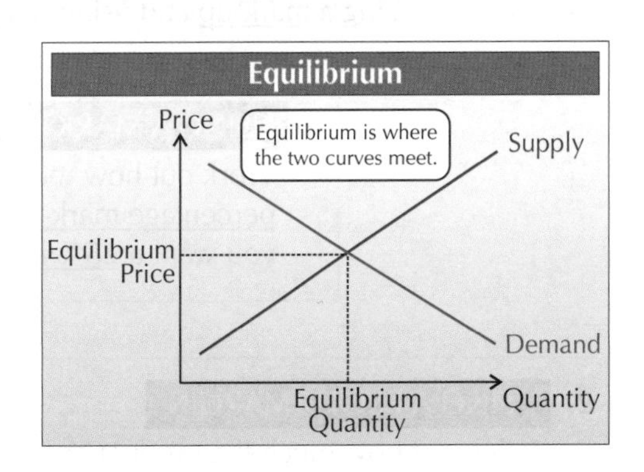

Commodity Markets are *Strongly Affected* by These Laws

1) A commodity is a product that's more or less the same whoever is selling it — e.g. petrol, steel, rice...
2) In a commodity market, it's hard for businesses to achieve product differentiation (see p21) — things like brand image and heavy promotion are less likely to influence customers. This means that the laws of supply and demand are powerful in a commodity market.
3) In a normal market (one where competing products are different from one another), a large business can use its brand image to charge higher prices than the competition. Supply and demand are still important, but smart businesses can work around them.

Supply, demand and price are all linked...

At low prices, demand is high but supply is low. At high prices, demand is low but supply is high. Equilibrium balances things out. Simple. Commodity markets provide the best examples of these laws.

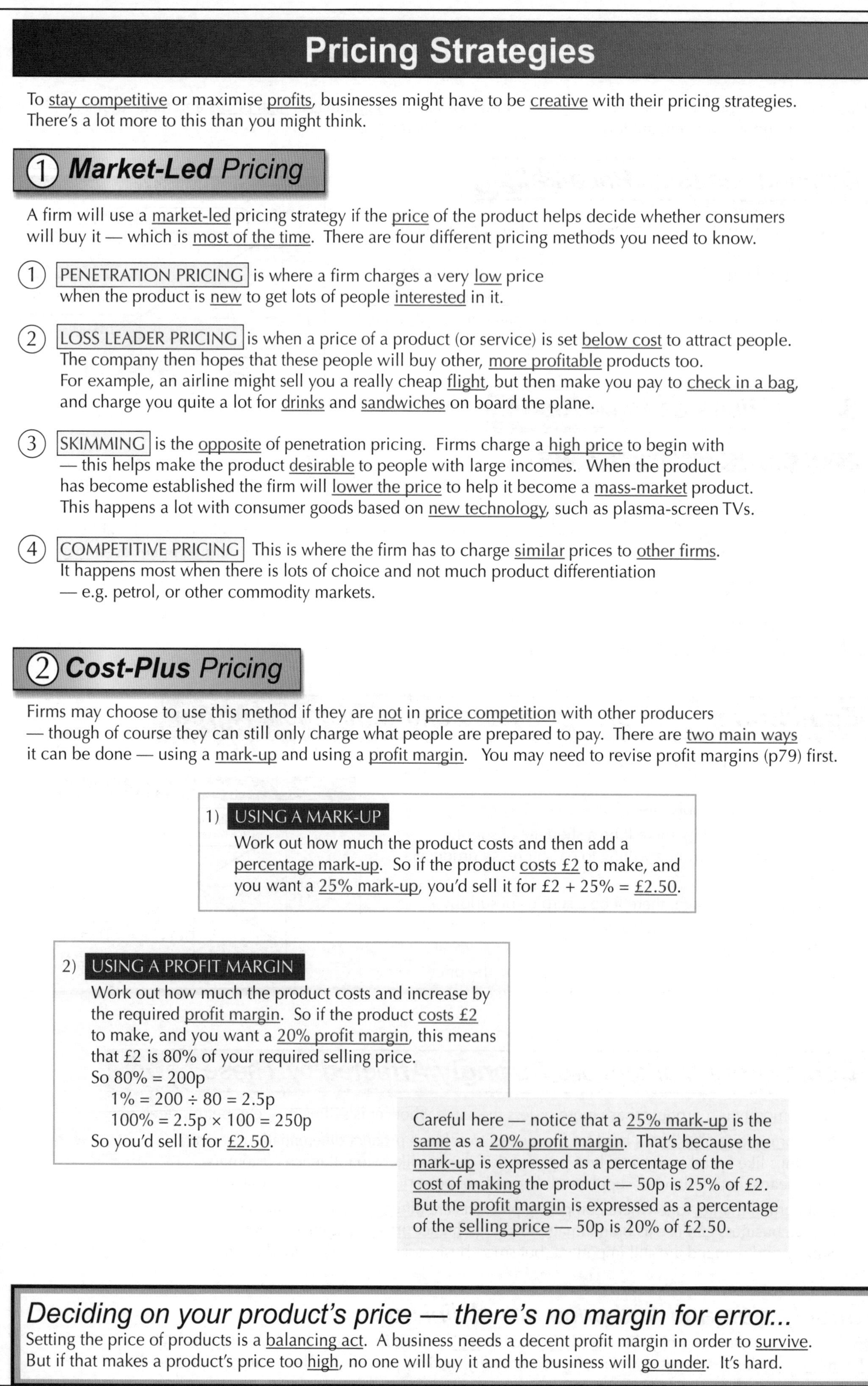

Pricing Strategies

To stay competitive or maximise profits, businesses might have to be creative with their pricing strategies. There's a lot more to this than you might think.

① *Market-Led Pricing*

A firm will use a market-led pricing strategy if the price of the product helps decide whether consumers will buy it — which is most of the time. There are four different pricing methods you need to know.

1. PENETRATION PRICING is where a firm charges a very low price when the product is new to get lots of people interested in it.

2. LOSS LEADER PRICING is when a price of a product (or service) is set below cost to attract people. The company then hopes that these people will buy other, more profitable products too. For example, an airline might sell you a really cheap flight, but then make you pay to check in a bag, and charge you quite a lot for drinks and sandwiches on board the plane.

3. SKIMMING is the opposite of penetration pricing. Firms charge a high price to begin with — this helps make the product desirable to people with large incomes. When the product has become established the firm will lower the price to help it become a mass-market product. This happens a lot with consumer goods based on new technology, such as plasma-screen TVs.

4. COMPETITIVE PRICING This is where the firm has to charge similar prices to other firms. It happens most when there is lots of choice and not much product differentiation — e.g. petrol, or other commodity markets.

② *Cost-Plus Pricing*

Firms may choose to use this method if they are not in price competition with other producers — though of course they can still only charge what people are prepared to pay. There are two main ways it can be done — using a mark-up and using a profit margin. You may need to revise profit margins (p79) first.

1) **USING A MARK-UP**
Work out how much the product costs and then add a percentage mark-up. So if the product costs £2 to make, and you want a 25% mark-up, you'd sell it for £2 + 25% = £2.50.

2) **USING A PROFIT MARGIN**
Work out how much the product costs and increase by the required profit margin. So if the product costs £2 to make, and you want a 20% profit margin, this means that £2 is 80% of your required selling price.
So 80% = 200p
1% = 200 ÷ 80 = 2.5p
100% = 2.5p × 100 = 250p
So you'd sell it for £2.50.

Careful here — notice that a 25% mark-up is the same as a 20% profit margin. That's because the mark-up is expressed as a percentage of the cost of making the product — 50p is 25% of £2. But the profit margin is expressed as a percentage of the selling price — 50p is 20% of £2.50.

Deciding on your product's price — there's no margin for error...

Setting the price of products is a balancing act. A business needs a decent profit margin in order to survive. But if that makes a product's price too high, no one will buy it and the business will go under. It's hard.

Promotion — Advertising

Advertising is any message about a firm or its products that the firm has paid for.
You need to know why and where firms advertise — and what the effects are on the consumer.

Firms **Advertise** for **Various Reasons**

These are some of the reasons why firms might want to advertise:

1) To make consumers aware of new products.
2) To remind consumers about existing products.
3) To persuade consumers to switch from rival products.
4) To promote the business' brand image.

The ultimate aim of all four, of course, is to sell more products and so help the business to grow.

Where They Advertise Depends on **Three Things**

Where the firm will place its advertising depends on three things:

1) The target audience. If you want to sell lace doilies to women over 55, don't place your advert in 'Which Skateboard' magazine.
2) The size and location of the market. If you are launching 'Death Cola' nationwide, don't just advertise in the 'Bognor Regis Morning Gazette'. In recent years e-commerce has become an important area of advertising — companies can now reach international markets much more easily (see p126).
3) The size of the advertising budget. A large business may be able to advertise in many different media — TV, radio, internet and newspapers. Smaller businesses will probably have to limit themselves to adverts in local newspapers or on their own websites. Handing out leaflets and business cards can also be a cost-effective way of advertising.

Advantages and **Disadvantages** of Advertising

The advantage to a firm in advertising is that it may increase sales. The disadvantage is that they could be spending the money making more products, or cutting prices. Advertising has costs and benefits for society as well — here are the main ones.

Advantages of Advertising

1) Advertising gives people information and helps them make a choice.
2) Advertising subsidises newspapers and magazines, so they cost less. And it subsidises television programmes and websites, so they're better quality.
3) Advertising is a big industry — think of all the people it employs.

Disadvantages of Advertising

1) Advertising makes people think they want things they used to be perfectly happy without.
2) Advertising costs money, so firms have to charge more for their products to pay for it.
3) Large firms with big budgets can gain a competitive advantage with huge advertising campaigns. This could mean smaller firms lose business and close down, leading to less choice for consumers.

Advertising — learn the pros and cons...

This page doesn't tell you whether advertising is good or bad — it's up to you to decide that. Write a mini-essay outlining the benefits and drawbacks of advertising for businesses and society, and then say whether you think it's a good thing or not. As long as you can justify your opinion, then there's no wrong answer to this question.

Promotion — Other Methods

Don't make the mistake of thinking promotion is just about advertising.
Here are three other ways the firm can remind you that they exist.

Sales Promotion — Learn These **Seven** Examples

These are called point of sale promotions — because that's where they happen.
Or below the line promotions because they don't depend on the media.

1) Buy One Get One Free (BOGOF). Or buy one get something else free.
2) Discounts. A good way to get people to notice the product is to stamp '10% off' on the label.
3) Competitions. Say why new Smello Baked Beans are good for you in less than twenty words — and win a year's supply free.
4) Free gifts. Buy a new skateboard and get a free MP3 Player with built-in toaster.
5) Product trials. Set up a stall and invite people to taste new Smello Baked Beans for free.
6) Point-of-sale advertising. Put tins of new Smello Baked Beans in a special display case at the front of the supermarket.
7) Use of credit. A good way to get someone to buy a product is to let them buy now but pay later — through hire purchase or a store charge card.

Direct Marketing Goes Straight to the Customer

1) In direct marketing, the business contacts the potential customer directly without going through other media. E.g. Saucy Co. might mail out vouchers for 10p off a bottle of their new Awfully Hot Sauce.
2) The customer is invited to make a direct response to the message — they might want to use their voucher next time they're at the supermarket.
3) The main benefit of direct marketing is that a business can measure its success. If they send out 20 000 vouchers and 4952 people use them at the shops, the promotion has had a success rate of nearly 25%.
4) The problem is that it creates junk mail and spam e-mail. Some people can't stand businesses that send out junk — but there's no way for a business to measure how many people they've annoyed.

Businesses Can **Sponsor** Organisations and Events

Businesses sometimes help to pay for events such as sports tournaments, TV shows and exhibitions.
In return, it can display its name at the event. This is called sponsorship, and examples are everywhere:

1) **SPORT** A large business might stamp its brand name all over an international competition. A smaller business will have to make do with the local Sunday League team, but the aim is the same.
2) **TELEVISION** Some soap operas and weather reports are sponsored by well-known brands.
3) **THE ARTS** Theatres, art galleries and concert halls are often short of cash — businesses can step in to sponsor them. It makes the business look classy — but some people think art and business don't mix.

Sponsorship can create a high profile for your business or brand name.
But if the thing you're sponsoring starts to get bad publicity, your company's image suffers too.

Firms use promotion to try and increase their sales...

So you see there's lots more to promotion than plain and simple advertising. Firms want you to know about their products — and will try and tempt you in lots of ways. The method of promotion depends on the type of product, size of budget, etc. Learn this page using the memorise, cover, and write a mini-essay method.

Place — Where the Product is Sold

There are two main decisions to be made here — how the product will reach the customer, and where the product will be sold. These questions are related, but not the same.

Distribution Channels Can be **Direct** or **Indirect**

Wholesalers buy products from a wide range of manufacturers and sell them to retailers.
Retailers specialise in selling to the consumer.

The diagram here shows four distribution channels — 1, 2 and 3 are indirect channels, 4 is a direct channel.

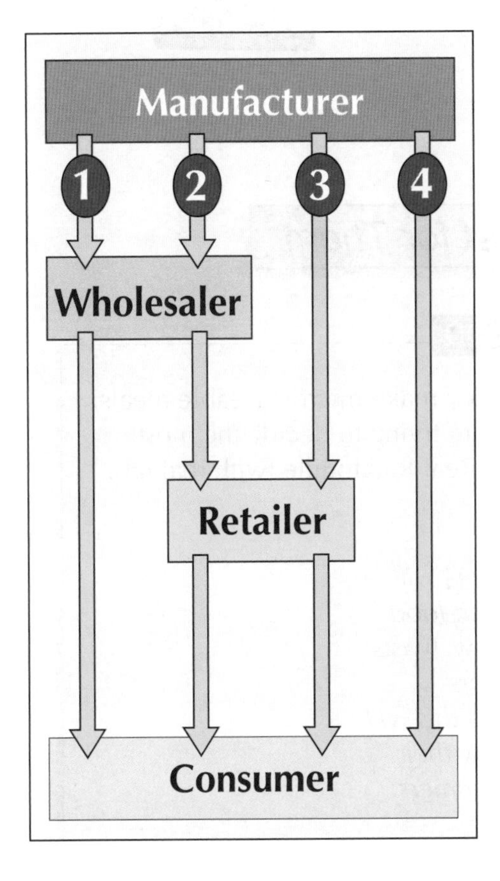

1 MANUFACTURER — WHOLESALER — CONSUMER

Here, consumers buy the product from a cash and carry warehouse. It's good for the manufacturer because they get bulk orders and the wholesaler takes on the cost of storing the products and the risk of not selling them. The consumer often pays lower prices than if they bought from a retailer — but levels of customer service may be lower.

2 MANUFACTURER — WHOLESALER — RETAILER — CONSUMER

This is the traditional route — it's still commonly used in the food and drink industry. The advantages to the manufacturer are the same as for channel 1. The retailer also benefits from dealing with a wholesaler — they reduce the risk by allowing retailers to buy in smaller quantities, and giving them a wide choice of goods. The problem is that goods can take a long time to get from manufacturer to consumer.

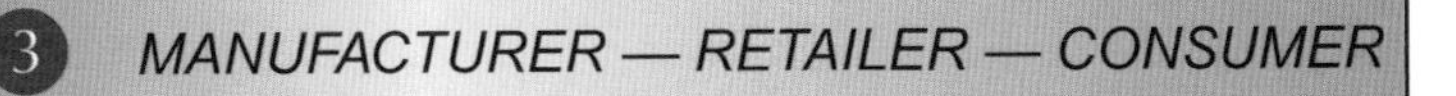

3 MANUFACTURER — RETAILER — CONSUMER

This route is becoming more common — e.g. it's often used in the clothing industry. It's faster than dealing with retailers through wholesalers, and the manufacturer gets better consumer feedback about the products. But it's harder for small retailers to avoid having to hold lots of stock.

The last distribution channel is on the next page...

Place — Where the Product is Sold

Here's the last of the distribution channels...

4 MANUFACTURER — CONSUMER

This is now very popular — examples include factory shops, mail order, telesales and internet selling. It's the fastest channel, and often cheapest for the consumer (and can be the most profitable for the manufacturer). But it can be more difficult for consumers to shop around, and customer service levels may not be as good.

Firms Must ***Decide*** *Which Channel is* ***Best*** *for Them*

A TYPICAL EXAM SCENARIO — SELLING FROZEN FOOD

New Twists Ltd. are a small frozen food manufacturer. They make microwaveable meals, based on traditional recipes, but with a new twist. They are trying to decide the most appropriate distribution channel for their new product of Real Ratatouille (with real rat). Explain what you would recommend to New Twists Ltd.

'Selling frozen food directly to consumers will be difficult, because you cannot post frozen food — it needs to be delivered quickly. New Twists should probably try to sell to wholesalers (or perhaps big supermarket chains), as this will reduce their delivery costs but still allow their products to reach a wide range of consumers.'

Where *a Product is Sold Affects a Product's* ***Image***

Some producers like to be careful where their product is sold.

For example, some perfume manufacturers market their products as expensive luxury items. They would not be happy if it was sold next to fresh fish on a supermarket shelf.

Channel all of your energy into learning these two pages...

The more 'middle men' there are in a distribution channel, the more people there are to make a profit, and so the higher the price for the consumer usually. But manufacturers might prefer fewer 'middle men' too — they can charge consumers higher prices than they might charge a retailer, and so make more profit.

Customer Service

It's important for firms to give their customers the right service — if they don't, customers might just lose their patience and take their business elsewhere.

Good Customer Service — **Six** Examples to Learn

1. Accurate product information: A business should know its products inside-out, and give its customers honest information about them.

2. Reliability: Products need to be reliable — customers don't want to have to keep phoning a helpline because their vacuum cleaner explodes every two weeks. The customer service also needs to be reliable — e.g. you'd expect to have your call answered and the problem resolved every time you phone a helpline.

3. Dealing with customer questions and concerns when buying a product. For example, a customer might need to be shown how a new product works.

4. Fulfilling the order requirements: If the order is for a ham and cheese pizza, don't send the customer a wooden spoon and a tube of toothpaste.

5. Delivering on time: If you've promised next-day delivery, deliver the next day. Don't turn up three weeks later saying you overslept.

6. After-sales support and warranties: Sometimes things go wrong, leading to customer questions and complaints — a good business will put the problem right. Some products, like cars and computers, might need to be serviced and updated throughout their life span.

Many businesses have a customer service department — others train all staff to provide a good level of customer service. Some businesses do both. Company websites can also provide customer service, such as answers to frequently-asked questions and contact information (see page 123).

Good Customer Service has **Benefits** for a Business

1) Good customer service leads to high levels of customer satisfaction. Satisfied customers are more likely to make repeat purchases from the business in the future.
2) Happy customers are also more likely to recommend the business to their friends and family. Word-of-mouth recommendation is a very important way for a business to expand. This is especially true for new small businesses.
3) If customers aren't satisfied, they won't come back. The business then has to work harder to find new customers. Unhappy customers are also less likely to recommend the business to others — they might even put people off it. The business ends up with a poor reputation and falling sales.
4) Of course, good customer service costs money — e.g. the wages of extra staff, and website running costs. However, most businesses recognise that the benefits of customer service outweigh this problem.

In business, the customer really is king (or queen)...

If a business wants to keep its customers, it needs to provide them with good service. Make sure you can explain why customer service is important, and list the different ways a company can provide it.

Warm-Up and Worked Exam Questions

Warm-up Questions

1) What does the law of supply say?
2) Explain the difference between skimming and penetration pricing.
3) Give four reasons why firms advertise.
4) Give five different sales promotion methods.
5) What is meant by direct marketing?
6) Which distribution channel is the traditional route for most goods?

Worked Exam Question

There's lots to get to grips with here. Have a look at the questions and answers below.

1 Really Big Supermarket is launching a new luxury range of microwaveable meals.

a) Each meal costs £2.09 from the manufacturer. The supermarket wants a mark-up of 15%. What will be the selling price of each meal?

Mark-up of 15% on 209p = 1.15 × 209p = 240.35p = £2.40 ✔[1 mark]

✔[1 mark for any correct method]

(2 marks)

b) State two advantages to consumers of buying the microwave meals from Really Big Supermarket, rather than buying them direct from the manufacturer.

It is more convenient for consumers to buy the meals from the supermarket along with their other grocery shopping. ✔[1 mark] *Customers are also able to buy the meals singly rather than in bulk.* ✔[1 mark]

(2 marks)

c) Explain one method of sales promotion Really Big Supermarket could use to launch the range of meals.

They could offer the meals at a special introductory discounted price, ✔[1 mark] *this would be a good way to encourage people to try the products.* ✔[1 mark]

The question asks you to explain, so you need to say how your choice of method would help successfully launch the product.

(2 marks)

d) When the meals are approaching their 'Use by' date, Really Big Supermarket reduces the price of the meals. Suggest why the supermarket does this.

The law of demand states that as the price decreases, the quantity demanded increases. ✔[1 mark] *This predicts that at the lower price, more people will want to buy the meals,* ✔[1 mark] *so the supermarket will not have to throw them away.* ✔[1 mark] *For the supermarket, getting some money for the products is better than getting no money.* ✔[1 mark]

Remember to relate the general law to the particular example of the meals in the supermarket.

(4 marks)

Exam Questions

1 Read the text below and answer the questions that follow.

> Matt and Nida are planning to open a restaurant *The Bakehouse,* in their local town centre. There are already many competing restaurants in the town. They plan to offer a number of 3-course set menus, priced at £35 each.

a) Describe **one** way Matt and Nida could use **direct marketing** to help launch the restaurant.

....

....

(2 marks)

b) Explain **one** potential disadvantage of direct marketing for Matt and Nida.

....

....

(2 marks)

c) Discuss how Matt and Nida could use customer service to increase their market share once the restaurant is open.

....

....

....

....

(Continue your answer on a separate piece of paper) *(6 marks)*

d) Matt used cost-plus pricing to calculate the amount they should charge for the set menus. Explain what is meant by the term "cost-plus" pricing.

....

....

(2 marks)

e) Nida thinks they should use penetration pricing rather than cost-plus pricing. Recommend one of these pricing methods to Matt and Nida. Explain your answer.

....

....

....

....

(Continue your answer on a separate piece of paper) *(9 marks)*

Revision Summary for Section Two

Marketing gives businesses plenty to think about. It's not just the product they need to get right — the whole marketing mix is dead important if they want to succeed. Well now... you know what the end of a section means — time to make sure you've learned the stuff you need to know.
You'll need your calculator for some of them. Answers to all number questions are at the bottom of the page — so you can cheat if you want to, but it won't do you any good because you won't learn a thing that way. There... that's you told.

1) List the five main ways that markets are segmented.
2) What is SWOT analysis? Why is it useful?
3) Give three advantages and three disadvantages for field research and desk research.
4) What is the difference between quantitative and qualitative data?
5) What's the difference between a product trial and a repeat purchase?
   How can a business try to get more repeat purchases?
6) Why is brand image important? And product differentiation?
7) Draw a sketch of the product life cycle. Explain what happens at each of the five main stages.
8) When are a product's sales highest?
   a) development; b) maturity; c) January.
9) What is an extension strategy?
10) What is meant by 'balanced product portfolio'?
11) Describe how the Boston matrix can help a firm analyse its product portfolio.
12) Why does the demand curve slope downwards?
13) Why does the supply curve slope upwards?
14) Sketch a demand and supply diagram using the data on the right.
    a) What is the equilibrium price and quantity?
    b) Which of the following is happening at a price of £6?
       i) consumers are desperate to buy and there's a shortage.
       ii) producers are making too much and there's a surplus.
    c) How about at a price of £21?

Price (£)	Demand (thousands)	Supply (thousands)
3	18	2
6	16	4
9	14	6
12	12	8
15	10	10
18	8	12
21	6	14
24	4	16
27	2	18

15) Describe four different market-led pricing strategies.
16) A firm works out it costs £4.50 to make each basketball.
    What price should it charge if it uses the following cost-plus methods?
    a) a 15% mark-up; b) a 20% profit-margin; c) a 30% mark-up; d) 40% profit-margin.
17) Describe three things that influence where a firm will advertise.
18) Give seven examples of point-of-sale promotions.
19) What is direct marketing? Explain the advantages of direct marketing to a business.
20) Why might manufacturers like dealing with a wholesaler?
21) What are the advantages and disadvantages of a direct distribution channel?
22) Describe six features of good customer service.
    What benefits are there to a business of providing good levels of customer service?

14. a) £15, 10;
b) i); c) ii)
16. a) £5.18; b) £5.63;
c) £5.85; d) £7.50

Primary, Secondary and Tertiary Industry

Production is all about where and how goods and services are produced.
There are three sectors of industry — you need to know what they are.

① The **Primary** Sector Produces **Raw Materials**

Raw materials are any natural resources which are used to produce goods or services.

1) They can be extracted from the ground. The mining industry provides coal, oil, gas, and metals like iron. The quarrying industry provides stone.
2) They can be grown. The forestry industry chops down rainforests and grows timber on plantations. The farming industry grows food (both animals and crops are classed as natural resources).
3) They can be collected. The fishing industry "collects" fish from the sea.

② The **Secondary** Sector Manufactures **Goods**

Manufacturing is the turning of raw materials into finished goods — either capital goods or consumer goods.

1) CAPITAL GOODS are used to make other goods or provide services — e.g. welding equipment or delivery vans.
2) CONSUMER GOODS go straight to the final consumer. There are two types...
   - consumables get used up, like pencils and cans of beans,
   - consumer durables last a longer time, like TVs.
3) The building and construction industries are also in the secondary sector. And so are the utilities — companies that supply water, gas and electricity.

③ The **Tertiary** Sector Provides **Services**

Services are provided for the benefit of others.

1) Some services are provided for businesses — like warehousing, advertising and distribution of goods.
2) Some services are provided for consumers — like hairdressers, shops and restaurants.
3) Financial services like banking and insurance are used by both businesses and consumers.

The **Tertiary** Sector is Now the **UK's Largest** Sector

In the UK, the tertiary sector is now the biggest of the three. There are two main reasons...

1) As people become wealthier they tend to spend more money on services.
2) The number of manufacturers in the UK has shrunk, affecting the primary and secondary sectors. This is because it's hard to produce goods in the UK as cheaply as they can be produced abroad.

As well as shrinking, the secondary sector has changed in other ways.
- Manufacturing in high-tech industries such as computing has increased, while traditional industries like shipbuilding have declined.
- Machines (e.g. robots) have become a lot more important, meaning fewer people are needed.

In the jargon, manufacturing is now capital-intensive — you need lots of money up front to buy and equip a modern factory. (Both money and equipment can be referred to as capital.)

Learn about sectors — and get in the zone...

This is a pretty easy page — especially if you do geography as well. Make sure you know all three sectors and try to come up with some more examples of industries in each of them — there'll be loads of possibilities.

Specialisation and Interdependence

It's a simple idea — if I'm good at cooking but can't count, and you're good at accounting but your cooking stinks, then our catering business will do much better if I do all the cooking and you do all the accounting. It's a lot more sensible than us both spending half our time on each.

Specialisation Leads to Division of Labour

Firms use specialisation to make their production more efficient. It's called division of labour — that means they divide up their workers and get each one of them to do a specific job.

1) Workers can play to their strengths — you might be a naturally gifted brain surgeon, say, or a drummer.
2) Skills are improved. If you spend all your time doing brain surgery or drumming, you get better.
3) Firms always try to break up complex production techniques into a series of simple tasks, and get workers to specialise in those tasks.
4) Workers may do the same task hundreds of times a day — so they get very efficient at it. And this improves the firm's productivity.

Division of Labour has its **Problems**

It's not all good news, though. Often you have to specialise in something more boring than brain surgery, like screwing the same little bolt onto an endless production line of mopeds.

1) Workers may get bored doing the same thing every day — resulting in low job satisfaction.
2) This can lead to poor quality products, more absenteeism and frequent industrial action.
3) A problem with one group of workers may halt production in the whole business.
4) Workers can become over-specialised — they have difficulty finding another job if their skills are no longer in demand. Unemployment due to occupational immobility may result.

Specialisation Makes Firms **Interdependent**

- It's not just workers in firms who specialise. Firms themselves specialise too. One firm will grow cocoa, another will process it, another will ship it. One firm will make chocolate bars, another will sell them. You generally don't get one firm trying to do all these things — it's not very efficient.
- Firms specialise in what they're best at. This means they don't just supply goods and services to consumers — they also supply each other.
- Firms are interdependent with businesses in the same production chain. If there's a crisis in the cocoa growing industry, Chocs-R-Us are in trouble too.

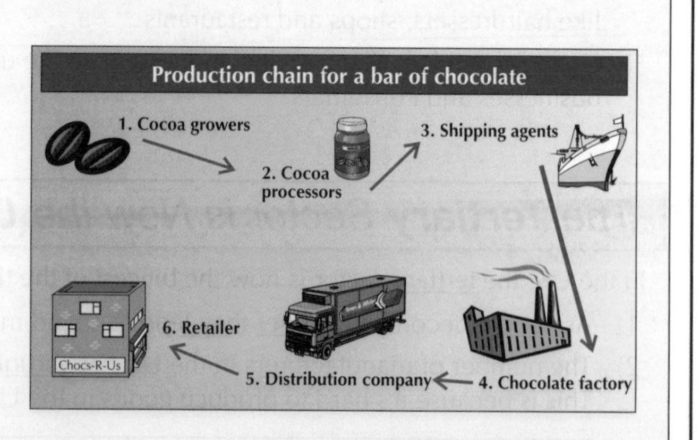

1) Some stages of production make the product more valuable than before — this is called adding value.
2) Other stages of production provide vital services, for example, transporting the product.

Specialisation leads to interdependence...

You can take this further than just production chains. For example, that chocolate retailer will depend on all sorts of other businesses — banks, other suppliers, etc. If you were to draw all the connections between interrelated businesses, you'd end up with something more like a spider's web. All those businesses are interdependent.

Location of Production

All firms, whether they produce goods or provide services, have to decide where to locate. It's usually a compromise between producing where it's cheapest and being where they would generate the most income. There are other factors which are also important — depending on the industry.

Location is Influenced by Nine Main Factors

Suppose a new startup company Granite King are looking for a location for their new kitchen worktops manufacturing business. They'll want to think about these things...

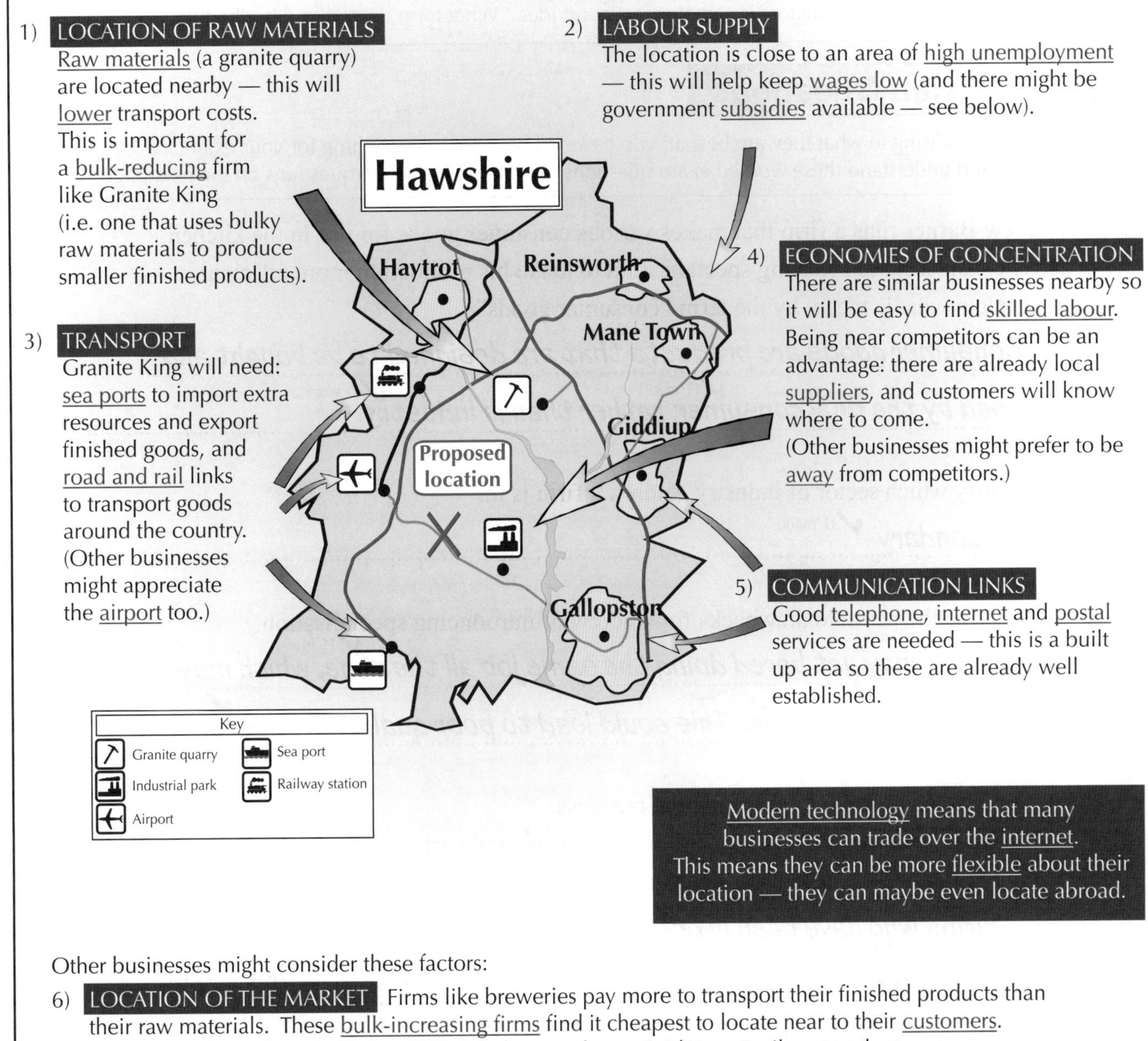

1) **LOCATION OF RAW MATERIALS** Raw materials (a granite quarry) are located nearby — this will lower transport costs. This is important for a bulk-reducing firm like Granite King (i.e. one that uses bulky raw materials to produce smaller finished products).

2) **LABOUR SUPPLY** The location is close to an area of high unemployment — this will help keep wages low (and there might be government subsidies available — see below).

3) **TRANSPORT** Granite King will need: sea ports to import extra resources and export finished goods, and road and rail links to transport goods around the country. (Other businesses might appreciate the airport too.)

4) **ECONOMIES OF CONCENTRATION** There are similar businesses nearby so it will be easy to find skilled labour. Being near competitors can be an advantage: there are already local suppliers, and customers will know where to come. (Other businesses might prefer to be away from competitors.)

5) **COMMUNICATION LINKS** Good telephone, internet and postal services are needed — this is a built up area so these are already well established.

Modern technology means that many businesses can trade over the internet. This means they can be more flexible about their location — they can maybe even locate abroad.

Other businesses might consider these factors:

6) **LOCATION OF THE MARKET** Firms like breweries pay more to transport their finished products than their raw materials. These bulk-increasing firms find it cheapest to locate near to their customers. Some services, such as dentists and florists, locate where people can easily get to them.

7) **GOVERNMENT POLICY** Governments often pay big multinationals to locate in their country. Or they may give subsidies or tax breaks to firms locating in areas of high unemployment.

8) **INDUSTRIAL INERTIA** Firms who have been in one place for a long time might find that high costs of relocation put them off moving, even though it might be cheaper in the long run.

9) **CLIMATE** It's obvious but important — especially in agriculture.

It's all about location, location, location...

Only nine factors to learn here — that isn't too bad. Each of these factors will be important in some industries but not in others. Think of a few industries — decide what location factors would be important for them.

Warm-Up and Worked Exam Questions

Warm-up Questions

1) In which sector of industry is banking?
2) Which sector of industry produces raw materials?
3) The process of turning raw materials into finished goods describes which sector?
4) Why do firms use specialisation?
5) What word describes the way in which firms rely on each other?
6) Being near your competitors is sometimes a good idea. What term is used to describe this?

Worked Exam Questions

Unlike firms specialising in what they are best at, you have to know about everything for your exam. Look through and understand these worked exam questions, then try the practice questions on the next page.

1 Andrew Barnes runs a firm that makes various consumer goods for use in the kitchen. He is considering introducing specialisation to make his production more efficient.

a) Explain what is meant by the term "consumer goods".

Consumer goods are products that are designed to be bought and used by the final consumer, ✔[1 mark] *rather than in industry.* ✔[1 mark]

(2 marks)

b) Identify which sector of industry Andrew's firm is in.

Secondary ✔[1 mark]

(1 mark)

c) Describe the possible drawbacks for Andrew of introducing specialisation.

Workers may get bored doing the same job all the time, ✔[1 mark] *which may result in low job satisfaction.* ✔[1 mark] *This could lead to poor quality products.* ✔[1 mark]

(3 marks)

d) Andrew is considering relocating the business. He knows that some firms are said to suffer from "industrial inertia".

(i) Explain what is meant by "industrial inertia".

Firms who have been in one place for a long time ✔[1 mark] *might find that the high costs of relocation put them off moving,* ✔[1 mark] *even if it might be cheaper to relocate in the long term.* ✔[1 mark]

(3 marks)

(ii) Identify three factors that Andrew might consider when deciding where to relocate.

1. *Location of suppliers* ✔[1 mark]
2. *Location of the market* ✔[1 mark]
3. *Labour supply* ✔[1 mark]

Other possible answers: transport and communication links, economies of concentration, government policy.

(3 marks)

Exam Questions

1 Read Source A and then answer the questions that follow.

Source A

Karen owns a small business that manufactures knitwear. Her business is currently based in the small village where she has lived all her life. Karen uses local wool in her products. She sells her products to local retailers. She is planning on expanding the business and is considering relocating to the nearest city, seventy miles away.

a) Karen's business is part of a production chain.
Give two reasons why production chains exist.

....

....
(2 marks)

b) Karen's business is interdependent with other firms.
(i) What does the term "interdependent" mean?

....

....
(1 mark)

(ii) Unfortunately, Karen's wool suppliers did not produce as much wool this year as they expected. What effect might this have upon Karen's business?

....

....

....

....

....
(5 marks)

c) Do you think Karen should relocate to the city? Give reasons for your answer.

....

....

....

....

....
(Continue your answer on a separate piece of paper) *(8 marks)*

Methods of Production

Production can take place in three different ways. You need to learn what each one is and which types of products it is best suited for. This is a favourite topic for examiners.

① Job Production is Making One Thing at a Time

1) Job production is used when a firm manufactures individual, unique products. Each product has a unique design based upon the customer's specification. If they're made in a factory, the firm will need to retool its factory each time it makes a new product.
2) These products often require highly skilled labour and have a high labour-to-capital ratio (i.e. lots of workers are needed, but relatively little financial investment) — they can be very labour intensive.
3) They're usually expensive and take a long time to make. But they're also high quality.
4) Examples include building ships, bridges and handmade crafts such as furniture making and made-to-measure clothes.

② Flow Production is Making Lots of Things Continuously

1) This is the opposite of job production. All products are identical and the aim is to produce as many as possible. To be efficient, production has to be continuous with no stoppages — many flow production factories operate 24 hours a day with workers rotating in shifts.
2) The aim is to gain from economies of scale (see p.93) and so produce at minimum unit cost to allow competitive prices. Modern flow production techniques use robots, not people, to do most of the work. Flow production is highly capital intensive (it needs a lot of money — to buy machinery, for example).
3) It is used for mass-market products. Most modern consumer goods are produced this way — chocolate bars, mobile phones, televisions... and so on.
4) Flow production is also sometimes called mass production.

The first modern mass producer of identical products was Henry Ford with his Model T car. He joked that his customers could have any colour Model T they liked — as long as it was black.

③ Batch Production is a Mixture of the Two

1) This is a combination of job and flow production. Firms use flow production techniques to make a batch of one thing then stop, reorganise, and make a batch of something else.
2) It is suited to products that are identical to each other, but which are only produced in limited quantities — or for a limited amount of time.
3) Examples include furniture (where producers make a limited number of many different designs), and house-building (where a batch of identical houses is built on a new housing estate).

Job production — it'd solve the unemployment crisis...

The type of production you should choose depends on what you're making. Learn these three methods and the types of products they're best suited for. Cover the page, write down the headings, then scribble about each.

Productivity

Businesses need to be competitive — and lean production is one strategy they can use to help achieve this.

Lean Production Uses as Few Resources as Possible

Lean production is a Japanese approach to making products that aims to use as few resources as possible. Waste and stocks of raw materials are kept to a minimum and workers are encouraged to think about ways to improve their productivity.

Three Stock Control Methods...

Stock Control Graphs

A traditional method is to use stock control graphs.

- Here the firm has set the reorder level at 1000 widgets.
- When stocks fall to 1000 widgets they will reorder 500 more.
- The hope is that by the time the new stock arrives the firm's stock level won't have fallen below the minimum level.

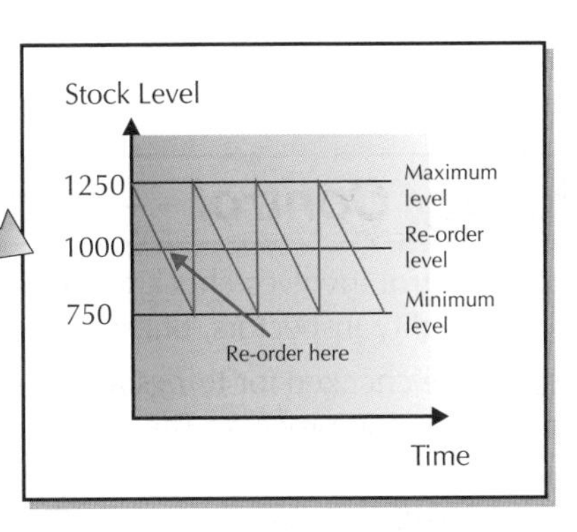

A computerised stock control system can calculate stock levels and place orders automatically.

Just-in-time (JIT)

This is a Japanese method that aims to keep stock levels to the bare minimum — ideally zero.

- The aim is that stock arrives in the factory immediately before it is used.
- The main benefit is that it reduces the cost of having to keep stocks (you need less warehouse space, fewer warehouse workers, and so on).
- The main problem is that it requires a lot of coordination between the firm and its suppliers — otherwise the firm could run out of stock.
- Extra training might be needed if JIT is to be successful — workers need to get used to working with very little stock.
- Another problem with JIT is some workers find it stressful if they are always on the verge of running out of stock. Some workers have called the system "Just too late".

Just-in-case (JIC)

This involves operating a production and distribution system with buffer stocks of items at every stage of the process — from raw materials to finished products — just in case there is a supply shortage or customer demand increases unexpectedly.

- The idea is that even if there's a problem with deliveries of any raw materials, the buffer stocks will mean there can still be continuous production.
- The main problem is that firms can be left with big stockpiles of items.
- JIC has tended to be replaced by JIT and other stock control methods.

Rationalisation — Reorganising to Increase Efficiency

1) This is another method that firms can use to increase efficiency. Firms use rationalisation when they need to reduce overhead costs in order to reduce their break-even point (see page 64).
2) Methods include
   - closing an administrative department and delegating their work elsewhere
   - closing a factory and moving the production to another site
   - reducing the number of managers
3) Rationalisation can be bad news for some workers as it often results in redundancies.

Revise Just-in-time — not two weeks after the exam...

Don't be put off by all the text above — there's nothing that's totally impossible to learn on this page. The main thing is to know how all the various methods work to improve the efficiency of a business.

Quality Management

Even the most productive business in the world won't get far if its products aren't up to scratch.

Quality Assurance is all about Satisfying Customers

Quality Assurance is the attempt to satisfy customers by making sure that quality standards are agreed and met throughout the organisation.

Quality awards are evidence of high standards — these show customers that certain standards have been met.

① Quality Control — Spotting Problems Before it's Too Late

1) Quality control involves checking products to make sure quality standards are being met. This used to be done by quality inspectors, but some firms now encourage workers to check their own quality.
2) Products are checked for things like design, appearance, defects and safety, usually at three different stages of the production process. The aim is to stop faulty goods from reaching the customer.

STAGE 1		STAGE 2		STAGE 3
Check the raw materials and components from suppliers.	→	Random samples taken to check quality of work in progress.	→	Random sample taken of finished products — items removed if they don't meet required quality.

3) Defects are spotted as they happen rather than waiting until products are finished — this reduces waste.
4) Quality control can be expensive (sometimes whole batches of goods might need to be scrapped). But the cost to the business would be greater if dissatisfied customers stopped buying their products.

② Total Quality Management — a Culture of Quality

1) The Total Quality Management (TQM) strategy aims to make quality the responsibility of every employee in an organisation. Employees are encouraged to think about the needs of the customer. The emphasis is on getting things right first time — to help reduce costs by cutting down on waste.
2) Quality Circles are an important TQM feature. Groups of workers from various departments meet regularly to identify quality problems and offer solutions — this can lead to increased motivation as workers feel more involved in the production process.
3) There is an emphasis on the quality of after-sales service as well as on the quality of production.
4) A downside of TQM is that it takes a long time to introduce. Workers need training so that they see quality as their responsibility — employees can get demotivated as it may seem like a lot of extra work.

Rapid Growth Makes it Hard to Maintain High Quality

1) A growing business is good — but success can bring its own problems.
2) A business can be overwhelmed by orders and cut corners to get products made more quickly. It may also become expensive to carry out all the necessary quality inspections.
3) One solution is to take on more employees — but it takes time to train new workers.
4) The business might outsource some tasks — pay another company to do them. It can be expensive to outsource to a company that delivers high quality (but using a cheaper company can mean quality will fall).

Quality circles — a well rounded idea...

It's a tough old world in business — the customer is king, and they expect satisfaction. No business can afford to let down its customers, and definitely not a small one — they might not get a second chance.

Warm-Up and Worked Exam Questions

Warm-up Questions

1) What is the name given to the production method which is used to make one thing at a time?
2) Batch production is a mixture of which two production methods?
3) What is lean production?
4) Describe the main purpose of the just-in-time (JIT) stock control system.
5) What is rationalisation?
6) What do the initials TQM stand for?

Worked Exam Questions

Revision's a bit like a production line — read, understand and learn the information, then go through these worked exam questions, then try some questions on your own.

1 British Sweets and Chocolates plc produce luxury hand-made confectionery. The company mainly uses batch production methods to produce its products.

a) Explain what is meant by the term "batch production".

Batch production means making a limited quantity of identical ✔[1 mark] *products* ✔[1 mark]*, then making another limited quantity of another product.*

(2 marks)

b) Identify two advantages of batch production over job production.

1. *Products can be produced more quickly.* ✔[1 mark]
2. *Workers become more efficient as they repeat certain tasks.* ✔[1 mark]

(2 marks)

c) The directors of the company are considering switching to flow production. Discuss the potential advantages and disadvantages of this for the company.

Flow production will require a lot of investment initially, ✔[1 mark] *but will reduce the direct costs of producing each item.* ✔[1 mark] *However, if products are no longer hand-made, they may seem less of a luxury item,* ✔[1 mark] *which could affect sales.* ✔[1 mark]

(4 marks)

2 Just-in-case is a method of stock control which involves keeping 'buffer stocks'.

a) Give two advantages to a manufacturing firm of using the just-in-case method.

1. *The manufacturing firm will be able to satisfy a sudden rise in demand.* ✔[1 mark]
2. *The firm can still meet its orders if delivery of raw materials is delayed.* ✔[1 mark]

(2 marks)

b) Explain one advantage and one disadvantage of switching to just-in-time (JIT) stock control.

JIT stock control can make a firm more efficient, ✔[1 mark] *as it reduces storage costs.* ✔[1 mark]
But a late delivery will cause production delays, ✔[1 mark] *which could be expensive.* ✔[1 mark]

(4 marks)

Exam Questions

1 The managing director of John's Manufacturing and Retail Limited has told his departmental managers that he is very worried about the firm's quality control processes. He also feels that the company will need to cut its costs in response to falling customer demand.

a) Explain the purpose of quality control.

....

....

(2 marks)

b) A manager recommends reducing the number of quality checks made, since the cost of making those checks is greater than the value of the faulty products they find.
Explain one danger in this approach.

....

....

(3 marks)

c) A different manager suggests introducing Total Quality Management (TQM).

(i) Explain what is meant by Total Quality Management.

....

....

(2 marks)

(ii) Quality circles are an important feature of TQM.
What are quality circles? Briefly explain their main purpose.

....

....

(2 marks)

d) A third manager suggests that it might be cheaper to outsource some production.
What is meant by "outsourcing"? Explain one potential problem with outsourcing.

....

....

(2 marks)

e) Recommend how you think the firm should deal with its quality control problem.
Give reasons for your answer.

....

....

....

....

....

(7 marks)

Revision Summary for Section Three

This is quite a short section, but don't let that fool you into thinking you can ignore it. There's lots of important stuff to learn. Remember that examiners love to test you on whether you know about the various ways that production takes place — and which methods are suitable for particular goods.

It's all too easy to think you know it all after one quick read, but don't be fooled — one quick read won't do the trick. So keep going over these questions until you can answer them in your sleep.

1) Write down definitions of the primary, secondary and tertiary sectors.
   Give two examples of each.
2) What is the difference between a capital good and a consumer good?
3) Give two reasons why the tertiary sector is now the UK's largest sector.
4) Why does division of labour lead to more efficiency?
5) Describe three problems with division of labour.
6) "Firms in the same production chain are interdependent." What does this mean?
7) Draw a production chain for chocolate.
8) Where do bulk-reducing firms ideally locate?
   a) near their raw materials; b) near their market; c) Norwich.
9) Why might a firm locate in an area of high unemployment?
10) Explain two benefits of economies of concentration.
11) What does industrial inertia mean?
12) What is the difference between job production and flow production?
13) What is the production method that combines elements of job production and flow production?
14) Which method of production should be used in the following examples?
    a) making T-shirts of varying colours and styles.
    b) making tins of baked beans.
    c) building luxury cruise ships to order, so each ship is a different design.
15) What does lean production aim to eliminate?
    a) wasted raw materials b) fatty foods c) workers standing upright
16) Draw a stock control graph for baked beans to show a maximum stock level of 300 cans, a minimum stock level of 100 cans and a reorder level of 200 cans.
17) Explain one benefit and one problem of JIT.
18) Give three methods a firm might use to rationalise the business.
19) What might happen to a business if they allow faulty goods to reach their customers?
20) What does TQM stand for?
21) Give one advantage and one disadvantage of TQM.
22) Give three reasons why a growing business might find it hard to maintain high quality.

Employment and the Law

These next two pages are crammed full of facts about the law. The most important thing here is the effect of the different laws rather than their names. So concentrate on learning that stuff first.

1 Contracts of Employment and the Minimum Wage

1) All employees must be given a written contract of employment within two months of starting work. This is covered by the Employment Rights Act 1996.
2) All staff should have a copy of the business's discipline procedure. This explains which offences would lead to a warning, and which would lead to dismissal. This is covered by the Employment Act 2002.
3) In 1998 the Working Time Regulations were introduced — these limit the working week to 48 hours.
4) The Government sets a National Minimum Wage for all workers, depending on their age. The amount is regularly increased, usually on 1st October every year.

- The national minimum wage means that businesses can't cut costs on their wage bills by paying workers less than the legal minimum. If they do, they're breaking the law.
- Companies sometimes argue that the minimum wage increases costs. These increased costs can lead to increased prices, meaning a possible fall in sales and a reduced income for the firm.
- The minimum wage can have benefits for companies though — it can lead to better motivated staff and increased productivity.

2 Anti-Discrimination Laws

1) Recruitment procedures must not discriminate against men or women, ethnic minorities or the disabled. This is covered by the Sex Discrimination Act 1975, the Race Relations Act 1976 and the Disability Discrimination Act 2005.
2) Apart from recruitment, the other main equal opportunities issue is pay. The 1970 Equal Pay Act says that a woman must be paid the same as a man doing the same job for the same employer.
3) Men and women often do different jobs, so exact comparisons of men and women's work are difficult. But businesses should give both sexes the same pay for work of equal value.
4) It's also illegal to discriminate against employees because of their age, religion or sexual orientation — this is covered in the Age Discrimination Act 2006 and the Employment Equality Regulations 2003.

3 Leaving Employment

1) The Employment Act 2002 protects employees against unfair dismissal. They can only be dismissed if they're incapable of doing their job — like if they're incompetent or have shown gross misconduct.
2) Employees can only be made redundant if the job they're employed to do no longer exists — e.g. if there is a drop in demand, or automation. The firm cannot re-advertise a redundant job.
3) Employees who think they have been unfairly dismissed or made redundant can usually appeal to an employment tribunal. The tribunal can award compensation or reinstate the employee.

Don't discriminate — learn about *all* these laws...

Staying within the law is expensive — keeping up to date with new laws costs money and creates a lot of paperwork (and small firms have to meet all the same requirements as large ones, remember).

Employment and the Law

All these regulations can cause firms problems (you often hear business folk complaining about "red tape"). But usually the rules are designed to make life safer and fairer overall.

④ Health and Safety Legislation

Health and safety legislation is designed to make sure that risks to people at work are properly controlled. A safe working environment should mean fewer accidents, and so fewer injuries. And hopefully it means a more productive workforce too — since people should need less time off work to recover as a result.

1) You need to know what these acts meant for companies and their employees...

   i) The 1961 Factories Act set minimum requirements including toilets, washing facilities, lighting and fire escapes.

   ii) The Health and Safety at Work Act of 1974 requires all employers and their employees to take responsibility for health and safety.

   iii) The 1992 Workplace Regulations introduced European Union rules including the safe use of computers.

2) These are some of the things that firms must do to comply with the acts...

   - Firms need to carry out risk assessments to identify possible dangers.
   - They need to take reasonable steps to reduce the risks.
   - Accident books need to be kept, and first-aiders trained.
   - All staff must receive health and safety training.
   - Health and safety equipment must be provided — e.g. hard hats on building sites.

Businesses that don't follow health and safety laws can be prosecuted, fined and even closed down.

⑤ Legislation about Leave for New Parents

1) New mothers are legally entitled to 39 weeks of paid maternity leave to look after their babies. Employers have to pay the mother during her leave, but not usually her full salary. New fathers can now take up to two weeks' paternity leave.
2) While the new parent is on leave, somebody else has to do their job at work. Sometimes existing staff can do this — this saves money on extra wages, but it may mean that staff have less time to concentrate on their usual tasks. This could reduce productivity.
3) If existing staff can't cover the job, an extra worker will have to be employed on a short-term contract. This increases costs as the firm has to pay for the extra worker's wages and the new parent's paid leave.
4) Maternity leave sometimes causes problems for businesses — it can be expensive, and leaves a gap in the workforce. But new parents are more likely to return to work for the business if it has been supportive. This can save a business money on recruiting and training a new employee to replace the parent.

It's all about giving employees a fair deal...

Employers can't pretend they don't know these laws exist — and neither can you. Cover these last two pages and scribble down everything you can about the five lots of legislation. Repeat until you've got all the details .

Motivation Theory

Keeping staff motivated is important for any business. Workers want to feel valued and that they're doing their jobs well. This page covers some of the ways that a business can improve the motivation of their workers.

Maslow's **Hierarchy of Needs**

Maslow believed that all people are motivated by the same things. The three lower needs at the bottom of the pyramid have to be achieved before the two higher needs can be met.

SELF-ACTUALISATION — people want to feel they are achieving something. Managers should help staff set and reach their own personal targets.

SELF-ESTEEM — people want to feel valued by others. Managers should praise and encourage, and give financial rewards for good performance.

LOVE AND BELONGING — people enjoy the company of others. Managers should encourage teamwork and social contact.

SAFETY — people want to feel safe and secure from harm. Managers should give their workers job security.

PHYSICAL SURVIVAL — people need food, water, shelter, clothing and warmth. These should be met by a basic wage.

Training Can Boost Motivation...

1) The main purpose of training (see page 57) is to help staff become better at their jobs.
2) But training can also improve motivation — being good at your job will boost your self-esteem.
3) Employees can also be trained to learn new skills. This means they can start to take on new tasks, which may stop them from becoming bored and frustrated.
4) Training can help staff meet their personal targets on the way to self-actualisation.

...And **Styles of Management** Can Also Have an Effect

1) Authoritarian (or autocratic) managers make decisions alone, without consulting staff.
2) Paternalistic managers make decisions themselves, but only after consultation with workers.
3) Democratic managers allow the workforce some influence over decisions.
4) Laissez-faire managers allow workers to perform tasks as they see fit, offering help if needed.

No single approach is perfect for all employees and all situations. For example...

- The authoritarian style can make workers feel their views aren't valued — which can demotivate able staff. (It can be very effective during crisis management though.)
- At the other end of the scale, laissez-faire management leaves workers to work things out for themselves — great for independent, motivated workers, but it could be a problem for staff who need support.

Motivated Staff are **Good for Business**

1) Motivated workers perform better. They'll produce more and better-quality products.
2) They'll also stay with the company for longer. This reduces staff turnover and saves money — the business spends less on recruiting and training new workers.
3) In the end, motivation comes from within. If an employee feels inspired and wants to work hard and improve at their job, then that's usually better than a manager telling them to work hard and do better.

Motivate yourself to learn everything on this page...

There's nothing surprising about this — happy staff are more productive than miserable staff. Managers play an important role in keeping staff motivated — their style and decisions have a big effect on workers.

Financial Rewards

There are a lot of facts on this page but it all boils down to two things — the different ways of paying people and the incentives each method gives them.

Workers can be Paid **Wages** or a **Salary**

1) Wages are paid weekly or monthly — usually to manual workers. Wages are paid in one of two ways:

A time rate pays workers by the hour. It encourages people to work long hours — the problem is they also have an incentive to work slowly. Time rate is best for jobs where measuring output is difficult — like driving a bus.

A piece rate is used if the output of each worker can be easily measured (such as a worker who sews sleeves onto shirts in a factory). Piece rates encourage people to work quickly — but if they work too fast, quality may suffer.

2) A salary is a fixed amount paid every month. It is usually paid to office staff who do not directly help to make the product. A salary of £24,000 means you are paid £2000 per month.
3) The advantage of a salary is that the firm and workers both know exactly how much the pay will be. A problem is that it does not link pay directly to performance.

Employers can Give Staff **Extra** Payments

1) With performance-related pay (PRP) the amount employees earn depends on how well they work.

Commission is paid to sales staff. They earn a small basic salary and then earn more money for every item they sell.

A bonus is a lump sum added to pay, usually once a year. It's paid if the worker has met their performance targets.

2) Some businesses make payments into a pension scheme for employees. Others offer a profit sharing scheme — where a percentage of the company's profits is divided up between employees, for example.

Temporary Workers can Help With **Short-Term** Tasks

1) Temporary staff are paid for a fixed period of a few weeks or months. Employment agencies often supply firms with temporary staff — for a fee.
2) Freelance workers are also temporary — but they're usually self-employed. A business might bring them in to help with a particular task.
3) These types of staff give businesses flexibility — they can get extra staff for a short time according to the work that needs to be done.
4) A problem is that the workers may not feel committed to the business — they may not be as motivated as permanent employees.

Employees are Paid What They're **Worth** to the Business

1) In most businesses, different staff will be given different pay.
2) Jobs that need a lot of skills and qualifications usually pay more than unskilled jobs. The age and experience of the worker can also have an effect — most people earn more as they get older and progress through their careers.
3) Businesses aim to make a profit — managers have to work out how much each employee is worth to the business and pay them accordingly.

Different methods of payment give workers different incentives...

Staff can be paid wages or a salary — but businesses give the highest pay to the employees that are most valuable to the company. Cover the page and jot down the benefits and drawbacks of the different payment methods.

Non-Financial Rewards

Money is nice to have — it's useful for buying essential products like food and video games. But if your job is boring and you never get a break, you probably won't be happy with money alone. This page is about methods of motivating staff without throwing cash at them.

① *Job **Rotation** — a **Change** is as Good as a Rest*

1) Thanks to the wonders of division of labour, a lot of production jobs are boring and repetitive. Job rotation reduces this by occasionally moving workers from one job to another.
2) The benefits are that workers don't get so bored, and learn to do different jobs — so if someone's ill, someone else will be able to cover.
3) The problem is that one boring job is replaced by another — it doesn't improve job satisfaction.

② *Job **Enlargement** — Give Them **More** Things to Do*

1) When a worker becomes good at their job, productivity increases — they can do the same work in less time. Job enlargement is when the person is given more tasks to do. This will increase the size of their job description.
2) The advantage is that extra tasks should make the job more varied and interesting. It can also make the worker feel more valued.
3) The problem is that if the person thinks they're just being given more work, it can be demotivating.

③ *Job **Enrichment** — Give Them **Better** Things to Do*

1) The idea of job enrichment is to stop the worker from feeling that their productivity is being punished with more work. The worker is given greater responsibility — for example supervising the work of new staff. This may mean the worker needs more training.
2) A benefit is that the worker may become more motivated and work harder.
3) A problem is that they may expect a pay rise as well.

④ ***Fringe** Benefits — Those **Extra** Little Perks*

1) A fringe benefit is any reward that is not part of a worker's main income.
2) Examples include the use of a company car, gym membership, a daily meal allowance or free health insurance.
3) All of these perks cost money for the business, and save it for the worker — you could argue that they were a type of financial reward.

- Small businesses with limited budgets won't be able to pay their staff huge salaries or dish out massive bonuses.
- Job rotation, enlargement and enrichment are cheaper options for keeping workers happy and motivated.

The reward for revision — better exam results...

Whether firms like it or not, employees are people too. They like to feel appreciated and be given variety and responsibility in their jobs. Learn the four ways to motivate staff without giving them any extra money.

Warm-Up and Worked Exam Questions

Warm-up Questions

1) The Working Time Regulations limit the working week to how many hours?
2) Under the Health and Safety at Work Act 1974 who has responsibility for safety in the workplace?
3) What is the only reason that an employee can be made redundant from their job?
4) In the context of salaries, what do the letters PRP stand for?
5) What are fringe benefits?
6) Name the management style of a manager who makes all the decisions on his own.

Worked Exam Question

There's plenty to learn in this section — loads of theories and definitions. You have to make sure you can apply them all to the real world, though, because that's what you'll have to do in the exam.

1 GeeWhizzz is a computer retailer with branches nationwide. Each shop has a manager and a number of sales assistants. Shop managers are paid a salary of £18,000. Sales assistants are paid a weekly wage based upon a time-rate system of £6.20 per hour.

a) State one difference between a salary and a wage.

A salary is a fixed monthly payment, but a wage can change depending upon how much work is done in the month. ✔ [1 mark]

(1 mark)

b) Calculate how much a full-time member of the sales staff would earn in one week if they worked 37 hours. Show your working.

37 hours x £6.20 per hour ✔ [1 mark] *= £229.40* ✔ [1 mark]

Don't forget your units.

(2 marks)

c) State one possible drawback to GeeWhizzz of a time-rate system of payment.

It doesn't reward the sales assistants who sell the most computers. ✔ [1 mark]

(1 mark)

d) The managers of GeeWhizzz want to introduce a performance-related pay system where staff are paid commission for each computer they sell. Give two advantages and two disadvantages for the business of doing this.

The sales staff may feel more motivated. ✔ [1 mark] *This should lead to greater sales and profits.* ✔ [1 mark] *However, the company will not know its wage costs in advance, making cash-flow forecasts difficult.* ✔ [1 mark] *Also, sales assistants may start to pressurise customers into buying computers, which could lead to the firm getting a poor reputation.* ✔ [1 mark]

(4 marks)

Exam Questions

2 Read **Item A** and then answer the questions that follow.

> **Item A**
> Heath Insurance Services is a medium-sized business that employs several office staff.
> Office staff are currently paid the national minimum wage.
> The board of directors has noticed that productivity is falling and wants to find a way of motivating the office staff to work harder.

a) What is meant by "national minimum wage"?

....

....

(2 marks)

b) Explain how poor motivation can lead to reduced productivity for a firm.

....

....

....

(4 marks)

c) Identify and explain the effect on motivation of **two** different management styles.

....

....

....

....

(Continue your answer on a separate piece of paper) *(6 marks)*

d) One of the firm's directors thinks the best way to motivate workers is by increasing wages. Another director thinks it would be better to introduce a bonus scheme.

Recommend which method the firm should use to increase the motivation of its office workers. Explain your answer.

....

....

....

....

....

....

(Continue your answer on a separate piece of paper) *(8 marks)*

Recruitment — Job Analysis

Recruitment is about appointing the best person to do the job. A business needs to understand what the job will involve so that it can decide what the right person will be like.

A Good Employee Needs a Balance of **Attitude** and **Skill**

1) Skills are things a person has learnt (such as being able to program a computer).
2) Attitudes are personal qualities a person has (such as being able to work in a team).
3) A highly-skilled person will probably be very good at the technical parts of a job. But they may still cause problems for other reasons — e.g. not cooperating with other staff or demanding higher pay.
4) A candidate with a good attitude may fit in better. But they might need extra skills training.

Businesses Need to Find the **Right Person** for the Job

1) To find the best candidates, a firm produces a job description and a person specification.
2) The job description is a written description of what the job involves. It includes the formal title of the job, the main purpose of the job, the main duties plus any occasional duties.

   It will also state who the job holder will report to, and whether they will be responsible for any other staff.
3) The person specification lists the qualifications, experience, skills and attitudes needed for the job.

   Essential criteria are qualities the candidate must have. Desirable criteria are qualities the candidate would ideally have.
4) The business must also say if the job is full-time or part-time.

- Employing staff full-time is expensive, but it means that they're available for the whole working week.
- Part-time workers are less expensive if there's not enough work to fill a full-time position. They may also be better rested and more motivated than staff who work 9 to 5 every day.

The Necks Directory Ltd. — Job Description

Job Title: Full-time Vampire Operative.
Reports to: Vampire Team Leader.
Responsible for: Trainee Vampire Operatives.
Main purpose of job: To climb through people's windows at night and suck their nourishing blood.
Duties and Responsibilities:
— to bite the necks of humans while they sleep;
— to wear a large black cape and cackle menacingly;
— to meet neck-biting targets set by Vampire Team Leader.

Vampire Operative — Person Specification

Essential: 5 GCSEs including Business Studies, NVQ Anatomy Level 3.
Desirable: Two years of vampiring experience.
Skills: Ability to climb through windows, bite necks, turn into a bat, etc. Good communication skills.
Attitudes: Fear of daylight, willingness to work unsocial hours, must enjoy meeting new people.

Businesses will often have a mixture of full-time and part-time staff.

5) A firm might first try to fill the vacancy with someone personally recommended by a friend or an existing worker. This can be cheaper and less hassle than advertising, and it's especially useful for small companies.

The Job Can Be Advertised **Internally** or **Externally**

1) The purpose of a job advert is to get as many suitable people as possible to apply for the job.
2) A firm might decide to advertise internally — it's much cheaper, the post can be filled more quickly, and the candidates will already know a lot about the firm. On the downside, there will be no 'new blood' and ideas, and the promotion will leave a vacancy to fill.
3) If the job is advertised externally, the firm has to decide where to advertise. Locations include local and national press, job centres, trade journals and employment agencies. Only specialist and senior jobs get advertised in the national press — because it's very expensive.

Recruitment is all about finding the best person to do a job...

Although it can sometimes be tricky to find that person — having a clear job description and person specification can help a firm find the best candidates. The firm also has to decide where to advertise the job — internally or externally. Cover the page, and write down the benefits and drawbacks of both. Check you got them all.

Recruitment — the Selection Process

The second part of recruitment is the selection process. This means reading all the applications and shortlisting the best candidates. Interviews and other methods help pick the best applicant.

Written Applications Help the Firm Make a *Shortlist*

A written application helps firms to decide which candidates meet the person specification.

1) In a letter of application the candidate writes about him- or herself — it gives the firm an idea of the applicant's personality as well as their written communication skills. These letters can take a long time to read, though — a business probably wouldn't ask for one if they expected a lot of applications.
2) A curriculum vitae (CV) is a summary of a person's personal details, skills, qualifications and interests. It's written in a standard format to give the firm the basic facts. Almost all firms ask for a CV.
3) An application form is designed by the firm and filled in by the applicant. It gives the firm the information it wants — and nothing else. Application forms are popular with large companies that don't have time to filter out irrelevant information.

Shortlisted candidates will usually be asked for references. These are statements about the character of the candidate written by someone who knows them — often a previous line manager. References are usually confidential — the candidate won't see what's written about them.

An *Interview* is the Traditional Selection Method...

1) Shortlisted candidates are invited for an interview with a manager. For senior jobs there's usually a panel interview, where the candidate is interviewed by two or more people.
2) Interviewers should ask the same questions to all candidates so that the process is fair. They should not ask questions that are irrelevant to the job or that discriminate unfairly.
3) Interviews are used to assess a candidate's confidence, their social and verbal skills, and whether they'll be compatible with existing workers. Businesses also want to find out about the candidate's general attitude.
4) Some people think that interviews are not a good way to select — people don't behave naturally in a formal interview. The skills needed to be good at interview are often different from the skills needed to do the job.

...But *Tests* are Increasingly Being Used

Because of the problems with interviews, many firms also use tests to help them assess candidates' skills and attitudes.

1) Skills tests or in-tray exercises test whether the candidate has the abilities to do the job.
2) Aptitude tests find out whether the candidate has the potential to learn how to do the job.
3) Personality tests such as handwriting analysis are used to assess the candidate's personal qualities.
4) Group tests find out whether the candidate can work as part of a team — and whether they have good leadership and decision-making skills.

Recruitment is so important that some firms hire recruitment consultants to do it for them. These consultants are expensive though — they're mostly used by large firms recruiting for highly-paid jobs.

Make a short list of the main points on this page...

You need to know about each stage of the recruitment process. Employing the wrong person is a waste of time and money, and you can't just sack them if you don't like them. That's employment law for you...

Staff Training

Training is the main way that a firm invests in its human resources (i.e. its workers).
A well-trained workforce will usually be more productive and better motivated.

Induction Training is for New Staff

1) Induction training introduces the new employee to their workplace. It usually starts on the first day of the new job.
2) It includes introducing them to their fellow workers and telling them about company rules — including health and safety rules. They should be given a tour of the site so they don't get lost. It may also include some initial training on how to do their new job.
3) It should help to make the new employee feel welcome and meet Maslow's need to belong (see page 50).

On-the-Job Training is Learning by Doing

1) This is the most common form of training. The person learns to do their job better by being shown how to do it — and then practising. It is also sometimes called internal training.
2) It is cost-effective for the employer because the person continues to work while learning.
3) A problem is that it is often taught by a colleague — so bad working practices can be passed on.

Off-the-Job Training can be Internal or External

1) This happens when the person learns away from their workplace. If the firm has its own training department, off-the-job training can be done internally (or in-house). Training that happens outside the business is called external training — for example, a course at a college.
2) It's more expensive than on-the-job training, and sometimes not as directly related to the actual job. But it's often higher quality because it's taught by people who are better qualified to train others.

Appraisal Helps to Identify Training Needs

The appraisal process helps managers to keep track of employees' progress and needs. There are three stages:

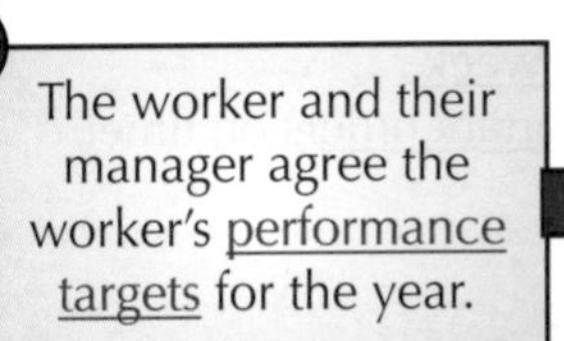

1
The worker and their manager agree the worker's performance targets for the year.

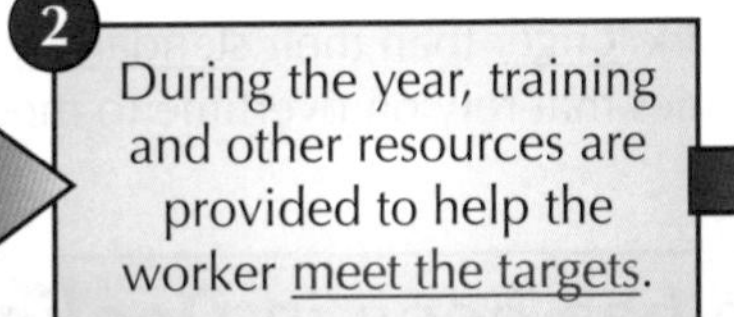

2
During the year, training and other resources are provided to help the worker meet the targets.

3
At the end of the year they meet again to discuss how well the targets were met.

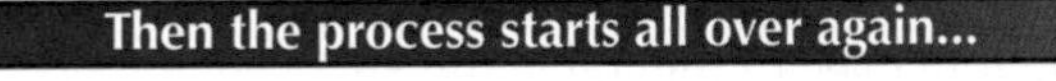

Then the process starts all over again...

1) People who meet or beat their targets could be rewarded with higher pay or a promotion. If a worker does not meet their targets, the manager can decide what action to take to help them improve.
2) Appraisal meetings can cause problems if they're badly managed. If a worker's targets aren't realistic they probably won't meet them — this can demotivate staff. And lack of honesty can be a problem — employees sometimes just say what they think managers want to hear, while some managers just try to avoid upsetting people.

Improve your productivity — train yourself to revise in your sleep...

Your teachers can't really expect you to get your GCSEs without teaching you something first.
It's the same in business — a company can't expect staff to do their jobs properly without training. Easy.

Trade Unions

Trade unions are organisations that try to protect the interests of their members. To join a union, you have to pay a subscription. The union will then do what it can to make your life better.

Trade Unions **Represent** their Members' **Interests**

1) A trade union can sometimes negotiate on behalf of all its members. This is called collective bargaining — members can get a better deal this way than by acting individually.
2) The trade union can help its members to get higher pay, better working conditions, shorter working hours, and legal help in disputes with employers.
3) Not all employers are willing to negotiate with unions. But some employers like collective bargaining as it makes it easier to deal with the workforce.
4) Trade unions can also offer their members social facilities, training and general legal advice.

There are **Two Main Types** of Trade Union

1) **INDUSTRY-SPECIFIC UNIONS** usually only accept members who work in a particular type of job (e.g. teachers, or workers in the retail industry). They're sometimes also called sector-specific unions.

   Some of these unions are very large. USDAW (Union of Shop, Distributive and Allied Workers) has more than 300 000 members, and Unison (a public sector workers' union) has over 1.3 million.

   More specialist unions have relatively few members. Examples include the Association of Flight Attendants and the National Union of Journalists.

2) **GENERAL UNIONS** negotiate for workers in any job from any industry. Examples include the GMB and Unite, Britain's largest trade union (2 million members).

Industrial Disputes Can **Lose Money** for Businesses

An industrial dispute happens when employers and unions can't agree about something important. Trade unions can then organise industrial action — and the business will lose money until the dispute is settled.

1) STRIKE: A group of workers stop working — this costs the firm in lost output and disruption to orders. Striking workers don't get paid by their employer.
2) WORK-TO-RULE: Workers do exactly what their job description says — and nothing more. Some rules are very detailed — workers may be slowed down if they follow them all exactly.
3) GO SLOW: Workers deliberately do their jobs as slowly as possible — again productivity will suffer.
4) OVERTIME BAN: Workers refuse to work longer than their standard working week. This is especially damaging for companies that rely on overtime to meet important orders on time.

Trade Union Membership has been in **Decline**

1) Trade union membership is down from over 12 million in the 1970s to around 7 million today.
2) Laws passed by the Thatcher Government in the 1980s reduced the power of unions. Also, fewer people now work in manufacturing — the sector with the largest number of union members.
3) But the Employment Relations Act (1999) increased union power, forcing some firms to deal with unions.
4) Modern businesses often behave in ways that make it less likely that workers will want to join a union. For example, they might consult their workers about management decisions. And many large businesses now have a works council where workers can discuss their concerns with the management.

You'll have to show some interest in unions to learn this page...

Individual workers can't usually influence a large business, but as part of a trade union they have more power. There are also laws encouraging unions and businesses to cooperate to resolve their differences.

Warm-Up and Worked Exam Questions

Warm-up Questions

1) What is the purpose of a job advertisement?
2) What is the difference between a job description and a person specification?
3) List three kinds of written job application.
4) What is induction training used for?
5) What is the purpose of a trade union?
6) Name four types of industrial action employees may take during an industrial dispute.

Worked Exam Questions

You know the drill by now. Work through these examples, then try the questions on page 60.

1 When Securepath Stores Ltd was taken over by Buy-Right Supermarkets plc, all Securepath employees were invited to apply for jobs in the new Buy-Right stores. Jobs were also advertised in the local press.

a) State the advantages for Buy-Right of recruiting old Securepath employees.

Recruiting would be cheaper ✔[1 mark] and training could be done more quickly ✔[1 mark] because the workers would already know the job.

(2 marks)

b) Suggest the information that should be included in the local press advertisement.

Adverts should describe the jobs available ✔[1 mark] and skills required. ✔[1 mark] Also essential is how and where to ✔[1 mark] apply for the jobs. Rates of pay, training and other ✔[1 mark] benefits offered can be included.

(4 marks)

2 KillAllPests plc uses various training methods for its workforce of pest control operatives.

a) Distinguish between on-the-job training and off-the-job training at KillAllPests plc.

On-the-job training is learning to do the work by being shown how, and then practising ✔[1 mark] e.g. by accompanying existing KillAllPests employees as they work. ✔[1 mark] Off-the-job training means learning away from the workplace, ✔[1 mark] e.g. attending courses on health and safety. ✔[1 mark]

Make sure you apply your answer to KillAllPests plc.

(4 marks)

b) State one problem associated with each type of training.

On-the-job training is often taught by a colleague, so bad habits can be passed on. ✔[1 mark] Off-the-job training can sometimes be too general, and not linked directly to the job the employee will be doing. ✔[1 mark]

It's usually more expensive as well.

(2 marks)

Exam Questions

1 Read **Item B** and then answer the questions that follow.

Item B

Riveted is an engineering firm. They are currently recruiting new operatives to their manufacturing department. Applicants complete an application form and shortlisted candidates are interviewed by the department manager. All candidates invited to interview are also given a number of tests to complete.

a) Explain the advantages of using interviews during the recruitment process.

....

....

....

(3 marks)

b) Suggest one benefit of testing applicants as well as interviewing them.

....

....

(1 mark)

c) Explain **two** benefits to *Riveted* of training all new employees.

....

....

....

....

(4 marks)

d) Many of the company's workers are members of an industrial union. Currently the firm does not negotiate with the union.

Do you think the firm's directors should choose to negotiate with the workers' union? Explain your answer.

....

....

....

....

....

....

(9 marks)

Revision Summary for Section Four

This section is about making sure that the people who work for a business are being treated fairly, and are generally happy and productive.

You need to know about the law, motivation methods, rewards, recruitment, training and trade unions. If you can answer all these questions, you're well on your way...

1) Which of these must all employees be given within two months of starting work?
   a) a contract; b) a pay rise; c) the sack.
2) What information should a business's discipline procedure give to employees?
3) What did the Equal Pay Act of 1970 say?
4) List five things that it's illegal for employers to discriminate on the basis of when employing staff.
5) In what circumstances is it legal for a business to dismiss an employee?
6) Describe some steps that a business must take in order to comply with health and safety legislation.
7) Explain the pros and cons of maternity and paternity leave for a small business.
8) Starting at the bottom, list the five human needs on Maslow's hierarchy — and say what firms can do to help meet each one.
9) If you make decisions alone, but only after consulting your staff, what type of manager are you?
   a) Authoritarian; b) Paternalistic; c) Democratic; d) Quite nice.
10) Give two reasons why motivated staff are good for a business.
11) What's the name of the method of payment when workers are paid by the hour?
12) Explain one problem with the piece rate method of payment.
13) Give an advantage of paying staff a salary.
14) Give one advantage and one disadvantage of employing temporary staff.
15) Give two reasons why different staff in a business might be given different pay.
16) Explain the difference between job rotation, job enlargement and job enrichment. Give one advantage and one disadvantage of each.
17) Give three examples of fringe benefits.
18) Explain the difference between skills and attitudes.
19) Explain the difference between a job description and a person specification.
20) Why might a business want to employ part-time staff?
21) Why do businesses sometimes employ staff that have been personally recommended?
22) Explain the pros and cons of advertising a job: a) internally, b) externally
23) Describe three documents you might be asked to include in a written application for a job.
24) List three things that are assessed in a job interview.
25) Name three types of test a firm might use to help them decide who to employ.
26) Give two advantages of having a well-trained workforce.
27) What should happen during induction training?
28) Explain the difference between on-the-job and off-the-job training.
29) Give one advantage and one disadvantage of on-the-job training.
30) Describe the three stages of the appraisal process.
31) Explain the benefits a trade union gives to its members.
32) Describe the two main types of trade union.
33) Describe four methods of industrial action.

Revenue, Costs and Profit

The stuff on this page is really important — it all hinges on one simple sum: profit = revenue – cost.

Revenue is the Income Earned by a Business

quantity sold
× price
= revenue

1) Businesses earn most of their income from selling their product to customers.
2) Revenue can be calculated by multiplying the quantity sold by the selling price.
   If Britney's Spheres Ltd. sell 20,000 tennis balls at £2 each — their total revenue will be £40,000.

Costs are the Expenses Paid Out to Run the Business

Costs can be divided into Direct and Indirect Costs...

1) Direct costs are expenses that can be attributed to making a particular product.
   Examples include costs of factory labour and raw materials.
2) Indirect costs are the general expenses of running the business.
   Examples include management salaries, telephone bills and office rent.
3) Firms that make more than one product will want each one to earn enough sales revenue to cover its direct costs and make a contribution to indirect costs.
   If all the products together make enough contribution then the business will make a profit.

direct costs
+ indirect costs
= total costs

...or Fixed and Variable Costs

1) Fixed costs do not vary with output. They're mostly indirect costs.
   They have to be paid even if the firm produces nothing.
2) Variable costs are costs that will increase as the firm expands output.
   They're mostly direct costs — factory labour, raw materials and machinery.
3) Some costs are semi-variable — they only vary a little because they have a large fixed element.
   E.g. some workers receive a fixed basic salary — the rest of their pay varies depending on their output.
4) Fixed costs are only fixed over a short period of time — an expanding firm's fixed costs will increase.
5) Firms can work out their break-even level of output if they know fixed and variable costs (see p63).

variable costs
+ fixed costs
= total costs

Average Cost is How Much Each Product Cost to Make

1) To find the average cost of making a product, divide the total cost by output (number of products made).
   To make a profit the firm must charge a higher price than this.

> Britney's Spheres Ltd. output 20,000 tennis balls — the total cost was £30,000.
> The average cost = £30,000 ÷ 20,000 = £1.50 per ball.
> The selling price should be more than £1.50 per ball.

total cost
÷ output
= average cost

2) Average costs usually fall as the firm gets bigger because of economies of scale (see p93).

Profit = Revenue – Costs

Profit is the difference between revenue and costs over a period of time.

> Britney's Spheres Ltd. sells 20,000 tennis balls in a month at £2 each.
> Over the same month its total costs are £30,000.
> Profit = (20,000 × £2) – £30,000 = £40,000 – £30,000.
> So the business makes £10,000 profit in the month.

Average cost — it's neither good nor bad...

Revenue is the money a business earns from selling its products — it's also sometimes called turnover. Price and cost are different things — price is the amount paid by a customer, cost is the amount paid by the producer. Learn all the different types of costs — and how to use all the formulas too.

Break-Even Analysis

The break-even point is the level of output where the firm will just cover its costs. If it sells more, it'll make a profit — if it sells less, it'll make a loss. You need to know how to draw and calculate the break-even point.

A **Break-Even** Chart Shows How Much You Need to **Sell**

To draw a break-even chart you need to know: the fixed costs, the variable costs per unit and the selling price.

1) Pin-Chit Ltd. make padlocks. They have fixed costs of £2000, and the variable cost per unit is £2. The selling price is £4.

Output	Fixed cost	Variable cost	Total cost	Total revenue	Profit
0	2000	0	2000	0	-2000
200	2000	400	2400	800	-1600
400	2000	800	2800	1600	-1200
600	2000	1200	3200	2400	-800
800	2000	1600	3600	3200	-400
1000	2000	2000	4000	4000	0
1200	2000	2400	4400	4800	400
1400	2000	2800	4800	5600	800
1600	2000	3200	5200	6400	1200
1800	2000	3600	5600	7200	1600
2000	2000	4000	6000	8000	2000

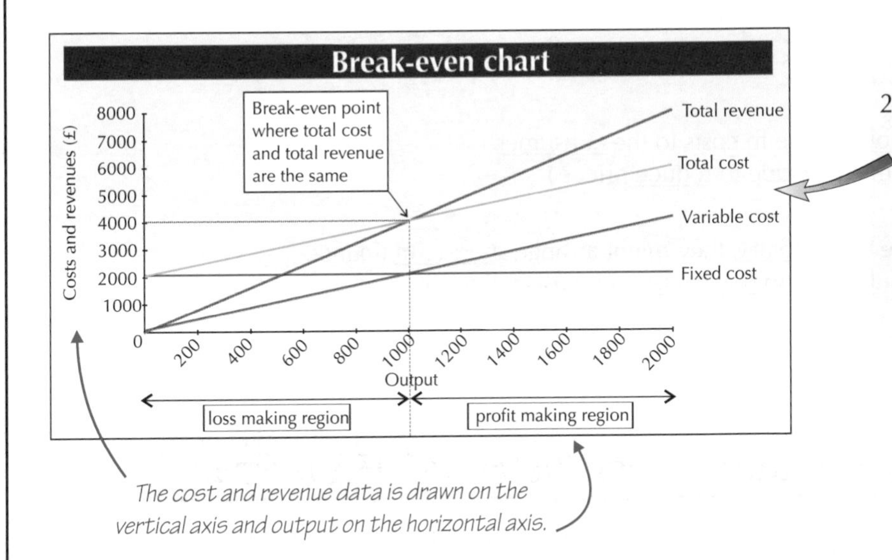

The cost and revenue data is drawn on the vertical axis and output on the horizontal axis.

2) The numbers in the table have been plotted on a graph. The break-even level of output is where total revenue and total costs are equal (the point where the two lines cross on the graph). The firm breaks even if it makes and sells 1000 units.

3) The margin of safety is the gap between the current level of output and the break-even point. If the current output is 1800 units then the margin of safety is 800 units — this means the firm's output will have to fall by 800 units before it starts making a loss.

Break-even charts tell you how much you need to sell, sell, sell...

For your exam, you'll need to know how to draw and read a break-even chart. Make sure you're happy with how to work out the break-even point and the margin of safety as well. A ruler might be handy for some of this.

Break-Even Analysis

It'd be nice and easy for firms if their break-even point always stayed the same — in the real world it varies over time as costs and prices change. It's important to know how these changes affect the break-even point.

Cost Increases or Price Falls Raise the Break-Even Point

1) A rise in costs or a fall in product prices means a firm must sell more products to cover its costs.
2) For example, a rise in rent increases the fixed costs of a business — so they must sell more to cover these higher fixed costs.
3) Pin-Chit Ltd. (see p63) have had their fixed costs increased from £2000 to £3000. The firm must now sell 1500 units instead of 1000 units in order to break even.

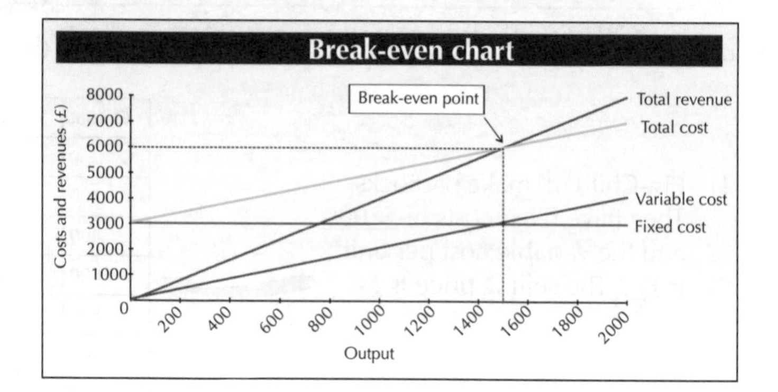

When costs rise, a business can respond in a few different ways.
They can...

1) Keep prices the same, but cut their profit margin (see pages 28 and 79) — this means they will make less money.

2) Try to reduce costs in other ways — improve efficiency, reduce expenses, and so on.

3) Increase prices — this will pass on the rise in costs to the consumer. (If external costs decrease, they might decide to reduce prices.)

4) If the cost increase is temporary, they might arrange short-term finance — which they would hope to pay back when costs fall again.

Cost Decreases or Price Rises Lower the Break-Even Point

1) If a firm gets more money for each product sold, it needs to sell fewer of them to cover its costs.

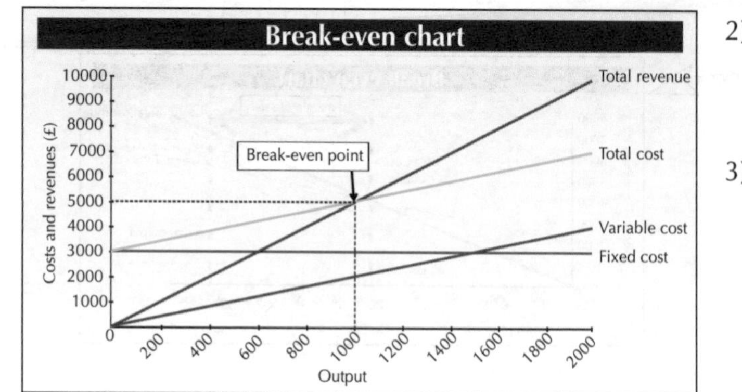

2) The same is true when costs fall. For example, a reduction in raw material costs will lower the variable costs — again, fewer products need to be sold to break even.
3) Pin-Chit Ltd. decide to increase the price of their padlock from £4 to £5. As a result, the firm's break-even output falls back to 1000 units — the level it was at before the increase in costs (see above).

Pin-Chit raise prices to help meet rising external costs — this is Option 3 in the purple box above.

This page charts the rise and fall of costs and prices...

The main thing to take away from this page is how costs and prices can affect the break-even point. It'd be useful to scribble down the four ways a business could respond to their rising costs.

Break-Even Analysis

Drawing a break-even chart can be a bit time-consuming — luckily the break-even point can also be calculated using a cunning formula.

You Can **Calculate** the Break-Even Point

The break-even chart looks pretty, but you don't always need to draw it.
You just need to know:
a) the variable cost per unit,
b) the selling price,
c) the total fixed costs.

In the Pin-Chit example from page 63, these were:
a) the variable cost per unit = £2
b) the selling price = £4
c) the total fixed costs = £2000

This is what you then need to do:

1) First find what's called the contribution per unit.
This is the selling price minus the variable cost per unit.
So here it's £4 – £2 = £2.

2) Now divide the total fixed costs by the contribution per unit.
Fixed costs are £2000 so this calculation is £2000 ÷ £2 = 1000.
And hey presto, that's the right answer.

break-even output = fixed costs ÷ contribution per unit

Break-Even Analysis has its **Benefits** and **Drawbacks**

Break-even analysis makes it relatively simple for a business to estimate the level of output needed in order to make a profit.

This analysis is great in theory but it has problems when used in the real world.

1. It can be difficult to get realistic estimates of revenue and cost figures. E.g. as output increases, the firm may need more machines, bigger offices, etc.

2. It assumes that the firm can sell any quantity of the product at the current price. In reality, the firm may need to reduce prices to sell at high levels of output. It also assumes all products are sold — this doesn't always happen.

Theoretical analysis — not as bad as the name makes it sound...

Make sure you can write about both the benefits and drawbacks of break-even analysis — that'll show the examiners that you really understand the theory. And should pick you up a hefty stack of marks too.
Learn how to use the formula as well — it's another favourite exam topic, so make sure you've got it sussed.

Sources of Finance — Small Firms

You need to know why firms need to raise finance, how they can do it and what each method is best used for.

Firms Need Finance for Five Reasons

Assets are valuable items owned by the business (e.g. equipment, buildings), or money owed to the business.

1) New firms need start-up capital to buy the assets needed to run the business.
2) New firms also need to finance their poor initial cash flow — they'll need to pay their suppliers before they receive money from their customers.
3) All firms need enough cash to meet the day-to-day running of the business — this is called working capital. If a business is struggling, it may need help from finance.
4) Sometimes customers delay payment — finance is needed to cover this shortfall in liquidity (see page 77).
5) Firms may need finance to fund expansion — e.g. they may be moving to larger premises.

Small Firms Have Five Main Sources of Start-up Finance

Small firms may be given money in the form of grants, or they may be able to borrow it — either over a short period or a longer period.

1) GRANTS are often given to qualifying new or small firms — e.g. businesses in areas of high unemployment. Grant providers include the EU, local and national government and charities, e.g. Prince's Youth Trust. Unlike loans they don't have to be repaid.

Short-term sources will lend money for a limited period of time. Examples of short-term sources include:

2) TRADE CREDIT — Rather than expecting the customer to pay cash on delivery, most businesses will issue them with an invoice — this usually gives the customer one or two months to pay. This is useful for a small firm as they have up to 60 days to earn the money needed to pay the debt.
3) OVERDRAFTS let the firm take more money out of its bank account than it currently has in it. However, banks will usually charge interest or fees while the account is overdrawn.

Long-term sources lend money for longer periods, usually more than one year. For example:

4) LOANS — there are three types of loans a small business might take out:
   - Bank loans are often quick and easy to take out — but will need to be repaid with interest. The bank may require collateral — assets the bank can repossess if the loan is not repaid.
   - Loans from friends and family. It can be hard to persuade a bank to lend money to a new business. Borrowing from a friend or family member (or using your own savings) can be a useful alternative.
   - Mortgages are long-term loans (usually more than five years) used to finance buying property. The property is used as collateral. Interest payments are relatively low compared to other borrowing types. A sole trader might use their own house as collateral to borrow money — they risk losing their home if their business fails.
5) VENTURE CAPITAL is money lent by individuals or businesses who specialise in giving finance to new or expanding small firms. In return they often take a stake in the ownership of the business.

New and Small Firms Can Find it Hard to Raise Finance

1) Banks can be reluctant to lend to new or small firms — compared to larger firms, there is a greater risk that they will be unable to repay the loan.
2) New firms that haven't yet made much profit may not have enough spare cash to fund new investments.

Learn these sources of finance — it'll help you in the long term...

Lots of facts on this page — make sure you can write down every source of finance for a small firm and try to remember one problem with each. Learn, cover the page and start scribbling.

Sources of Finance — Large Firms

Larger firms find it easier to raise finance than smaller firms. Being bigger and more established means they are less likely to go bankrupt — so they are less of a credit risk to banks.

Established Firms Have Other Sources of Funds Available

As well as the sources on page 66, established firms can use these methods to get funds:

1) RETAINED PROFITS are profits that the owners have decided to plough back into the business after they've paid themselves a dividend. But larger companies (e.g. PLCs — see page 4) are under pressure from shareholders to give large dividends, reducing the amount of profit they can retain.
2) FIXED ASSETS Firms can raise cash by selling fixed assets (e.g. machinery/buildings) that are no longer in use. There is a limit to how many assets you can sell, though — sell too many and you can't go on trading.
3) SHARES A limited company (see page 4) can issue more shares. The money raised does not have to be repaid to shareholders — but more shares means less control for the existing owners.
4) DEBENTURES Limited companies can issue debentures to the public. These are long-term loans which the firm commits itself to repay with interest — for up to 25 years or so. People who are issued with debentures don't own any part of the business — they only lend the business money.

Finance can be Classed as Internal or External

1) Internal finance comes from inside the business. It can be a quick and easy way to get money. It saves borrowing and having to pay back interest.
2) External finance comes from outside the business. It usually needs to be paid back (e.g. loans) — sometimes with high interest.

Internal Sources include...
- Personal or business savings
- Retained profits
- Selling fixed assets

External Sources include...
- Bank loans and overdrafts
- Venture capital
- Debentures and new share issues
- Trade credit
- Grants

Four Factors Affect the Choice of Finance

1. SIZE AND TYPE OF COMPANY — not all companies have access to all types of finance:
   - Some types of business may not have fixed assets available to sell.
   - Small businesses are unable to issue new shares and may also find it hard to get loans or overdrafts.

2. AMOUNT OF MONEY NEEDED — a company wouldn't issue more shares to buy a toaster. Small amounts of money usually come from internal sources. For larger amounts of money (e.g. for new property or machinery), the firm is more likely to need an external source of finance.

3. LENGTH OF TIME the finance is needed for — it'd be daft to take out a mortgage because a customer is a week late paying an invoice. Using savings or an arranged overdraft from a bank should be able to see a business through a short-term lack of finance.

4. COST OF THE FINANCE — some sources, e.g. bank loans and overdrafts are more expensive than others as the money has to be paid back with interest.

The source of finance depends on what the money's for...

Examiners love to test whether you can identify the right source of finance to meet the needs of a business. You need to know the different sources of finance and the factors that affect which source a firm will choose.

Warm-Up and Worked Exam Questions

Warm-up Questions

1) Give three examples of indirect costs in business.
2) Complete the following formula: **"variable costs + fixed costs = ... "**
3) Give the formula used to calculate average cost.
4) Why is the break-even point important to a firm?
5) What is meant by working capital?
6) Give four factors that affect the type of finance a company chooses.

Worked Exam Questions

The types of finance available to businesses are a popular topic with examiners.
Have a look at the worked exam questions below.

1 Bird Homes Ltd is a small business selling luxury bird boxes to gardeners.
Each box is sold for £25. Fixed costs are £15,000 and variable costs are £15 per box.

a) How many bird boxes must the company sell to break even?

Unit contribution = selling price – variable costs: £25 – £15 = £10 ✔[1 mark]

Break-even point = fixed costs ÷ unit contribution:

£15,000 ÷ £10 = 1500 bird boxes ✔[1 mark]

It's always a good idea to state the formulae — that'll earn you marks even if you get some of the working wrong.

(2 marks)

b) With reference to Bird Homes Ltd, explain how break-even analysis is limited in the real world.

"With reference to Bird Homes Ltd" is the most important thing to notice here.

As output rises, more machinery and larger premises might be needed, so fixed costs can change. ✔[1 mark] *Break-even analysis assumes that Bird Homes Ltd can sell any quantity of the bird boxes at £25 each,* ✔[1 mark] *which is unlikely in the real world* ✔[1 mark] *— to sell large quantities they may need to reduce their price.* ✔[1 mark]

(4 marks)

2 Explain why retained profits can be a useful source of funds for a business.
Why might shareholders prefer profits not to be used in this way?

Using retained profits should be cheaper than using loans, ✔[1 mark] *which need to be paid back with interest.* ✔[1 mark] *It also avoids the complications of issuing new shares,* ✔[1 mark] *such as the loss of control for the existing shareholders.* ✔[1 mark] *However, shareholders might prefer profits to be paid out as dividends rather than reinvested in the business.* ✔[1 mark]

(5 marks)

Exam Questions

1 Joe Morris, a sole trader, owns a garden centre and sells 50,000 trays of bedding plants in a year. His total costs are £100,000 for the year.

a) Calculate the average cost of each tray.

....

....

....

(2 marks)

b) The following year, Joe's total costs are £110,000, but the average cost of each tray stays the same. How many trays does Joe make in that year?

....

....

....

(2 marks)

c) Joe wants to expand his greenhouse capacity. He owns the land, but the materials, heating, and watering facilities will cost £50,000. Explain two methods of external finance Joe could use for this project, and outline the risk each carries.

....

....

....

....

....

....

....

(6 marks)

2 Becky and her sister Gemma plan to start a small travel agency, organising holidays for disabled clients. Explain why they will need finance to set up the business.

....

....

....

....

....

(4 marks)

Cash Flow

One of the most important parts of any budget is the cash-flow forecast.
More profitable businesses go bankrupt because of poor cash flow than for any other reason.

Cash Flow is **More Than Just Profits**

1) Cash flow is the flow of all money into and out of the business. When a firm sells its products, money flows in. When it buys materials or pays wages, money flows out. It's a bit like water flowing into a bath through the tap and out through the plughole.
2) Net cash flow is the difference between cash inflow and cash outflow over a period of time.
3) Cash flow's important because if there's not enough money flowing in, you don't have enough to pay your bills.

Poor Cash Flow Means You've Got **Big Problems**

1) Poor cash flow means there is not enough cash in the business to meet its day-to-day expenses — there is a lack of working capital.
2) Staff may not get paid on time — this will cause resentment and poor motivation.
3) Some suppliers offer discounts for prompt payment of invoices — the business will not be able to take advantage of these.
4) Creditors may not get paid on time — they may insist on stricter credit terms in future.
5) Some creditors may not wait for payment — they might take legal action to recover the debt. If the business does not have the money it may go into receivership (a 'receiver' is appointed to reclaim money owed to the creditors by selling off a struggling firm's assets) or be forced to cease trading.

Cash Flow **Forecasts** Help Firms to **Anticipate Problems**

1) A cash flow forecast is a good way of predicting when the firm might face a liquidity problem (lack of cash). It lists all the inflows and outflows of cash that appear in the budget.
2) The firm will see when an overdraft or other short-term finance might be needed.
3) The forecast needs to be watched carefully — to monitor the impact of unexpected cash flows.
4) Here's an example of a cash flow forecast for a firm publishing football magazines. In summer, when the football season's over, the net cash flow is negative because more money flows out than in.
5) The firm can see it will need an overdraft to get it through from June to September.
6) It's useful to know this in advance because it means the firm can plan — it won't suddenly have to panic in June when it starts to run out of money.

Businesses forecast their sales volume to estimate what their revenue will be (over a given period of time) — these predictions are often based on sales from previous months or years, and the firm's best guess.

Cash Flow Forecast — Fanzines of Football Ltd.

	April	May	June	July	August	Sept
Total receipts (cash inflow)	15,000	12,000	5,000	5,000	16,000	16,000
Total spending (cash outflow)	12,000	12,000	10,000	10,000	12,000	12,000
Net cash flow (inflow – outflow)	3,000	0	-5,000	-5,000	4,000	4,000
Bank balance at start of month	1,000	4,000	4,000	-1,000	-6,000	-2,000
Bank balance at end of month	4,000	4,000	-1,000	-6,000	-2,000	2000

Cash outflow — it's just money down the drain...

Cash flow is quite easy — once you've understood how the figures are worked out, that is.
Make sure you can understand the figures in that table, and that you know why cash flow is important.

Cash Flow

Businesses have certain tricks that they can use to help improve their cash flow.

Credit Terms Can Affect Cash Flow

Credit terms tell you how long after agreeing to buy a product the customer has to pay. This can affect the timings of a business's cash flows.

1) Stuffin's Turkeys Ltd. sell most of their products in December.
2) This table assumes customers pay cash when they purchase the product.

Cash Flow Forecast — Stuffin's Turkeys Ltd.

	October	November	December	January	February	March
Total receipts (cash inflow)	800	1500	12000	300	500	300
Total payments (cash outflow)	3000	4000	2000	300	200	150
Net cash flow	-2200	-2500	10000	0	300	150
Bank balance at start of month	3000	800	-1700	8300	8300	8600
Bank balance at end of month	800	-1700	8300	8300	8600	8750

bank balance at end of month = bank balance at start of month + net cash flow

3) This table assumes customers are given 60 days credit to pay.

This table is a bit more complicated as the receipts come in two months after the sales are made.

Cash Flow Forecast — Stuffin's Turkeys Ltd.

	October	November	December	January	February	March
Total sales this month (for payment in 60 days)	800	1500	12000	300	500	300
Total receipts (cash inflow)	200	200	800	1500	12000	300
Total payments (cash outflow)	3000	4000	2000	300	200	150
Net cash flow	-2800	-3800	-1200	1200	11800	150
Bank balance at start of month	3000	200	-3600	-4800	-3600	8200
Bank balance at end of month	200	-3600	-4800	-3600	8200	8350

Payment made in 2 months

In February, the total receipts are for the turkeys bought in December. So net cash flow is 12000 – 200 = 11800

4) The main differences are:
   - when customers pay cash there is only one month where short-term finance is needed.
   - when they pay on 60 days credit the business will need to arrange short-term finance for 3 months.

Businesses Can Improve Cash Flow in Three Ways

1) Businesses can give their customers less generous credit terms or insist they pay by cash.
2) They can try to get better credit terms from their suppliers — ideally, the credit period given to customers should be less than the credit period obtained from suppliers.
3) Most firms carry a stock of unsold products — they could simply sell these instead of making more.
   - By destocking, the cash inflows will be the same — but cash outflows will be reduced as less will be spent on raw materials.
   - It's only a short-term solution, though. Eventually they'll run out of stock and will have to start paying out money to make more products.

Take your time with this page — just go with the flow...

Ultimately, all solutions to cash flow problems come down to doing two things — reducing cash outflows and increasing cash inflows. Make sure you can list the tricks used by businesses to help their cash flow.

The Trading, Profit and Loss Account

The trading, profit and loss account records the difference between the firm's income and the cost of running the business over a period of one year. The next two pages describe the three sections it contains.

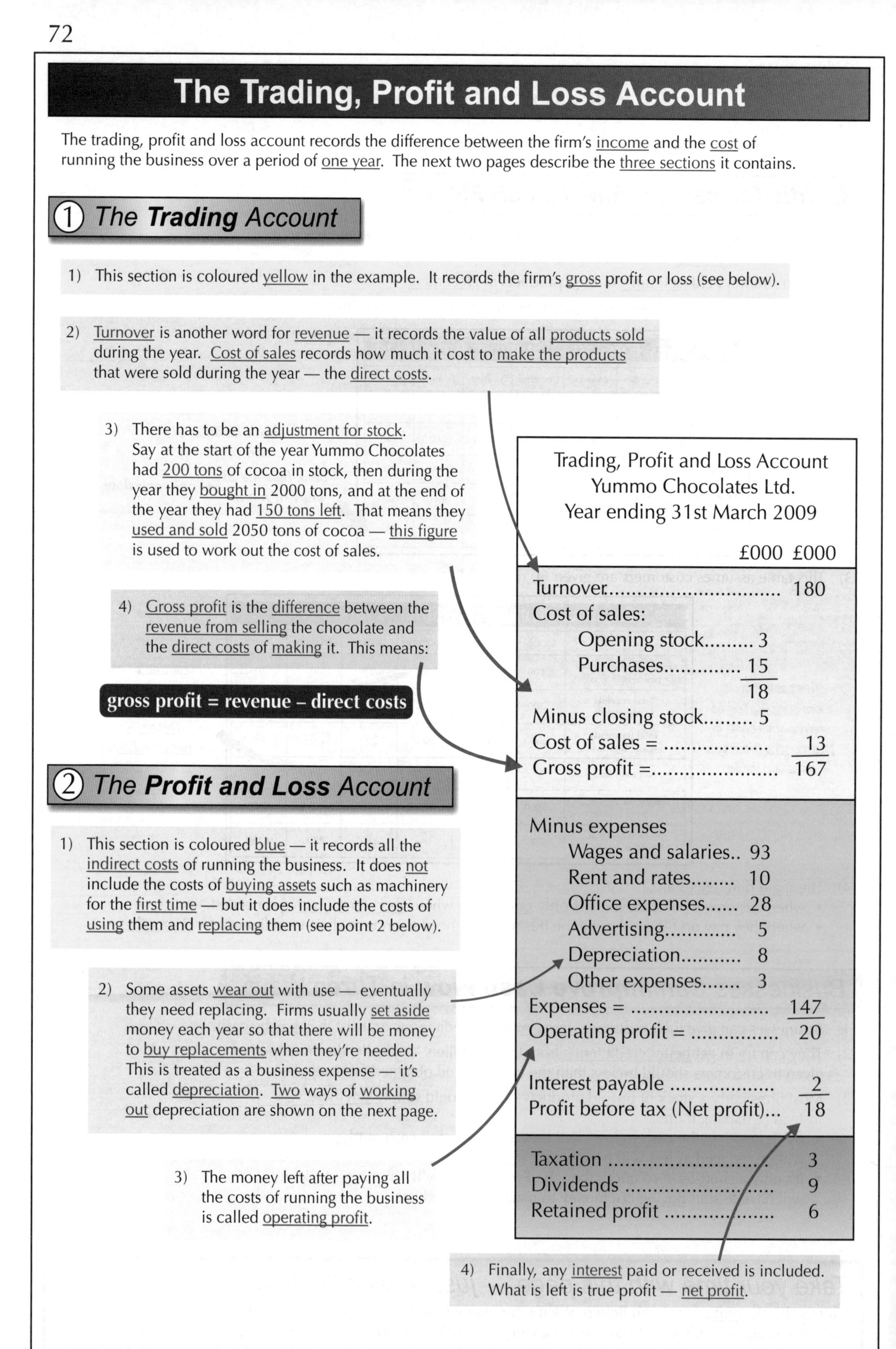

① The Trading Account

1) This section is coloured yellow in the example. It records the firm's gross profit or loss (see below).

2) Turnover is another word for revenue — it records the value of all products sold during the year. Cost of sales records how much it cost to make the products that were sold during the year — the direct costs.

3) There has to be an adjustment for stock. Say at the start of the year Yummo Chocolates had 200 tons of cocoa in stock, then during the year they bought in 2000 tons, and at the end of the year they had 150 tons left. That means they used and sold 2050 tons of cocoa — this figure is used to work out the cost of sales.

4) Gross profit is the difference between the revenue from selling the chocolate and the direct costs of making it. This means:

gross profit = revenue – direct costs

② The Profit and Loss Account

1) This section is coloured blue — it records all the indirect costs of running the business. It does not include the costs of buying assets such as machinery for the first time — but it does include the costs of using them and replacing them (see point 2 below).

2) Some assets wear out with use — eventually they need replacing. Firms usually set aside money each year so that there will be money to buy replacements when they're needed. This is treated as a business expense — it's called depreciation. Two ways of working out depreciation are shown on the next page.

3) The money left after paying all the costs of running the business is called operating profit.

4) Finally, any interest paid or received is included. What is left is true profit — net profit.

Trading, Profit and Loss Account
Yummo Chocolates Ltd.
Year ending 31st March 2009

	£000	£000
Turnover		180
Cost of sales:		
Opening stock	3	
Purchases	15	
	18	
Minus closing stock	5	
Cost of sales =		13
Gross profit =		167
Minus expenses		
Wages and salaries	93	
Rent and rates	10	
Office expenses	28	
Advertising	5	
Depreciation	8	
Other expenses	3	
Expenses =		147
Operating profit =		20
Interest payable		2
Profit before tax (Net profit)		18
Taxation		3
Dividends		9
Retained profit		6

The Trading, Profit and Loss Account

3 The Appropriation Account

1) Coloured purple on the example. This is only included for limited company accounts.
2) It records where the profit has gone — to the government as tax, to shareholders as dividends, or kept in the business as retained profit.

There are Two Methods of Calculating Depreciation

1. Straight-line method. This is the easy way. If a machine costs £5000 and will wear out after about 5 years, the depreciation is simply £1000 each year.

2. Reducing-balance method. This depreciates the machinery by a percentage of its value each year — a £5000 machine might depreciate by 25% each year.
   - Depreciation in year 1 = 25% of £5000 = £1250. The value is now £5000 – £1250 = £3750.
   - Depreciation in year 2 = 25% of £3750 = £938. The value is now £3750 – £938 = £2812. And so on.

Profit and Loss Accounts are Useful for a Firm's Stakeholders

Profit and loss accounts can show how well a business is doing — a firm's stakeholders will be interested in this information for lots of different reasons...

1) Existing shareholders are usually entitled to a share of the profits (called the share dividend). Potential shareholders will look at how much profit the business makes to help them decide if the business is worth investing in.
   Shareholders may also use the profit and loss account to assess the performance of the directors who are responsible for running the business.

2) Employees will want to know if the business is making a profit or loss — a profitable business could afford to give them a pay rise, but a loss-making business might make some workers redundant.

3) The government receives corporation tax from the business. The profit and loss account is used to calculate how much tax the business needs to pay.

Remember the 3 sections of the trading, profit and loss account...

Some of this is a bit tricky, so take your time and make sure you know what is included in each part of the accounts and why. Memorise and copy out the headings — then explain what each one means. Covering the page and scribbling down all the people who might be interested in the profit and loss accounts will be useful too.

The Trading, Profit and Loss Account

Yep, you guessed it — another page all about profit and loss accounts. You need to know how you can use profit and loss accounts to see how a business is performing. This page points out some key things to look out for...

*Profit and Loss Accounts **Show** Business **Performance***

The profit and loss accounts from two consecutive years for a yacht-building firm are shown below:

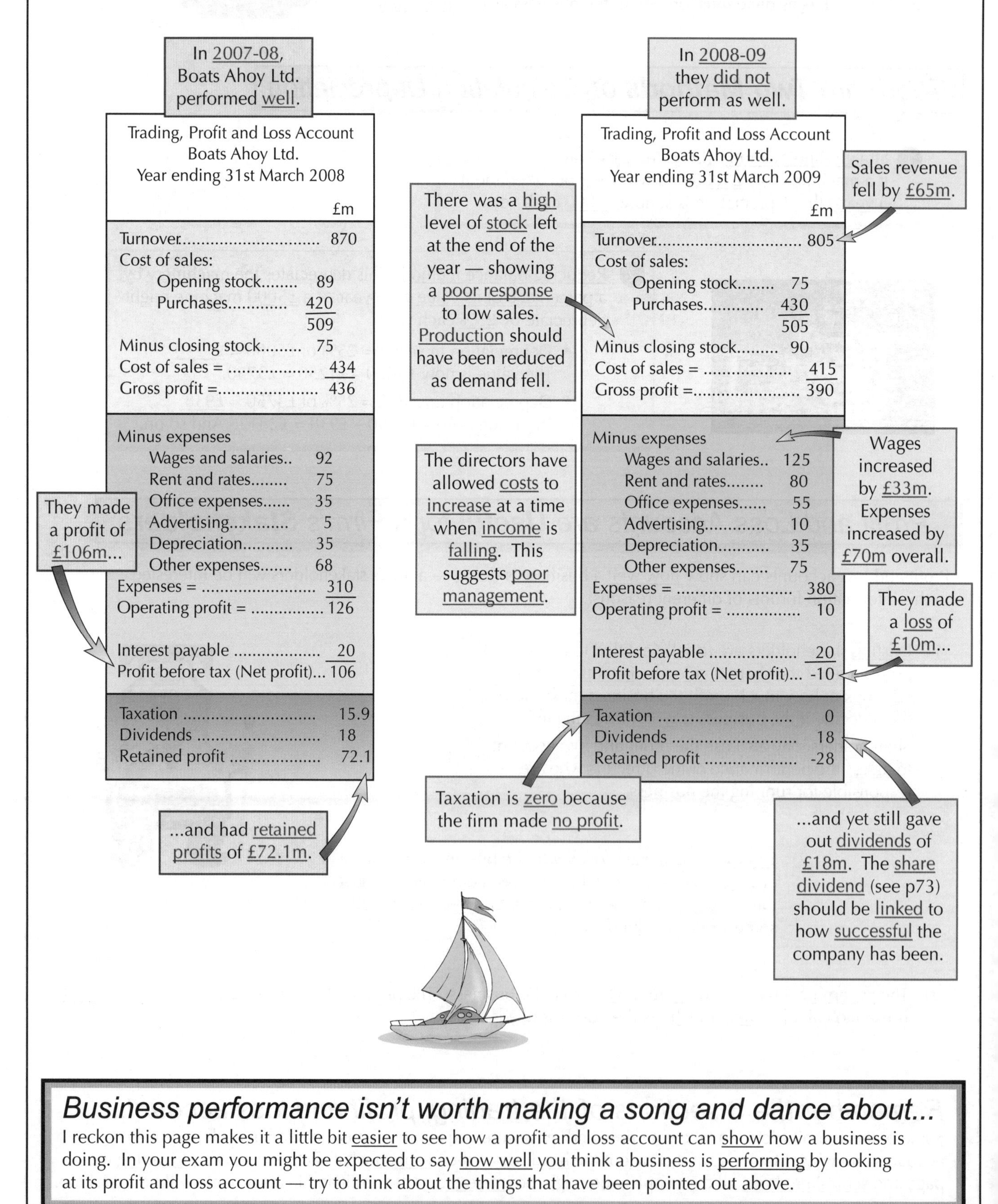

Trading, Profit and Loss Account
Boats Ahoy Ltd.
Year ending 31st March 2008

		£m
Turnover		870
Cost of sales:		
Opening stock	89	
Purchases	420	
	509	
Minus closing stock	75	
Cost of sales =		434
Gross profit =		436
Minus expenses		
Wages and salaries	92	
Rent and rates	75	
Office expenses	35	
Advertising	5	
Depreciation	35	
Other expenses	68	
Expenses =		310
Operating profit =		126
Interest payable		20
Profit before tax (Net profit)		106
Taxation		15.9
Dividends		18
Retained profit		72.1

Trading, Profit and Loss Account
Boats Ahoy Ltd.
Year ending 31st March 2009

		£m
Turnover		805
Cost of sales:		
Opening stock	75	
Purchases	430	
	505	
Minus closing stock	90	
Cost of sales =		415
Gross profit =		390
Minus expenses		
Wages and salaries	125	
Rent and rates	80	
Office expenses	55	
Advertising	10	
Depreciation	35	
Other expenses	75	
Expenses =		380
Operating profit =		10
Interest payable		20
Profit before tax (Net profit)		-10
Taxation		0
Dividends		18
Retained profit		-28

In 2007-08, Boats Ahoy Ltd. performed well.
They made a profit of £106m...
...and had retained profits of £72.1m.
There was a high level of stock left at the end of the year — showing a poor response to low sales. Production should have been reduced as demand fell.
The directors have allowed costs to increase at a time when income is falling. This suggests poor management.
Taxation is zero because the firm made no profit.
In 2008-09 they did not perform as well.
Sales revenue fell by £65m.
Wages increased by £33m. Expenses increased by £70m overall.
They made a loss of £10m...
...and yet still gave out dividends of £18m. The share dividend (see p73) should be linked to how successful the company has been.

Business performance isn't worth making a song and dance about...

I reckon this page makes it a little bit easier to see how a profit and loss account can show how a business is doing. In your exam you might be expected to say how well you think a business is performing by looking at its profit and loss account — try to think about the things that have been pointed out above.

Warm-Up and Worked Exam Questions

Warm-up Questions

1) "A cash flow forecast shows how much profit a firm is making." Is this statement true or false?
2) Which costs are included in the trading account — direct or indirect?
3) How is gross profit calculated?
4) What does an appropriation account show?
5) What is depreciation?
6) A firm buys a new van for £35,000. It expects to scrap it after five years. How much depreciation should be charged each year if the firm uses the straight-line method?

Worked Exam Question

Budgeting is crucial for all businesses, and it's really important for your Business Studies GCSE. Have a look at this worked exam question.

1 Amuse Yourself Ltd is an amusement arcade in a busy seaside town. It has drawn up the following cash flow forecast.

Cash Flow Forecast for Amuse Yourself Ltd (£000's)

	Jan	Feb	Mar	Apr	May	Jun
Revenue						
Sales	10	15	15	20	18	22
Total Revenue	10	15	15	20	**E**	22
Payments						
Rent	2	2	2	2	2	2
Wages	12	12	13	13	13	**F**
Other Payments	7	2	3	1	2	2
Total Payments	21	**B**	18	16	17	18
Net Cash Flow	**A**	–1	–3	4	1	4
Balance (start of month)	10	–1	–2	**D**	–1	0
Balance (end of month)	–1	–2	**C**	–1	0	4

a) Calculate the amounts of money represented by the letters A to F.

A = £10k – £21k = –£11 000. ✔[1 mark] *B = £2k + £12k + £2k = £16 000.* ✔[1 mark]

C = –£2k – £3k = –£5000. ✔[1 mark] *D = C = –£5000* ✔[1 mark] *E = £18 000.* ✔[1 mark]

F = £18k – £2k – £2k = £14 000. ✔[1 mark]

There are 6 marks available here — take care with your maths and you should get them all.

(6 marks)

b) Explain what the company could do to improve its cash flow.

The company could try either to increase the money coming in from sales, ✔[1 mark] *perhaps by having special promotions or changing their advertising.* ✔[1 mark] *Or it could decrease its outgoings,* ✔[1 mark] *perhaps by decreasing wages or making a worker redundant.* ✔[1 mark]

(4 marks)

Exam Questions

1 See-Saw plc manufactures playground equipment.
Use the information in this trading, profit and loss account to answer the questions below:

Trading, Profit & Loss Account for See-Saw plc

Year ending 31st March, 2009

		£000's	£000's
Sales	Revenue		120
	Cost of Sales:		
	Opening Stock	50	
	Purchases	35	
		85	
	Closing stock	35	
	Total Cost of Sales		50
	GROSS PROFIT		**A**
Expenses	Rent	6	
	Wages	40	
	Advertising	5	
	Other Expenses	8	
	Total Expenses		**B**
	NET PROFIT		11

a) Calculate the amounts of money represented by A and B.

A: ....

....

B: ....

....

(2 marks)

b) Explain the difference between gross profit and net profit.

....

....

....

(3 marks)

c) The directors of See-Saw plc have applied for a bank loan to finance a planned expansion. Why might the bank manager wish to see the company's trading, profit and loss account before granting See-Saw a loan? What information might they hope to gain?

....

....

....

....

(5 marks)

The Balance Sheet — Net Assets

The balance sheet is quite tricky — but the basic idea is pretty simple. It records where the business got its money from, and what it has done with it. The two balance out exactly — hence the name.

Balance sheets include the business figures that aren't covered on profit and loss accounts (and vice-versa). They show the values of assets and capital on a particular date — usually the last day of the financial year.

Fixed Assets will Last for *More Than One Year*

1) The business has used some money to buy fixed assets — premises, machinery, vehicles.
2) This figure is what they're worth on the date of the balance sheet — they'll have depreciated since they were bought, but that's all taken care of in the profit and loss account.

BALANCE SHEET

Yummo Chocolates Ltd., 31st March 2009

	£000	£000
Fixed Assets		
Premises		80
Machinery		40
Vehicles		30
		150
Current Assets		
Stock	5	
Debtors	12	
Cash	3	
	20	
Current Liabilities		
Creditors	14	
Unpaid Corporation Tax	1	
	15	
Net Current Assets (Working Capital)		5
Net Assets		155
Shareholders' Funds		
Share Capital		80
Retain		50
Long-term		
Bank L		20
Deben		5
Capital Employed		155

Current Assets – Current Liabilities

Fixed Assets + Net Current Assets

This purple bit is the Capital Employed section — see the next page.

Current Assets Last a *Few Months*

1) These are listed in increasing order of liquidity.
2) Stock is the least liquid. It includes raw materials and finished products that the firm has spent its money on but which have not yet been sold.
3) Debtors shows the value of products sold — usually on credit — that have not yet been paid for by the customers. What's happening here is that the firm is lending its money to customers so they can buy its products.
4) Cash is the most liquid. This is money the firm hasn't spent on anything yet — it's just kept it as cash.

The liquidity of an asset tells you how easy it is to convert into money.

Current Liabilities are Bills the Firm Has to *Pay Soon*

1) These are any payments the firm will have to make within one year of the date on the balance sheet. Creditors is the opposite of debtors — it is money the firm owes to its suppliers. Also included is any unpaid corporation tax — payable to the government out of the previous year's profits — as well as any unpaid dividends to shareholders (there aren't any for Yummo this year, so this figure's not shown).
2) This is all money which doesn't really belong to the firm, since it's going to have to pay it to someone else pretty soon. So you take this away from the current assets figure...

Current Assets – Current Liabilities = *Net Current Assets*

1) The net current assets figure is what you get when you subtract those current liabilities from the current assets. It's also called working capital (see page 66).
2) Add the net current assets to the fixed assets and you get the net assets, or net worth, of the business. This is the amount the firm would make if it sold all its assets (in theory) — it's what the firm is worth.

Both these calculations are labelled on the balance sheet above.

'Current' means 'due to be paid in the next year'...

I told you this was tricky. You're gonna finish this off on the next page — for now, make sure you know the names of all the headings and their meanings, and that you understand why current liabilities are taken away.

The Balance Sheet — Capital Employed

Now for the second part of the balance sheet — where did all the money come from to create the net worth of the business. Originally it came from shareholders buying the shares, and money loaned to it by other people — over the years this will be added to with profit that the firm has retained, and possibly more loans.

Shareholders' Funds Came from the *Firm's Owners*

1) **SHARE CAPITAL** is the money put into the business when shares were originally issued. This might have been years and years ago for long-established companies.

   This is not the same as what the shares are currently worth. Most shares traded on the stock exchange are second-hand — the person selling them gets the cash, not the firm.

   Firms can raise new capital by issuing new shares. The usual way is to have a rights issue. This is where existing shareholders are offered new shares at a reduced price.

This is the Capital Employed section from Yummo Chocolates' balance sheet (see previous page).

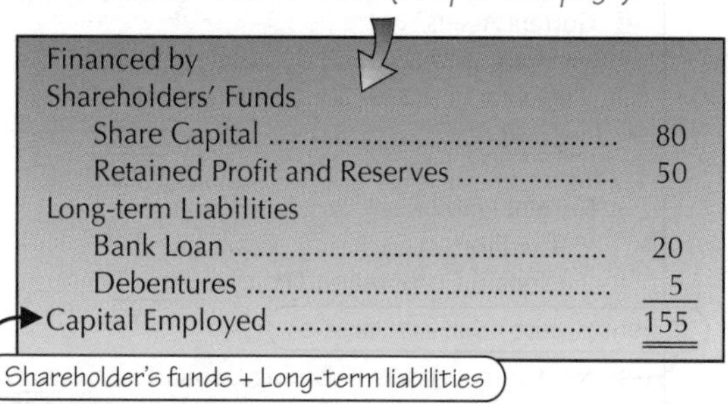

Financed by	
Shareholders' Funds	
Share Capital	80
Retained Profit and Reserves	50
Long-term Liabilities	
Bank Loan	20
Debentures	5
Capital Employed	155

2) **RETAINED PROFIT AND RESERVES** shows all the profit that the firm has made over the years that it has decided to retain instead of paying in dividends. Firms retain profit to finance future investment or to protect the firm against future problems.

   This comes under "shareholders' funds" because profits are really the shareholders' money — they've just decided to leave it in the firm rather than take it out as dividends.

Long-term Liabilities — Money *Owed to Others*

1) Firms don't just get money from their shareholders — they borrow it from other people as well. Included here are any debts that will take more than one year to repay — bank loans and debentures. They were covered in the stuff on sources of finance (pages 66-67).
2) Debts payable in less than a year come under current liabilities instead — see the previous page. It's all money the company owes, but it's conventional to split it up like that.

Capital Employed is the *Total* Put Into the Business

1) Capital employed is what you get when you add shareholders' funds and total liabilities (see diagram). This is equal to net assets because it shows where the money to fund them came from.
2) If you're confused, think about it this way — all the money the business has got (from shareholders and borrowing from other people) is accounted for by capital employed. And everything it's done with the money it got (bought premises, kept it as cash, etc.) is listed under net assets. They have to be the same — because money doesn't just vanish.

The *Balance Sheet* is Useful to *Stakeholders*

1) Stakeholders use the balance sheet to assess the financial health of a business.
2) The net assets figure from the balance sheet can show this. A business whose net assets are growing each year is probably healthy, because it's increasing the value of its fixed assets and its cash reserves.
3) On the other hand, a business with low or negative net assets may be unhealthy. It might be borrowing money to finance short-term assets — such as unsold stock, or debtors who may not pay their bills.

Share capital — but I want to keep it all for myself...

These two pages are worth struggling with until you've understood all of it. Explain what all the headings mean — then make sure you can explain why the whole thing is called a balance sheet.

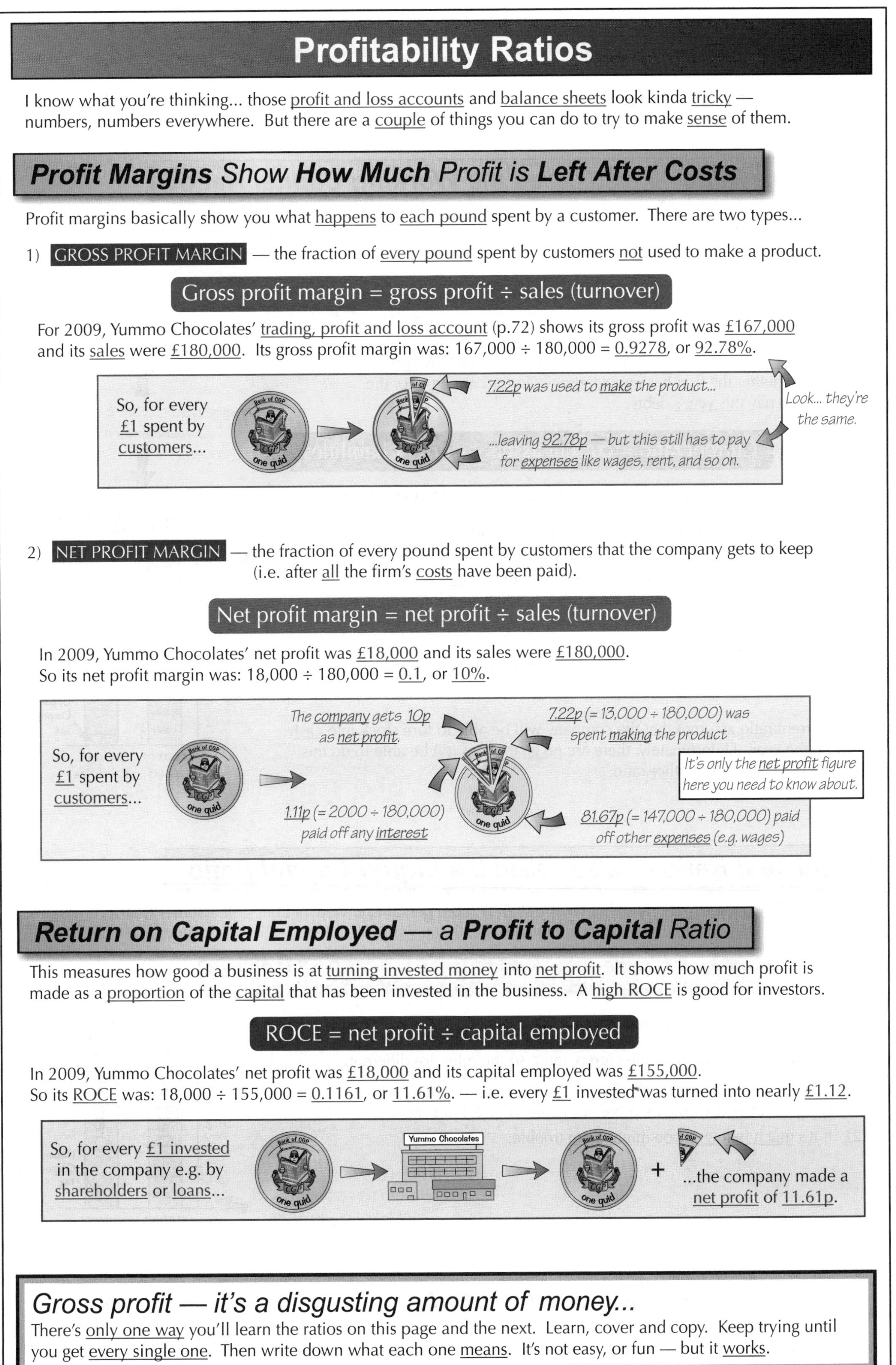

Profitability Ratios

I know what you're thinking... those profit and loss accounts and balance sheets look kinda tricky — numbers, numbers everywhere. But there are a couple of things you can do to try to make sense of them.

Profit Margins Show *How Much* Profit is *Left After Costs*

Profit margins basically show you what happens to each pound spent by a customer. There are two types...

1) **GROSS PROFIT MARGIN** — the fraction of every pound spent by customers not used to make a product.

Gross profit margin = gross profit ÷ sales (turnover)

For 2009, Yummo Chocolates' trading, profit and loss account (p.72) shows its gross profit was £167,000 and its sales were £180,000. Its gross profit margin was: 167,000 ÷ 180,000 = 0.9278, or 92.78%.

So, for every £1 spent by customers...
Bank of CGP
one quid
7.22p was used to make the product...
...leaving 92.78p — but this still has to pay for expenses like wages, rent, and so on.
Look... they're the same.

2) **NET PROFIT MARGIN** — the fraction of every pound spent by customers that the company gets to keep (i.e. after all the firm's costs have been paid).

Net profit margin = net profit ÷ sales (turnover)

In 2009, Yummo Chocolates' net profit was £18,000 and its sales were £180,000.
So its net profit margin was: 18,000 ÷ 180,000 = 0.1, or 10%.

So, for every £1 spent by customers...
Bank of CGP
one quid
The company gets 10p as net profit.
7.22p (= 13,000 ÷ 180,000) was spent making the product
1.11p (= 2000 ÷ 180,000) paid off any interest
81.67p (= 147,000 ÷ 180,000) paid off other expenses (e.g. wages)
It's only the net profit figure here you need to know about.

Return on Capital Employed — a *Profit to Capital* Ratio

This measures how good a business is at turning invested money into net profit. It shows how much profit is made as a proportion of the capital that has been invested in the business. A high ROCE is good for investors.

ROCE = net profit ÷ capital employed

In 2009, Yummo Chocolates' net profit was £18,000 and its capital employed was £155,000.
So its ROCE was: 18,000 ÷ 155,000 = 0.1161, or 11.61%. — i.e. every £1 invested was turned into nearly £1.12.

So, for every £1 invested in the company e.g. by shareholders or loans...
Bank of CGP
one quid
Yummo Chocolates
+
...the company made a net profit of 11.61p.

Gross profit — it's a disgusting amount of money...

There's only one way you'll learn the ratios on this page and the next. Learn, cover and copy. Keep trying until you get every single one. Then write down what each one means. It's not easy, or fun — but it works.

Liquidity Ratios

Liquidity ratios tell you how easy it is for a business to pay off this year's current liabilities (this year's bills) using their current assets (money and existing stock).

Current Ratio — also called the Working Capital Ratio

The middle part of a balance sheet shows a firm's current assets and current liabilities. ('Current' means 'this year', basically.)

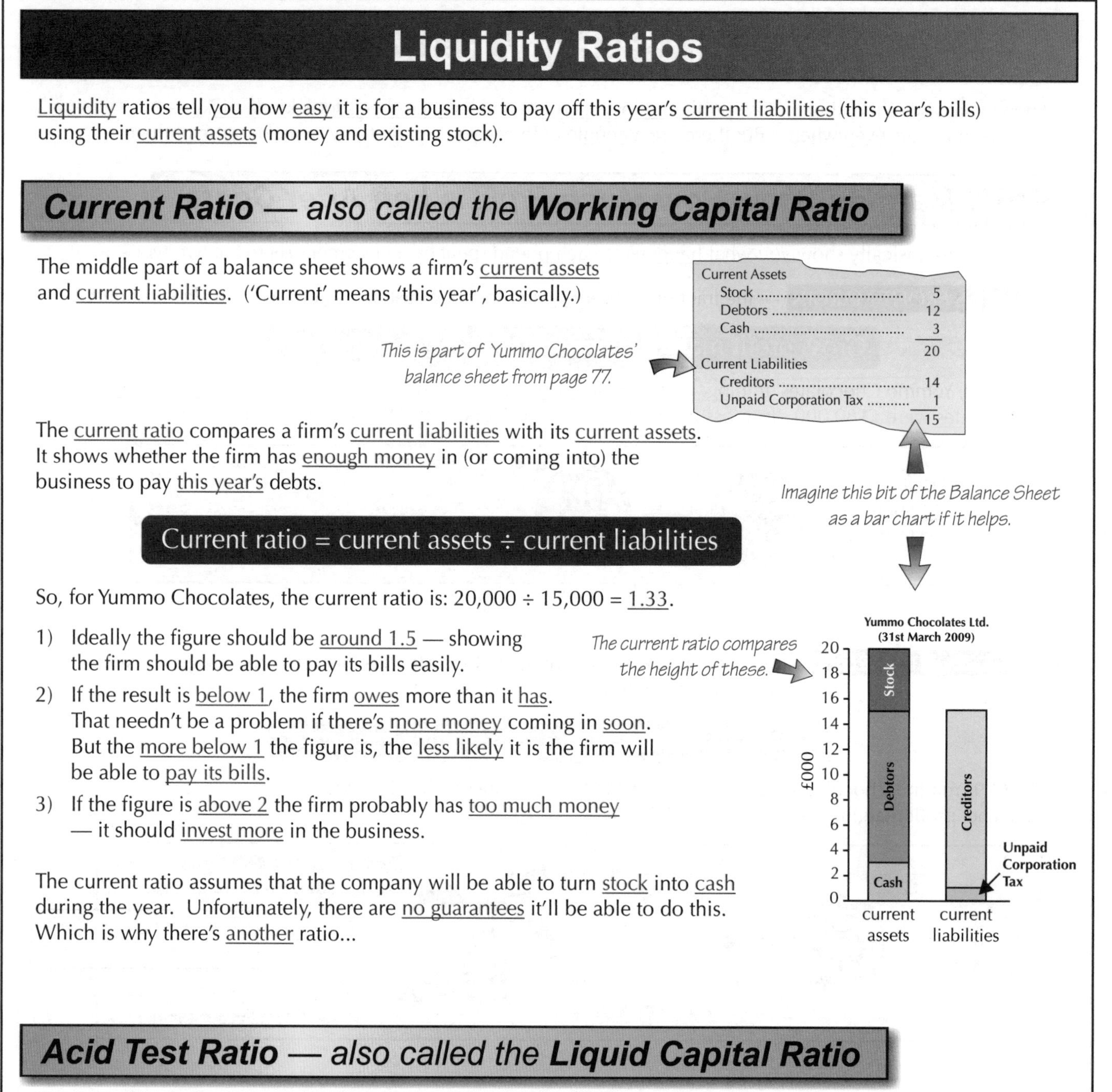

Current Assets	
Stock	5
Debtors	12
Cash	3
	20
Current Liabilities	
Creditors	14
Unpaid Corporation Tax	1
	15

The current ratio compares a firm's current liabilities with its current assets. It shows whether the firm has enough money in (or coming into) the business to pay this year's debts.

Current ratio = current assets ÷ current liabilities

So, for Yummo Chocolates, the current ratio is: 20,000 ÷ 15,000 = 1.33.

1) Ideally the figure should be around 1.5 — showing the firm should be able to pay its bills easily.
2) If the result is below 1, the firm owes more than it has. That needn't be a problem if there's more money coming in soon. But the more below 1 the figure is, the less likely it is the firm will be able to pay its bills.
3) If the figure is above 2 the firm probably has too much money — it should invest more in the business.

The current ratio assumes that the company will be able to turn stock into cash during the year. Unfortunately, there are no guarantees it'll be able to do this. Which is why there's another ratio...

Acid Test Ratio — also called the Liquid Capital Ratio

This is similar to the current ratio, but takes a slightly more pessimistic view of things. It assumes that the company won't be able to turn stock into cash (i.e. that it won't be able to sell its stock during the year).

Acid test ratio = (current assets – stock) ÷ current liabilities.

So, for Yummo Chocolates, the current ratio is: (20,000 – 5,000) ÷ 15,000 = 1.

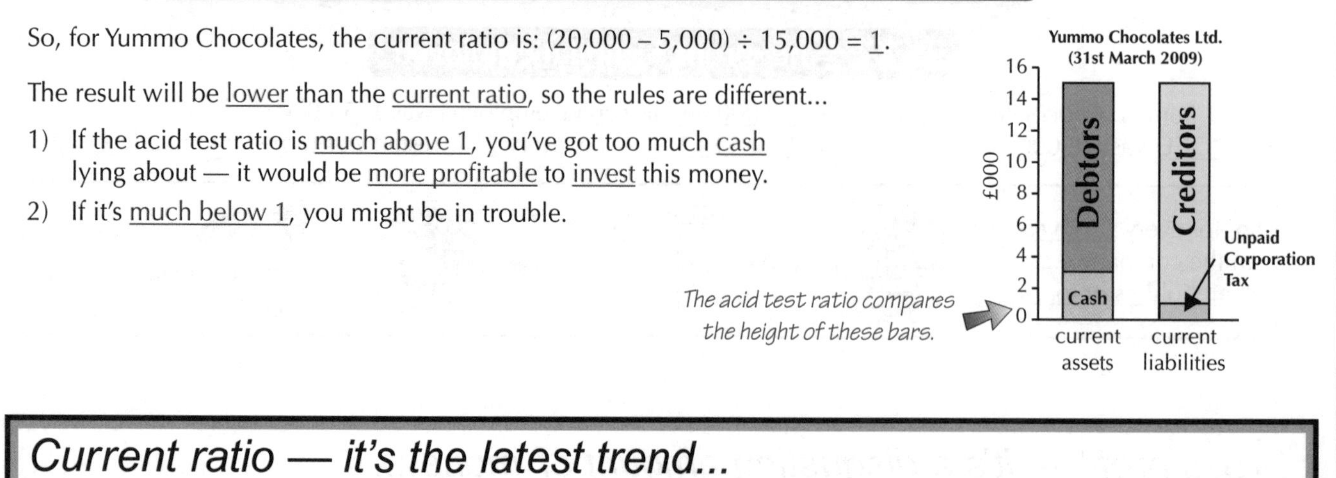

The result will be lower than the current ratio, so the rules are different...

1) If the acid test ratio is much above 1, you've got too much cash lying about — it would be more profitable to invest this money.
2) If it's much below 1, you might be in trouble.

Current ratio — it's the latest trend...

Phew, that's the last of the ratios. Learn, cover and copy these too — make sure you know what are good values for the current ratio and the acid test ratio. Oh, and remember it's the acid test that ignores stock.

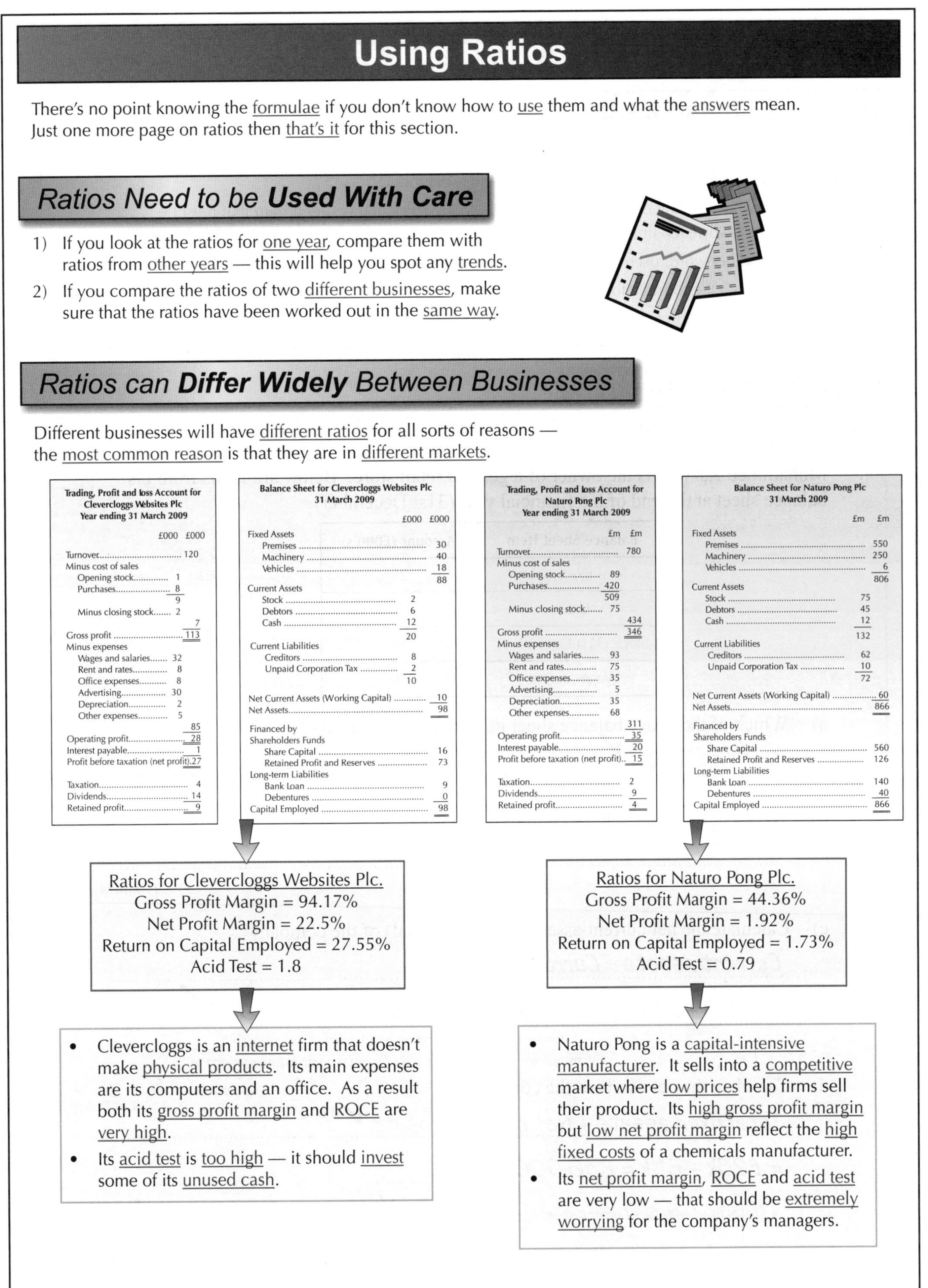

Using Ratios

There's no point knowing the formulae if you don't know how to use them and what the answers mean. Just one more page on ratios then that's it for this section.

Ratios Need to be **Used With Care**

1) If you look at the ratios for one year, compare them with ratios from other years — this will help you spot any trends.
2) If you compare the ratios of two different businesses, make sure that the ratios have been worked out in the same way.

Ratios can **Differ Widely** Between Businesses

Different businesses will have different ratios for all sorts of reasons — the most common reason is that they are in different markets.

Trading, Profit and loss Account for Cleverclogs Websites Plc
Year ending 31 March 2009

	£000	£000
Turnover		120
Minus cost of sales		
Opening stock	1	
Purchases	8	
	9	
Minus closing stock	2	
		7
Gross profit		113
Minus expenses		
Wages and salaries	32	
Rent and rates	8	
Office expenses	8	
Advertising	30	
Depreciation	2	
Other expenses	5	
		85
Operating profit		28
Interest payable		1
Profit before taxation (net profit)		27
Taxation		4
Dividends		14
Retained profit		9

Balance Sheet for Cleverclogs Websites Plc
31 March 2009

	£000	£000
Fixed Assets		
Premises		30
Machinery		40
Vehicles		18
		88
Current Assets		
Stock	2	
Debtors	6	
Cash	12	
	20	
Current Liabilities		
Creditors	8	
Unpaid Corporation Tax	2	
	10	
Net Current Assets (Working Capital)		10
Net Assets		98
Financed by		
Shareholders Funds		
Share Capital		16
Retained Profit and Reserves		73
Long-term Liabilities		
Bank Loan		9
Debentures		0
Capital Employed		98

Trading, Profit and loss Account for Naturo Pong Plc
Year ending 31 March 2009

	£m	£m
Turnover		780
Minus cost of sales		
Opening stock	89	
Purchases	420	
	509	
Minus closing stock	75	
		434
Gross profit		346
Minus expenses		
Wages and salaries	93	
Rent and rates	75	
Office expenses	35	
Advertising	5	
Depreciation	35	
Other expenses	68	
		311
Operating profit		35
Interest payable		20
Profit before taxation (net profit)		15
Taxation		2
Dividends		9
Retained profit		4

Balance Sheet for Naturo Pong Plc
31 March 2009

	£m	£m
Fixed Assets		
Premises		550
Machinery		250
Vehicles		6
		806
Current Assets		
Stock	75	
Debtors	45	
Cash	12	
	132	
Current Liabilities		
Creditors	62	
Unpaid Corporation Tax	10	
	72	
Net Current Assets (Working Capital)		60
Net Assets		866
Financed by		
Shareholders Funds		
Share Capital		560
Retained Profit and Reserves		126
Long-term Liabilities		
Bank Loan		140
Debentures		40
Capital Employed		866

Ratios for Cleverclogs Websites Plc.
Gross Profit Margin = 94.17%
Net Profit Margin = 22.5%
Return on Capital Employed = 27.55%
Acid Test = 1.8

- Cleverclogs is an internet firm that doesn't make physical products. Its main expenses are its computers and an office. As a result both its gross profit margin and ROCE are very high.
- Its acid test is too high — it should invest some of its unused cash.

Ratios for Naturo Pong Plc.
Gross Profit Margin = 44.36%
Net Profit Margin = 1.92%
Return on Capital Employed = 1.73%
Acid Test = 0.79

- Naturo Pong is a capital-intensive manufacturer. It sells into a competitive market where low prices help firms sell their product. Its high gross profit margin but low net profit margin reflect the high fixed costs of a chemicals manufacturer.
- Its net profit margin, ROCE and acid test are very low — that should be extremely worrying for the company's managers.

Warning — handle ratios with care...

Check that you can see where the answers for the ratios came from. Make sure you know why the two businesses have such different ratios — and why last year's figures would be interesting.

Warm-Up and Worked Exam Questions

Warm-up Questions

1) What type of asset is "stock" — a current asset or a fixed asset?
2) Explain the difference between a creditor and a debtor.
3) Under what heading on a balance sheet would an accountant enter a loan that must be repaid in two years' time?
4) Give another word, used in accounts, that means "sales" (i.e. the total income from sales).
5) Write down the formula for gross profit margin. And the formula for net profit margin.
6) Explain what the Return on Capital Employed (ROCE) shows.

Worked Exam Question

Here's a worked exam question on balance sheets and ratios.

1 Mohammed Razwan is the owner of a general retail store. Below are items from his balance sheet at the end of his financial year (31st December).

Balance Sheet Item	Amount (£000's)
Total fixed assets	25
Cash	2
Stock (31st December)	10
Wages owing	1

a) Which of the above balance sheet items are current assets?

Cash and stock ✔ [1 mark] You have to give both answers to get the mark.

(1 mark)

b) Which of these current assets is the most liquid?

Cash ✔ [1 mark]

(1 mark)

c) Calculate the net current assets (working capital) of the company.

Current assets – Current liabilities

= (Cash + Stock) – Wages ✔ [1 mark] *= £2k + £10k – £1k = £11 000* ✔ [1 mark]

Show the formula and as much working as possible. It may earn you marks even if you get the final answer wrong.

(2 marks)

d) Calculate the net assets of the company.

Total fixed assets + Net current assets ✔ [1 mark]

= £25k + £11k = £36 000 ✔ [1 mark]

or (Total fixed assets + Current assets) – Current liabilities ✔ [1 mark] *= (£25k + £2k + £10k) – £1k = £36k* ✔ [1 mark]

(2 marks)

e) State the total value of the capital employed in the business.

This is the same as net assets, which is £36 000. ✔ [1 mark]

(1 mark)

Exam Questions

1 a) State the formula used to calculate the current ratio.

....

....

(1 mark)

b) A firm has a current ratio that is below 1.
Why should the owner of the firm be concerned?

....

....

(2 marks)

2 Two fashion retailers, Now plc and Tops and Bottoms plc, are in competition in the same market. Summaries of their accounts are shown below.

NOW PLC		TOPS AND BOTTOMS PLC	
Turnover	£500 000	Turnover	£750 000
Cost of Sales	£200 000	Cost of Sales	£400 000
Expenses	£100 000	Expenses	£100 000
Capital Employed	£1 000 000	Capital Employed	£1 000 000

a) Calculate the net profit margin for Now plc.

....

....

(2 marks)

b) The net profit for Tops and Bottoms plc is £250 000.
Calculate the return on capital employed (ROCE) for this company.

....

....

(2 marks)

c) The ROCE for Now plc is 20%. Which do you think is the better company to invest money in? Give a reason for your answer.

....

....

(2 marks)

Revision Summary for Section Five

It's that time again, I'm afraid — time to check you've learned all the stuff in this section. I know it's a pain but believe me it's worth it. Finance is really important in Business Studies and you can almost guarantee it'll come up somehow or other in your exam. So no slacking — get your nose to the grindstone and check you can answer these questions.

1) List three examples of direct costs. And three examples of indirect costs.
2) If Tardy Ltd. output 30,000 alarm clocks at a total cost of £120,000, what is the average cost of making each clock?
3) What two things are equal at the break-even level of output?
4) What do you get if you deduct the break-even point from the current level of output?
   a) net profit; b) total costs; c) the margin of safety.
5) Describe three ways a business could respond to cost rises.
6) What happens to the break-even point if the price of a product is increased?
7) Calculate the break-even level of output given the following information:
   Variable costs = £3 per unit, selling price = £6 per unit, and fixed costs = £6000.
8) Explain two limitations of break-even analysis.
9) Give five reasons why firms need finance.
10) Give five sources of start-up finance for a small firm.
11) Why might a new or small firm find it hard to raise finance?
12) List three internal sources of finance. And five external sources of finance.
13) Explain four factors that affect the choice of finance for a business.
14) Dave's Dodgy Motors Ltd. is suffering from poor cash flow. Explain three problems that might result.
15) Give three ways in which a business can improve its cash flow.
16) In a trading, profit and loss account, how do you calculate the cost of sales figure?
17) A gym buys a new treadmill for £3000. The owner's accountant decides to depreciate it using the straight-line method, and assumes it will last for six years before it needs replacing.
   What allowance for depreciation will be in the accounts each year?
18) Name three groups of people who might look at a firm's profit and loss account.
19) Put these in order, most liquid first: debtors, stock, cash.
20) What do you get if you deduct current liabilities from current assets?
21) What are the two ways a firm gets funds from its shareholders?
22) In 2009, Tyler's Tidy Tiles Ltd. made a gross profit of £6,000 and had sales of £24,000.
   What was the firm's gross profit margin?
23) What do you get if you divide net profit by capital employed?
   a) gross profit margin; b) net profit margin; c) return on capital employed.
24) What do you get if you take away stock from current assets, and divide by current liabilities?
   a) current ratio; b) acid test ratio; c) a migraine.
25) Look at the information on the right, and work out these ratios:
   a) current ratio; b) acid test ratio.

sales (turnover) = £80,000
cost of sales = £25,000
current assets = £20,000
closing stock = £5,000
current liabilities = £18,000
debtors = £8,000
creditors = £3,750
net profit after tax = £7,000

2) £4. 5) 2000. 18) £500.
23) 0.25 or 25%.
26) a) 1.11; b) 0.83.

Starting a New Business

Some of the biggest businesses around started as just one person and a good idea. And that's what this section's about — why people start businesses, how those businesses grow, and some of the issues that growth causes.

Different People Start Businesses for Different Reasons

Here are some possible reasons why people might want to start a business...

1) Lots of entrepreneurs have the financial objective of becoming rich from their share of the profits.
2) There are also several non-financial objectives, like the freedom of being your own boss.
3) For many people, running a business is a challenge that they enjoy.
4) Some people start a business because they want to benefit others. This could be done by starting a charity, or by having social objectives for their business.

There's more about entrepreneurs and why they start businesses in Section One.

Successful New Businesses are Innovative not Inventive

1) If a new business is going to succeed it must provide something that other competitors do not.
2) An invention is a new idea — a new product or a new method for doing something, e.g. a new way to dry hair or make chocolate.
3) An innovation is a successful introduction of a new idea.
4) Creating a toaster that contains a portable radio would be an invention, but it would only be innovative if the idea was successful and people wanted to buy it.

Successful Businesses Add Value to their Products

Adding value is the way that a business increases its profits by making a product or service seem more desirable to the customer. Here are six ways a business can add value to a product:

① **CONVENIENCE** The product could be made more convenient — e.g. ready-grated cheese tends to cost more than blocks of cheese.

② **SPEED** Customers may pay more to have a product delivered quickly — e.g. some firms that offer next-day delivery charge more for their products.

③ **BRANDING** Having a strong brand image is important. Some brands of portable MP3 player are more expensive than others, but people are happy to pay more because they have a well-known and trusted name. Brands that are seen as fashionable or 'cool' also tend to be able to charge more for their products.

④ **QUALITY** People are often prepared to pay more for a high quality product. Some brands of car are better built than others and the manufacturers charge more to reflect this.

⑤ **DESIGN** Having a good design is important — e.g. clothes with an attractive, distinctive design are often more desirable than more basic clothes. This means customers may be prepared to pay more for them.

⑥ **USP** The secret is to have a unique selling point (USP) — something that makes your product different from your competitors. As long as customers value the USP they will pay more for your product.

The USP of this book? All these bits at the bottom of the page...

A nice page to start this section. Make sure you know the main reasons why people start businesses and the six ways successful businesses add value to their products. The trickiest bit here is the difference between invention and innovation — remember that innovation means bringing a new idea successfully to the market.

Succeeding as a New Start-up

You saw some of the skills an entrepreneur needs on page 2 — now you need a bit more detail...

Entrepreneurs Need to *Think Creatively*...

When you start a new business, you need to be able to see a gap in the market (see page 18) and come up with an innovative product to fill it. To do this, it's important that you think both analytically and creatively:

1) Thinking analytically means looking at things in the real world and trying to understand them. Some of the key questions to ask include:

   - *How do other businesses do things? What could we do that is better?*
   - *Why do customers buy from business X? What could we do to persuade them to buy from us?*
   - *What do customers want that no business currently provides? What would happen if we provided it?*

2) Thinking creatively (or laterally, also known as 'thinking outside the box') means trying to find answers to some of these questions that no one else has thought of before — looking beyond the obvious for new opportunities.
3) The aim of thinking creatively is to come up with a useful product or idea that nobody else has thought of — giving you an advantage over your competitors or helping a new business to be successful.
4) A mind map is a good way to record your ideas — it allows you to collect all your thoughts together and spot links that might not have been obvious otherwise.

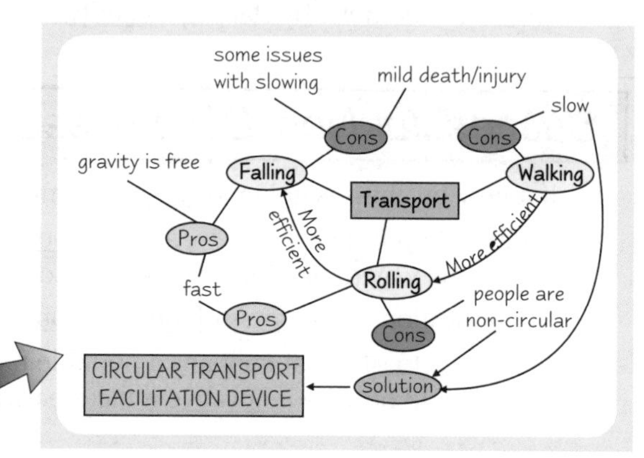

...But there are also *Practical Considerations*

It's all very good thinking creatively and drawing pretty mind maps, but if you're starting a business there are also more practical things you need to think about. For instance...

1) The location of your business. There's more about this on p39, but it boils down to two main questions:

   - *Where is the cheapest place to produce your products?*
   - *Where will your firm make the biggest income from sales?*

   These are unlikely to be in the same place so you must choose the location which is likely to be the best compromise, the most profitable in the long run.

There are loads of other practical considerations too — this is just a selection.

2) Protecting your ideas. It's important that a business protects its ideas from being copied by competitors. There are various ways you can do this, including:

   - Using your rights as a copyright holder. If you write or record something original, then you automatically own the copyright to it. Other people and businesses must seek permission (and possibly pay you) if they want to use your copyrighted material. Registering original work can be a useful thing to do — this way, you can prove when you made it if someone else claims they did it first.
   - Taking out a patent. If you have a patent for your product, or your method for producing it, no one else can copy it unless you give them a licence — and you can charge for the licence. Patents only apply to products or methods that are new and inventive in some way.

3) Choosing your type of business. Are you going to bring a new product to the market or should you become a franchise, selling an existing range of products? (See page 5 for more on franchises.)

Practical considerations — take a pen to your exam...

If a new business considers the issues covered on the last two pages then it should increase its chances of success. But don't forget that luck matters too — and it's often the things that the business can't predict or control that matter the most. I predict you'll need to know all this in the exam. Make sure you learn it.

The Business Plan

It's vital that the business has a clear idea of what it's going to do — that's what business plans are for.
You need to know why businesses have them and what they should contain.

The Plan is for the **Owner** and **Financial Backers**

1) It is important that the owner thinks carefully what the business is going to do and what resources are needed. This will help calculate how much start-up capital is needed.
2) Financial backers such as banks will need to be convinced that the new business is a sound investment.
3) The hope is that if the business is a bad idea, either the owner or the financial backers will realise this at the planning stage — before they've wasted lots of time and money on a business that was never going to work.

The Plan Needs At Least **Seven Sections**

There is no single correct way to write a business plan — but most good ones will include all of these:

1) PERSONAL DETAILS of the owner and other important personnel — like their CVs.
Financial backers will want to know who they are trusting with their money.

2) MISSION STATEMENT — a way of describing the broad aims of the company.
They usually use long words to say something general and obvious.
"To combine fresh bread and tasty fillings in popular combinations and become the market leading sandwich shop in Kent."

3) OBJECTIVES These are more concrete and specific aims.
"To average 160 sandwich sales each weekday lunchtime over the next four years."

Lots of these things are covered in greater detail elsewhere in this book — check the index if you're not sure.

4) PRODUCT DESCRIPTION — including details of the market and competitors.
It should explain how the firm will achieve product differentiation — also called its unique selling point (USP) (see page 85). It should describe its marketing strategy using the 4 Ps (page 17). All statements should be supported by field or desk research (page 19).

5) PRODUCTION DETAILS — how the firm will make its product or provide its service.
It should list all the equipment needed and where it will be located.

6) STAFFING REQUIREMENTS What personnel will be needed — how many people, their job descriptions and the expected wage bill.

7) FINANCE It should explain how much money is needed to start up the business.
There should be a cash-flow forecast and a projected profit and loss account and balance sheet.
There should also be ratios to show any backer the likely return on their investment.

A Good Business Plan is **No Guarantee** of Success

There are lots of risks and uncertainties involved in operating a business that even a good business plan can't protect you from. These include:

1) The health of the economy. The UK entered a sharp recession in 2009 that very few people predicted. Many businesses closed as a result.
2) The actions of competitors. Few businesses know exactly what their competitors are planning. Businesses can avoid being caught out by new threats by constantly monitoring the market — e.g. regularly carrying out market and competitor research.

Your plan should be to make sure you know all about plans...

Make sure you've learned the reasons for producing a business plan, and scribble down the seven things it should contain. Then write a brief business plan for a new home-delivery pizza firm.

Starting a Business — Help and Support

Starting a new business isn't easy — even if you've done GCSE Business Studies.
You need to know what help is available and why so many organisations are keen to help.

The **Government** Gives A Lot of Help

1) The government has a lot to gain by encouraging new businesses. Many people start businesses as an alternative to unemployment. This reduces the amount of state benefits the government has to pay out.
2) The government will also receive taxation revenue when the firm makes a profit. And successful businesses create employment for many people — helping both themselves and the government even more.
3) The government funds Business Link, which operates in each region of the country and offers financial support to businesses. It also provides guidance on how to produce a business plan, as well as more general information like advice on staff training.
4) Another body providing help is the government's Department for Business, Enterprise and Regulatory Reform (BERR) — it provides advice and leaflets, most of which are available on its website.
5) New firms can also apply to have bank loans underwritten by the government. This means the government will pay them back if the business fails — making it easier for the new firm to borrow money.

Private Firms also Offer Support

1) Some firms in the private sector aim to make a profit by providing help to new businesses. The most obvious example is banks. They publish guides on how to produce a business plan and have business advisors who will talk to potential entrepreneurs.
2) Banks do this for two main reasons. Firstly, to get the firm to open an account with them and not with one of their competitors. And secondly, to reduce the chances of the new business going bankrupt owing the bank lots of money.
3) Some firms exist to provide management services to other businesses — they charge for their help but sometimes provide free advice to new firms. This is because they hope the new firm will pay for their services once it is established.

A Few **Charities** Offer Advice and Money

1) Some charities help people start new businesses. These charities are usually started by people who believe that it is good for society to have lots of new firms starting up.
2) The most well known example is the Prince's Trust. The Prince of Wales set it up when he realised there were limited employment opportunities for young people living in inner-city areas. The charity gives advice, grants and low-interest loans to young entrepreneurs.

Chambers of Commerce Give Help to **Local Firms**

1) Chambers of Commerce are groups of business people in a city or town who work together to look after the interests of local businesses.
2) These groups provide information and support for small companies and act as an important link between local businesses and local and central government.

I'll get by with a little help from the Chamber of Commerce...

With all that help around it's a wonder why so many businesses fail. Still, your job's a lot easier — learn this page, cover it up and scribble down a list of who wants to help and why.

Warm-Up and Worked Exam Questions

Warm-up Questions

1) Give one non-financial incentive for running your own company.
2) What is meant by "lateral thinking"?
3) What are the two basic considerations when deciding where to locate a new business?
4) Describe seven kinds of information that should be included in every business plan.
5) Give three sources of information for people setting up their own business.

Worked Exam Question

Take a look at these worked examples, then try the exam-style questions on page 90.

1 Read **Source A** and then answer the questions that follow.

Source A

When Peter was made redundant recently he received a large redundancy payment. He is now considering starting his own business. He has been advised that the best ideas are innovative rather than merely inventive. He has also been advised to protect his original ideas in case someone tries to steal them.

a) Identify one form of legal protection for original ideas.

Copyright law (or patent law) can offer protection for original ideas. ✔[1 mark]

(1 mark)

b) Explain the difference between an "invention" and an "innovation".

The term "invention" can describe any new product or method. ✔[1 mark] *However, "innovation" is used to refer to the successful introduction of a new idea.* ✔[1 mark]

(2 marks)

c) A business advisor tells Peter that his product needs a USP. What is meant by "USP"?

A unique selling point ✔[1 mark] *— something that makes a product different from competing products.* ✔[1 mark]

(2 marks)

d) Describe the advantages of starting your own business, and some of the risks involved.

Advantages of starting up your own business include being independent ✔[1 mark] *and running the business the way you want to.* ✔[1 mark] *You also stand to gain financially if the business is successful,* ✔[1 mark] *and you can choose how any profits from the business are used.* ✔[1 mark] *However, new businesses often need a lot of investment, and if the business is unsuccessful, this investment can be lost.* ✔[1 mark]

✔[There is also 1 mark available for an answer that is well structured and well written.]

(6 marks)

Exam Questions

1 Eve wants to turn her hobby of candle making into a business. She has been told that she should write a business plan first, before approaching her bank about a loan.

a) (i) Explain what a business plan is, and the type of information it should contain.

....

....

....

(4 marks)

(ii) Explain why a business plan cannot guarantee that Eve's business will succeed.

....

....

....

(3 marks)

b) (i) Explain **two** ways in which the government could support Eve's business.

1. ....

2. ....

(2 marks)

(ii) Identify **two** other organisations that may be able to offer help to Eve.

1. ....

2. ....

(2 marks)

c) Eve believes that her design skills are important if her business is to add value.

(i) What is meant by "adding value"?

....

....

(2 marks)

(ii) Creating products with interesting designs is one way in which a company can add value. Identify and explain two other ways in which a company can add value to its products.

1. ....

....

2. ....

....

(4 marks)

Growth of Firms — Internal Expansion

There are two ways a firm can grow — internally, by expanding their own activities, and externally (see next page for more about external expansion). It's important to learn why firms grow as well as how they grow.

Firms Grow for **Five Main Reasons**

1) ECONOMIES OF SCALE — larger firms can produce at lower average cost (see page 93) than smaller firms. They can pass on these economies of scale to consumers as lower prices. This will help them increase their sales, their market share and their profits.
2) DIVERSIFICATION — larger firms can afford to produce more products than smaller firms. They can sell into different markets and so reduce the risks that a decline in sales of one product will harm the business. That means there's less threat to their profits.

See also page 24.

3) FINANCIAL SUPPORT — larger firms are less likely to go bankrupt than smaller firms. That's mainly because they can borrow money more easily from banks so they will find it easier to survive cash-flow problems. Larger firms can also receive more financial support from the government than smaller firms because they employ lots of people.
4) PERSONAL VANITY — some owners also enjoy the power and status that comes from owning a large business.
5) DOMINATION OF THE MARKET — the larger the market share a firm has, the more it can control prices. It will face fewer threats from competitors and may even be able to eliminate rivals by charging prices that they can't compete with.

There are **Three Main Methods** of **Internal Expansion**

Internal expansion is also called organic growth.

1) The firm can produce more of its current products to sell in its existing markets. For example Glugg Soft Drinks Ltd. could try to increase its market share in the UK fizzy cabbage juice market from 1% to 20%.
2) The firm can sell its current product into new markets. Glugg Soft Drinks could try to export its fizzy cabbage juice to the USA.
3) The firm could launch a new product. This could be a similar product to existing ones, like fizzy turnip juice — this is called line extension, because you're extending your line of products. Or it could be a completely new product, like sports cars — this is called diversification.

Internal Expansion has its **Benefits** and **Problems**

1) Internal growth is good in that it is relatively inexpensive to achieve. Also, with the exception of diversifying with a completely new product, the firm expands by doing more of what it is already good at — making its existing products. That means it's less likely to go horribly wrong.
2) The problem is that it can take a long time to achieve growth. Some owners are not prepared to wait that long — that's why they go for external growth.

Organic growth — expansion without pesticides...

Make sure you learn all the reasons for growth as well as the benefits and problems of internal expansion. Memorise the three types of internal expansion and find examples of firms that have grown in each of these ways.

Growth of Firms — Takeovers and Mergers

Takeovers and mergers are the two ways a firm can achieve external expansion — also called integration. A merger is when two firms agree to join together, a takeover is when one firm buys another. Sometimes that firm agrees to be taken over, sometimes it doesn't want to be.

There are Four Types of Integration

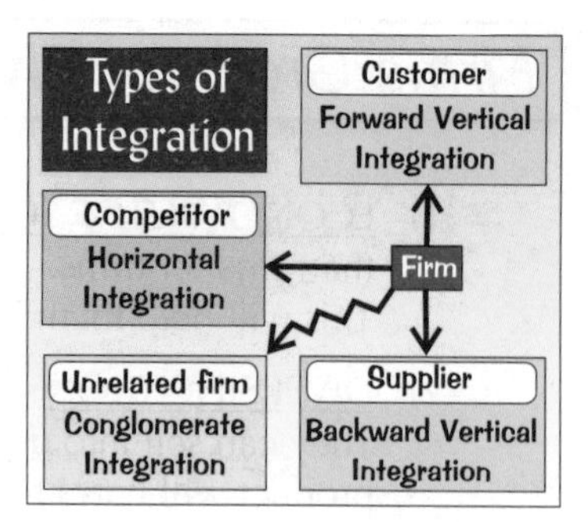

1 Horizontal Integration...

...is when two competitors join together — they make the same product at the same stage of the production chain. For example, Glugg Soft Drinks Ltd takes over another company which makes fizzy sodas.

- Horizontal integration creates a firm with more economies of scale and a bigger market share. It will be more able to compete than before.

2 Forward Vertical Integration...

...is when a firm takes over a customer. For example, Glugg Soft Drinks Ltd takes over a chain of juice bars.

- Forward vertical integration gives the firm greater access to customers. Owning its own retail outlets will make it easier to sell its products.

3 Backward Vertical Integration...

...is when a firm joins with a supplier. For example, Glugg Soft Drinks Ltd takes over a cabbage farm.

- Backward vertical integration gives the firm greater control over its supplies — it helps guarantee a supply of raw materials. It may also be able to obtain cheaper and better quality raw materials.

4 Conglomerate Integration...

...is when two firms with nothing in common join together.
For example, Glugg Soft Drinks Ltd takes over a clotheswear firm.

- Conglomerate integration means the firm will expand by diversifying into new markets. This reduces the risks that come from relying on just a few products.

Mergers and Takeovers Have their Problems

1) Less than half of all takeovers and mergers are successful. It is very hard to make two different businesses work as one. Management styles often differ between firms — the employees of one firm may be used to one company culture and not be motivated by the style used in the other.
2) Takeovers can create bad feeling. Often a firm agrees to be taken over, but sometimes the takeover bid is hostile and unpopular. And mergers usually lead to cost-cutting by making lots of people redundant, so they lead to tension and uncertainty among workers.

Firms Can also Grow through Franchising

See page 5 for more about franchising and how it works.

1) Franchising is a good way of rapidly increasing both brand awareness and the market share of a firm's products without the usual costs and risks of opening a new outlet — the franchisee has to pay to start the franchise and takes on most of the risk.
2) By franchising, a firm can achieve greater economies of scale (see next page) — they benefit from increased sales, while somebody else runs part of their business, saving them money on wages.

Don't let revision takeover — have a break now and then...

Loads of new stuff to learn here — but I don't reckon any of it's too tricky. Just make sure you know the four types of integration. Then scribble down a mini-essay on the advantages and problems of each type. Don't forget franchising as well — you should know why a business might choose to grow using this method.

Effects of Expansion — Economies of Scale

One of the main advantages of expansion is the reductions in average cost that come from producing on a large scale. These are called economies of scale — and examiners are always banging on about how kids know nothing about this stuff, so give it a good read and show them that you do.

There are Six Main *Internal* Economies of Scale

1) PURCHASING ECONOMIES happen when a large firm buys its supplies in bulk and so gets them at a cheaper unit price than a small firm.
2) MARKETING ECONOMIES arise because the cost of an advertising campaign is pretty much a fixed cost. A larger firm will need to spend less per unit advertising its products than a smaller firm.
3) MANAGERIAL ECONOMIES are where a large firm can afford to employ specialist managers who have expert knowledge, such as accountants and lawyers. This managerial division of labour means that management costs do not double every time the firm doubles in size.
4) FINANCIAL ECONOMIES result from banks being prepared to lend more money to larger firms at lower interest rates than smaller firms. This is because the banks know that larger firms are more likely to pay them back than smaller firms.
5) TECHNICAL ECONOMIES occur because a large firm can afford to operate more advanced machinery than smaller firms. Also, the law of increased dimensions means that, for example, a factory that's ten times as big will be less than ten times as expensive.
6) RISK-BEARING ECONOMIES are where the firm can afford to sell a range of products into many different markets. A decline in sales of one product will not significantly harm the firm's cash flow.

There are Four Main *External* Economies of Scale

These happen when a number of large firms locate near to each other.

1) When this happens suppliers will choose to locate near their customers. This reduces delivery times, transport costs and the need for the producers to hold large stocks of raw materials.
2) There will be a local workforce who already have the skills needed — they got these skills working for other firms in the area. This reduces firms' training costs.
3) Firms will receive support from the local council and national government — for example, motorways may be built which make distribution easier.
4) The area will build up a good reputation for particular products. This will benefit firms in the area and encourage other firms to locate there.

But There are also *Diseconomies of Scale*

It's not all good news for large firms though — growth brings with it some diseconomies of scale. These are areas where growth can lead to increases in a firm's costs. For example:

1) The bigger the firm, the harder and more expensive it is to manage it properly.
2) Decisions take time to reach the whole workforce, and workers at the bottom of the hierarchy feel insignificant. Workers can get demotivated, which may cause productivity to go down.
3) The production process may become more complex and more difficult to coordinate. For example, different departments may end up working on very similar projects without knowing.

Learn the six benefits of large-scale production...

This might seem a bit tricky at first, but it's not too bad. Basically, bigger firms can produce goods at a lower cost per item. And it's that per item bit that's important. Make sure you go over this page until it's all clear — examiners love asking you about this stuff and you don't need me to tell you it's a good idea to know it.

Effects of Expansion — Communication

Good communication is important for all firms — but it can be particularly difficult to achieve in large ones. You need to know what the different methods of communication are and the effects of poor communication.

The Choice of **Medium** Should Reflect the **Message**

There are three main methods of communication in a business — written, verbal and visual.

	Examples	Advantages	Disadvantages
Written	Letters, e-mails, faxes, messages on notice boards, memos and reports	There's a permanent record of the message. The reader can study complex information again and again. Copies can be seen by many people.	Feedback can be difficult to obtain. And if you don't understand what someone has written, it can be hard to check it with them.
Verbal	Telephone calls, one-to-one conversations, group meetings (in person or using video-conferencing).	Information can be given quickly. Body language and tone of voice can reinforce the message and feedback can be easily obtained.	There is no permanent record of the message and sometimes people forget what they have been told.
Visual	Films, posters, diagrams and charts. Also watching body language.	Complicated information can be summarised so the message is received quickly. Pictures can also communicate feelings and emotions better than words.	People will interpret images in different ways. Some people find complicated diagrams hard to understand.

There are **Barriers** to **Effective Communication**

There are many reasons why a message may not be understood by the receiver:

1) The message may be badly worded or use technical jargon, making it hard to understand.
2) There may be language or cultural differences between the sender and receiver of the message — particularly if a firm has operations in more than one country.
3) Staff may be physically separated (located in different buildings, or on different sites), meaning a less effective method of communication has to be used.
4) The receiver may be distracted (e.g. by noise) and so misinterpret the message, or fail to receive it altogether.
5) There could be a contradiction between the sender's body language and their words — this may confuse the recipient as to what the intended message is.
6) The sender or receiver may lack subject knowledge meaning that terminology is used or interpreted incorrectly.

Poor Communication is **Bad for Business**

Poor communication can affect the efficiency of a business and the motivation of the staff.

1) Excessive communication can mean that workers spend too much time passing on messages or replying to emails and not doing their actual job. This reduces their productivity and the efficiency of the business.

2) Insufficient communication can result in poor decisions being made and low morale if staff members feel that they are not being listened to. Workers can become demotivated and their productivity can go down.

It's good to talk (but make it effective)...

I hope this page has communicated effectively to you the things you need to know — that's the different methods of communication, the barriers to effective communication and the effects of poor communication.

Effects of Expansion — Communication

How a business communicates as it grows will be down to its organisational structure. You've already seen a bit about this on pages 10-11 but you also need to know how it can cause problems for communication.

A Long Chain of Communication is a Problem...

1) As firms grow, they tend to become more hierarchical, with many layers of management.
2) A chain of communication in a firm is the chain of people messages travel through to get from one layer of the firm's hierarchy to another.
3) Here, Dodgy Computers has six levels in its hierarchy, so its longest chain of communication (from the top of the hierarchy to the bottom) has six layers.
4) Long chains of communication mean messages can take a long time to travel up and down the hierarchy. This can leave people at the top and the bottom of the hierarchy feeling isolated and demoralised. There's also the danger that messages may not reach their intended destination — and even if they do, they might get distorted along the way (like in a game of Chinese whispers).
5) Some firms have tried to solve the problem of long chains of communication by de-layering — removing tiers of management, usually in the middle.

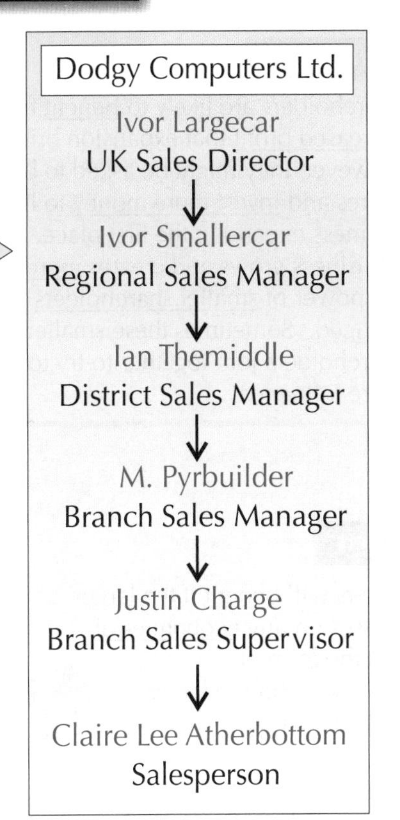

...and so is a Wide Span of Control

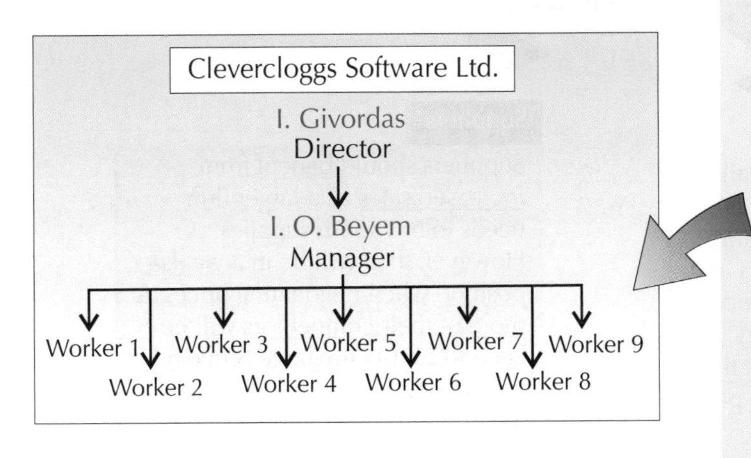

1) The span of control is the number of workers who report to one manager in a hierarchy.
2) The manager of Clevercloggs Software has a span of control of nine workers.
3) A wide span of control leads to a manager having to communicate with a lot of employees.
4) This means it can take a long time to pass messages to all the people under a manager's control (and for them all to pass messages back to the manager). It can also be difficult to manage a lot of employees effectively.
5) Firms must find balance between a short chain of communication and a narrow span of control.

Spam of control — managers sending hundreds of emails...

A good page this, I reckon — not too much to learn and a couple of pretty diagrams to look at. Make sure you know what chain of communication and span of control mean, and why having a long chain of communication or a wide span of control is a problem for firms.

Effects of Expansion on Stakeholders

Growing businesses have an impact on their stakeholders (see page 9) — and the effects aren't always good.

The Growth of a Business Affects its Stakeholders

Shareholders

Shareholders are likely to benefit from any increased profit that expansion brings. However, they might be asked to buy more shares and invest more money to help the business expand in the first place. Also, as a business grows and creates more shares, the power of smaller shareholders will be reduced. Sometimes these smaller shareholders join together to try to exert more influence.

Employees

Employees should benefit from greater job security as larger businesses are less likely to fail than small firms. On the other hand large firms tend to be more hierarchical, so employees may feel less involved in the running of the business. As a result, workers in large firms are more likely to join a trade union in order to protect their interests than workers in small firms.

Customers

Customers will benefit if the larger firm passes on any economies of scale in the form of lower prices. But the larger firm may have fewer competitors and so be able to charge higher prices. On their own, individual customers are often powerless to influence large businesses — but if a business upsets large numbers of its customers, it can be in trouble.

Government

The government will collect more taxes as the business becomes larger and more profitable. However, some businesses can become so powerful and influential that it can be hard for governments to pass laws that threaten the interests of the business. Governments can investigate large firms if it thinks they are behaving in an anti-competitive way (i.e. if they're using their power to unfairly squeeze other firms out of the market).

Local Community

Any negative impact the business causes locally, such as noise pollution or traffic congestion, is likely to be made worse as the business expands. On the other hand, it may make larger profits and so be able to invest in the community. The local community may try to protect its interests by forming pressure groups to campaign against the business and try to persuade governments to pass laws limiting its negative impact.

Suppliers

Suppliers should benefit from increased sales as a larger firm needs to buy more supplies. However, they will be in a weaker position when negotiating prices as more of their competitors will be keen to supply the large firm (and the large firm will be able to drive a hard bargain because of this).

Stakeholders — they all want a piece of the action....

All pretty straightforward here — when a business grows, it impacts on all the different stakeholders connected to that business. Make sure you know how each different set of stakeholders is affected by the growth of a business and how those stakeholders might react to protect their own interests.

Warm-Up and Worked Exam Questions

Warm-up Questions

1) Many businesses want to grow bigger. What are the two main processes for growth?
2) What is meant by "diseconomies of scale"?
3) List the four types of integration.
4) State any three of the six internal economies of scale.
5) Messages can be communicated visually. What are the other two main methods of communication?
6) What is meant by "span of control"?

Worked Exam Questions

Take a look at these worked examples, then try the exam-style questions on page 98.

1 Peter owns a fast food restaurant. Business is good, and Peter now wants to expand his business. He wants the business to "grow organically".

a) What is meant by "organic growth"?

Organic growth is "internal expansion", and happens when a firm grows by expanding its own activities, ✔[1 mark] *rather than joining with another company.* ✔[1 mark]

(2 marks)

b) Identify and explain two strategies for organic growth that Peter could use.

1. *He could try to attract more customers into his existing restaurant.* ✔[1 mark]
He would be trying to gain a larger share of his existing market. ✔[1 mark]

2. *He could open a second restaurant somewhere else.* ✔[1 mark]
Then he would be selling into a new market. ✔[1 mark]

(4 marks)

c) Explain two possible advantages to Peter of expanding his business.

As his firm grows, Peter will be able to buy supplies cheaper by buying in bulk, ✔[1 mark] *which should allow him to become more competitive* ✔[1 mark] *(if he passes these discounts on to his customers as cheaper prices). And if he opens a second restaurant,* ✔[1 mark] *then if business falls in one, the other may still do well.* ✔[1 mark]

(4 marks)

d) Peter has been advised that there are disadvantages to having a larger business. Identify and explain one possible disadvantage for Peter.

Expanding his business would probably mean Peter would require more staff, and possibly more premises. ✔[1 mark] *This could be difficult* ✔[1 mark] *and expensive to manage effectively.* ✔[1 mark]

(3 marks)

Exam Questions

1 Harry Blake runs a market garden, growing fruit and vegetables.

a) He decides to buy a fruit and vegetable shop in the small town nearby.

(i) Harry describes this as forward vertical integration. What does this mean?

....

....

(1 mark)

(ii) Identify **two** possible advantages of this integration, and a possible disadvantage.

....

....

....

....

....

(3 marks)

b) Harry is now the manager of both the market garden and the shop, and has to divide his time between the two sites.

(i) Identify one effect this may have on how Harry communicates with his workers.

....

(1 mark)

(ii) Identify and explain two ways that poor communication can be bad for a business.

....

....

....

....

(4 marks)

c) Harry worries that his shop might not be able to compete against the big supermarket on the edge of town. Briefly explain **four** economies of scale which the supermarket enjoys.

....

....

....

....

....

(4 marks)

Multinational Firms

Sometimes a firm decides to expand overseas, so it has operations in more than one country.
These firms are called multinational enterprises (MNEs) or transnational corporations (TNCs).

Firms **Become Multinational** for Many Reasons

1) By producing in various countries they can keep transport costs to a minimum.
2) They can increase their knowledge of local market conditions.
3) They can avoid trade barriers by producing inside a country.
4) They can reduce risks from foreign exchange fluctuations.
5) They can gain access to raw materials or cheap labour.
6) By employing expert accountants and shuffling money between countries, big companies can avoid paying tax.
7) They can win subsidies from governments and force workers to accept lower wages by threatening to relocate production to another country.

MNEs Can Benefit the **Host Country**...

1) MNEs often invest money in their host countries and create employment for locals.
2) MNEs bring their own methods of working, giving the host country access to foreign technology and working methods — like with Japanese car producers in the UK.
3) The profits of the MNE can be a source of tax revenue for the host country's government — in theory at least (see point 2 below).
4) The MNE will probably export goods from the host country to foreign markets. The revenue from these export sales may improve the host country's balance of payments (this is the difference between the money coming into a country from sales of exports, and money being spent by the country on imports).

...But They Can Cause Plenty of **Problems** Too

1) The jobs created by MNEs are often unskilled. Workers often work for long hours, with lower wages than they'd get in the MNE's home country. Some people argue that these workers are treated unfairly by the MNE.
2) In return for locating in their country, the MNEs may ask for reduced tax rates and even subsidies from the government — or ask the government to build roads and airport links. It could cost governments money to host an MNE if taxation revenue is less than they expected.
3) The MNE, benefiting from economies of scale, might drive out local industries.
4) They can exert a strong influence on the government to change laws that increase their costs. E.g. they might lobby for a reduction in environmental controls or worker protection laws.
5) MNEs can cause environmental degradation in developing countries that lasts for a long time. The company's owners probably don't live there, so they don't see the impact of the damage.
6) When MNEs locate in poorer countries, the benefits to the country are often much less than the benefits to MNE shareholders — after all, the point of locating there is to maximise profits.

But that's enough about MNE — let's talk about you...

You have to make up your own mind whether MNEs are good or bad — examiners think there's no right or wrong answer, it's how you argue it that counts. Learn everything on this page then think about it and scribble an answer to the mini-essay question: "Are MNEs good or bad?"

Competitive and Monopoly Markets

The basic aim of consumers is to buy as many goods as possible at the cheapest prices.
The basic aim of firms is to maximise profits for their shareholders. These aims are not the same.

Consumers Want Markets to be **Competitive**

1) A competitive market is one where there is a large number of producers selling to a large number of consumers. Nobody is powerful enough to dictate prices. If a firm charges too much then consumers will go elsewhere — this forces producers to be efficient.
2) If the prices charged by firms are as low as possible then consumers will be able to buy as large a quantity of products as possible. This gives them the highest possible material standard of living.
3) Firms compete by trying to convince the consumer that their product is better than their rivals' — this results in high quality products and good after-sales service.
4) Firms will rush to fill any gap in the market — supplying a previously unmet consumer need. This results in high levels of product innovation and the exploitation of new technologies.
5) However, competition means that sometimes all the firms end up making the same product — the result being fewer different products for the consumer. This also means that the only competition is over the selling price of the item — this drives down prices and reduces each firm's profits. If each firm makes smaller profits there may be less money available to develop new and better products.

Producers Want to be **Monopolies**

1) Being a competitive firm is hard work — businesses have to constantly strive to keep ahead of their competitors. They would much prefer to be a monopoly.
2) There are three different definitions of a monopoly:
   - To an economist a monopoly is the only supplier of a product or service.
   - To the government a monopoly is any firm which has more than a 25% market share.
   - To most people a monopoly is any firm that has a dominant position in the market — it can dictate prices to others.
3) A monopoly charges higher prices than a firm in a competitive market because the consumer has less choice about who to buy from. As a result the monopolist earns higher profits for its shareholders.
4) These higher prices mean that consumers end up with a lower standard of living — but the higher profits can be spent on the research and development of new products. A good example is the pharmaceuticals industry.

Governments Prefer **Competitive Markets** to Monopolies

1) Governments generally believe that the benefits to consumers of competitive markets are more important than the benefits to producers of monopoly markets.
2) One way the British Government promotes competition is by setting up organisations to monitor the amount of competition between businesses. For example, the Competition Commission investigates businesses it thinks are anti-competitive.
3) Some industries have an organisation of their own, for example the Office of Communications (Ofcom) monitors the behaviour of businesses in the communications industry (e.g. telephone network operators).

Consumers and producers want different types of markets...

Companies generally operate in a competitive environment, which can make life tough. Some companies may try to reduce the problem by using a clever strategy. For instance, they could take over a competitor, or innovate and bring a new type of product to the market — it could take a while for competitors to 'catch up'.

Business Failure

It's no use running from the truth. The sad fact is that a lot of firms go bust sooner or later. You need to know why this is and what their owners can do to avoid it.

Businesses Close Because of **Poor Cash Flow**

Most businesses fail because they become insolvent — in other words, they don't have enough working capital (that's cash to you and me) to pay their short-term liabilities (debts).

There are three main reasons for this.

1) POOR SALES — there's a lack of demand from consumers for the firm's products, so the firm has less money coming in and it cannot pay its creditors (the people the firm owes money to — e.g. its suppliers).
2) OVERTRADING The firm takes on too many orders — as a result it buys in too many raw materials and hires too many staff. Something goes wrong with the orders and the firm doesn't get the money from its customers quickly enough to pay its debts.
3) POOR BUSINESS DECISIONS — for example it decides to bring out new products or expand into new markets but they do not bring in as much money as forecast. Bad business decisions are usually caused by not doing enough planning or market research.

In each case eventually either the business sells off its assets and closes voluntarily, or one or more of the firm's creditors don't get paid and decide to take legal action to get their money back.

Businesses can do **Certain Things** to avoid **Failing**

Nobody wants their business to fail. Luckily, there are a few things that business owners can do to help make sure that their business is a success.

1) **PLANNING** Doing a proper business plan at the start makes a new business less likely to fail.
2) **A GOOD PRODUCT OR SERVICE** Businesses are only successful if people buy their products — if they try to sell products that nobody wants or needs, they won't get very far. They can make sure that they sell the right products by doing market research to find out what customers want, and by making their product better than or different from what's already around.
3) **THE RIGHT PRICE** Businesses have to make sure that their prices are high enough to make a profit, but low enough for customers to be prepared to pay them. Their prices also have to compete with similar competitor products.
4) **MARKETING** Advertising campaigns and offers like "buy one get one free" encourage more customers to buy particular brands, so good marketing decisions can make a business more successful.
5) **THE RIGHT LOCATION** If a business has a good location, it'll probably attract more customers and make more money (e.g. a clothes shop is more likely to be successful if it's on a busy high street than if it's down a back alley).

Even if a business does all these things, it can still fail — sometimes success is just down to luck.

You too can do certain things to avoid failing...

Make sure you remember why firms fail and what happens to them when they do. Scribble down a mini-essay telling the whole sad story. Then make sure you know the things they could have done to prevent failure.

Warm-Up and Worked Exam Questions

Warm-up Questions

1) What do the letters MNE stand for?
2) Suggest two ways in which MNEs can benefit a host country.
3) How would an economist define a monopoly?
4) Why might a company's shareholders quite like the company to be operating in a monopoly market?
5) Explain the term "overtrading".

Worked Exam Questions

There's a lot to think about in business. Make sure you think about it, then look at these questions.

1 EnviroDrivo is a multinational enterprise (MNE) which manufactures electrical cars.

a) What is meant by a multinational enterprise (MNE)?

A company that has operations in more than one country. ✔[1 mark]

(1 mark)

b) Explain why companies may choose to become multinational enterprises.

Operating in different countries can reduce costs. ✔[1 mark] *For example, locating production facilities in different countries can reduce transport costs,* ✔[1 mark] *and labour costs may also be lower in certain countries.* ✔[1 mark] *Firms may also be able to generate higher revenues by selling in various countries,* ✔[1 mark] *since this means the overall size of the market is greater.* ✔[1 mark]

(5 marks)

2 Julie Price opened Crusties, a sandwich shop, a year ago. Unfortunately, the business has become insolvent and Julie has been forced to shut down.

a) Explain what is meant by "insolvent."

A business is insolvent when it doesn't have enough working capital (cash) ✔[1 mark] *to pay its short-term liabilities.* ✔[1 mark]

(2 marks)

b) Identify and explain three vital factors that entrepreneurs should consider in order to reduce their firm's likelihood of failure.

Entrepreneurs should carry out enough market research ✔[1 mark] *to be confident that there is sufficient demand for their product or service.* ✔[1 mark] *The location for a business* ✔[1 mark] *has to be chosen so that potential income is maximised while costs are reduced.* ✔[1 mark] *Marketing* ✔[1 mark] *needs to convince target customers of the usefulness of the firm's product.* ✔[1 mark]

(6 marks)

Exam Questions

1 Read **Source A** and then answer the questions that follow.

Source A

Global MegaComms plc manufactures telecommunications equipment. It has recently opened two new factories in the Far East. The company says it bases its operations in various countries because that is the only way it can compete in today's very competitive market.

a) (i) What is meant by a competitive market?

....

....

(2 marks)

(ii) Explain why governments usually encourage competitive markets.

....

....

....

(3 marks)

b) Explain how a country in the Far East could benefit from the company's presence.

....

....

....

....

(4 marks)

c) Summarise the problems Global MegaComms plc might cause the host country.

....

....

....

....

(4 marks)

d) A pressure group asks you whether you think that, on balance, multinational enterprises do more harm than good. What answer would you give? Explain your reasoning.

....

....

....

(Continue your answer on a separate piece of paper) *(9 marks)*

Revision Summary for Section Six

Well, there you are, the whole story of a firm from birth to death. Probably an easier section than Section Five but you've still gotta learn it all. And the way to make sure you've learned it is to check you know the answers to these questions. Note down any questions you find tricky and then go over the stuff again until you can do them easily. I know it's a pain but trust me, it's the only way...

1) Give four reasons why people start their own businesses.
2) Describe the difference between an invention and an innovation.
3) Explain what is meant by a product having a unique selling point.
4) Explain the main differences between analytical thinking and creative thinking.
5) Describe two ways an entrepreneur can protect their ideas.
6) Describe seven sections that should be in a business plan.
7) Explain three ways that the British government helps new businesses.
8) Why do banks give help to new firms?
9) What's the difference between internal and external expansion?
10) Explain three reasons why firms choose to expand.
11) If a firm making statues of Mozart starts making statues of Beethoven as well, what is this an example of?
    a) diversification; b) line extension; c) the world going mad.
12) Smellsbad Rhubarb Chutney Ltd., a well known rhubarb chutney manufacturer, merges with the following firms. Which type of integration is each an example of?
    - a) Quality Rhubarb Chutneys Manufacturers Ltd.
    - b) Exotic Chutney Shops Ltd.
    - c) Megalarge Knickers Producers Ltd.
    - d) Rhubarb Farms Ltd.
13) Explain the benefits to a business of growing through franchising.
14) Give six examples of internal and four examples of external economies of scale.
15) What is meant by diseconomies of scale? Give an example.
16) What are three main methods of communication? Explain one advantage and one disadvantage of each method.
17) Give three examples of barriers to effective communication.
18) What problems can result from poor business communication?
19) Explain how a business can solve the problem of a long chain of communication.
20) Explain a problem of having a wide span of control in a business.
21) Describe how a firm's employees are likely to be affected by the firm's growth.
22) Explain how a firm's suppliers could benefit as the firm grows. Why might the firm's suppliers be disadvantaged by the firm's expansion?
23) Explain five advantages in operating as an MNE.
24) Give two benefits and two problems for a country of hosting an MNE.
25) Explain three benefits to consumers of a competitive market.
26) Explain why governments prefer competitive markets to monopolies.
27) Give five ways that a business can protect itself against failure.

The Business Cycle

This section is about factors that take place outside the firm which influence what the firm does. They are known as external influences. One of the biggest influences is the economy.

The *Size* of the Economy is measured by *GDP*

1) Gross Domestic Product (GDP) is a measure of the total output of the economy over one year. It's calculated by adding together the value of all goods and services produced by businesses in the UK.
2) To produce their output, businesses have to pay suppliers and workers — and the profits the firm makes are paid to the owners. That means GDP is also a measure of the total income generated by the UK economy. In 2008 the UK's GDP was about £1,800 billion (give or take a few tens of billions of pounds).

Economic *Growth* is an *Increase* in GDP

1) Economic growth is defined as the yearly percentage change in GDP. An increase in GDP means that, on average, people's material living standards are rising.
2) This doesn't necessarily mean that their quality of life is better — an increase in GDP can also mean an increase in pollution. And it doesn't mean everyone's living standards increase equally — some groups of society may benefit a lot while others lose out. Economic growth isn't always a good thing for everyone — though people often assume it is.
3) The United Kingdom's GDP is much higher than it used to be — about 50% greater than it was twenty years ago.
4) Growth rates in the last twenty years have varied a lot. In the late 1980s the economy grew by more than 4% a year. But in the early 1980s and early 1990s there were periods of negative growth — when GDP was getting smaller.
5) In 2008, another period of negative growth started. It's almost as if there's some kind of pattern...

Changes in Economic Growth Result in the *Business Cycle*

1) Economic growth seems to move in a regular pattern. It grows, then declines, then grows again. This regular pattern is called the business cycle — also known as the trade cycle or economic cycle.
2) Periods of high growth are called booms. GDP is increasing a lot, consumer demand is strong and firms will have healthy sales and make big profits.
3) Times of negative growth are called recessions. During a recession GDP is falling — consumer demand is weak and firms will struggle to sell their products. Some firms will make losses and have to close down.
4) Small businesses are especially vulnerable in recessions — they often don't have enough money saved to help them through the hard times.

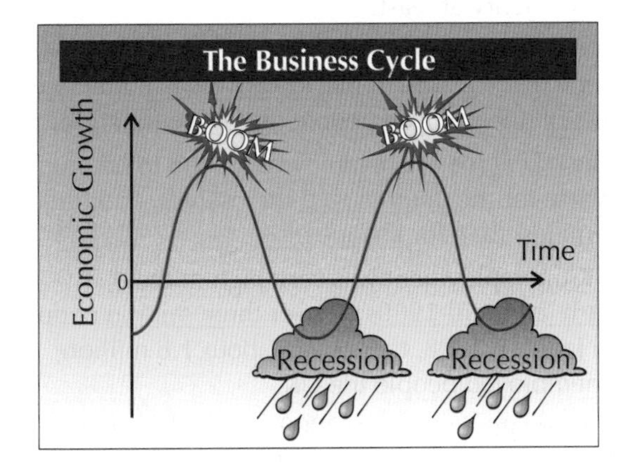

The economy — there's highs and there's lows...

The economy seems to go around in a cycle of good times and bad times. Businesses need to take this into account during the boom times — they can't assume that the economy will keep growing forever.

Population and Unemployment

Generally, businesses like to see the population increasing — it means they have more people to sell to. Other factors like age and the number of people in employment can also have an impact.

The **Population** of a Country Can **Change**

1) A country's total population can rise if more people are born than die each year.
2) Population can also rise if more immigrants enter the country than emigrants leave to live abroad.
3) An increased population means more demand for products and a bigger selection of potential workers. Both these factors can help to increase profits.
4) A higher proportion of immigrants in the population can increase the demand for particular goods and services (e.g. Halal food products for Muslim customers). Firms that are able to meet these demands will increase their market share and profits.

A country's population can also fall (e.g. if deaths outnumber births, or emigration is greater than immigration). This would lead to less demand and a smaller workforce — both of these factors are bad news for businesses.

The **Average Age** of the Population Can Also Change

1) A country's average age can increase if people are healthier and live longer, and people choose to have fewer children.
2) If people begin to die at younger ages, and the birth rate stays high, the average age will decrease.
3) Any change in the average age will affect demand for various goods — people of different ages usually want different products and services.
4) For example, if your product is aimed at teenagers, an increase in average age could mean that your market is getting smaller.

Unemployment is a **Big Problem**

People are unemployed when they're able to work but can't find a job.

1) Unemployment means the economy as a whole produces less output than if everyone was employed. So everyone suffers from unemployment — in theory at least.
2) Some firms can actually benefit from unemployment. They may be able to pay lower wages if there are lots of unemployed people desperate for a job.
3) The problems of unemployment tend to be much worse for the unemployed themselves, and their families, than for anyone else.
4) UK unemployment was very high in the early and mid-1980s — over three million people. In January 2008, there were about 1.6 million unemployed people the UK.
5) A year later in January 2009, unemployment figures had gone back over the 2 million mark.

PROBLEMS FOR INDIVIDUALS

- Loss of income leads to less spending power and a fall in living standards.
- Loss of status, self-respect and social contact that may come from having a job.
- May find it hard to find another job if their skills are no longer needed by firms.

PROBLEMS FOR BUSINESSES

- Lack of demand for products from the unemployed.
- Unemployed workers may lose skills — businesses may need to retrain them.

PROBLEMS FOR THE GOVERNMENT

- Less taxation revenue from the unemployed.
- Need to pay out more welfare payments to the unemployed — Jobseeker's Allowance, etc.

Population changes can have a major impact on a firm's market...

The market might grow or shrink, or the mix of people within it could change, including the level of unemployment. Make sure you know the effects of different types of population change, and the problems unemployment causes.

Government Spending and Taxation

The British government spends hundreds of billions of pounds in the economy every year.
Government has to decide how to raise money, and what to spend it on — these decisions affect businesses.

Government Spending Goes **Up** in a **Recession**

1) In a recession, more people become unemployed — so the government has to pay out more in social security to support these people.
2) The effect of this is not only to give the unemployed enough money to live on — it also helps to maintain demand for the economy's businesses.

Public Spending Benefits **Most Firms**

1) Firms benefit from the financial support the government gives to people on low incomes, but some more than others. A firm making food will get more business from the unemployed than one making luxury yachts.
2) Governments spend billions of pounds building new roads, schools and hospitals. This spending is very important to construction firms and civil engineers such as bridge-builders, but all firms benefit from having good roads, facilities and public services.
3) The defence industry employs hundreds of thousands of people — it would be much smaller without government spending on the military.

The Government Raises Money through **Taxation**

1) The main tax paid by firms is Corporation Tax — basically it's a tax on the firm's profits.
2) The biggest tax paid by employees is called income tax — the more you earn the more tax you pay.
3) Another tax is National Insurance — paid by both the employer and employee. People have to pay this throughout their working lives to qualify for the State Pension and other benefits.
4) Households also pay Council Tax — this helps to pay for local services like waste collection and street repairs.
5) A tax that everyone pays is Value Added Tax (VAT) — it's added to the price of most products. VAT was set at 17.5% for a long time, but in recent years the rate has varied.
6) Excise duties are similar to VAT — the government puts taxes on specific products such as petrol and beer.

Tax **Cuts** Give People **Extra Income** to Spend

1) If the government cuts taxes, it has a similar effect to an increase in government spending — people's incomes are higher and so they demand more products from businesses.
2) This means firms need to increase output — and they usually take on more workers, which helps to reduce unemployment.
3) As a result, governments sometimes cut taxes in a recession to 'kick-start the economy'. They may increase taxes during a boom.

Tax doesn't have to be taxing...

That's what the government tells us, anyway. And it's not too bad — just make sure you understand taxation and government spending, and the effects that changes in these can have on businesses.

Interest Rates

Most businesses borrow money to finance their activities. The amount of money they have to pay back depends on the interest rate. Consumers are also affected by interest rates, so this is an important topic.

Interest is **Added** to Loans and Savings

1) When you borrow money, you usually have to pay it back with interest — this means that you pay back more than you borrowed.
2) If you save money, you earn interest — the amount of money in your savings account will increase over time.
3) The amount of interest you pay or earn depends on the interest rate — it's usually given as a percentage. The higher the interest rate, the more you pay or earn.
4) In the UK, the Bank of England sets the base rate of interest — most other interest rates are linked to this. The base rate changes depending on economic conditions.

Low Interest Rates Lead to **Increased** Spending

1) When the interest rate is cut, it's cheaper to borrow money. But you get less interest when you save money at a bank.
2) When rates are low, firms and consumers borrow and spend more, and save less.
3) This increases spending just like a cut in taxes, and it has similar results — bigger company profits and reduced unemployment.
4) Small businesses often use overdrafts and loans to finance their spending — The repayments on small firms' loans will be smaller when interest rates are low. This means they have more money to spend on other parts of the business.

High Interest Rates Lead to **Decreased** Spending

1) Increases in interest rates have the opposite effect to cuts — borrowing money becomes expensive, but savers get good returns on their investments.
2) Many consumers will also have less disposable income — they'll be paying higher rates on their credit cards and mortgages.
3) As a result, firms and consumers spend less than when interest rates are low.
4) This reduces demand for products and services, which can lead to lower profits and higher unemployment.
5) It's also bad news for small firms that have borrowed a lot to help them invest — they're going to have to pay more back in interest.

High Interest Rates are Bad for **Exporters**

1) Interest rates affect the exchange rate between the pound and other currencies (see page 115). Higher interest rates in the UK result in savers from abroad putting their money in UK banks. To do this they need to buy pounds — and this demand for pounds makes them more expensive.
2) This makes it more expensive for foreign consumers to buy goods exported from the UK (see page 115) — and cheaper for UK consumers to buy imports. UK manufacturing firms can then suffer, as they become uncompetitive.

Not the most interesting page — but a really important one...

Interest rates go up and down — you need to know how these changes affect businesses and consumers. Remember that interest rates also affect exchange rates, so any businesses selling overseas will be affected.

Government Policy — Consumer Protection

There are laws restricting how firms sell their products — the aim is to protect the consumer.
If these laws weren't in place, some businesses might be tempted to be a bit dishonest.

Sale of Goods Legislation Sets Conditions for Products

This legislation includes the Sale of Goods Act (1979), Supply of Goods and Services Act (1982) and Sale and Supply of Goods Act (1994). These acts state that goods should meet three criteria:

1) The product should be fit for its purpose.

- The product has to do the job it was designed for.
  — if you buy a mug, say, it's not much use if it leaks water out of the bottom.

2) The product should match its description.

- It's illegal for a retailer to give a false description of something being sold.
- This includes the size or quantity of the product, the materials it's made from, and its properties.
- It's also illegal to claim that a product has been endorsed or approved by a person or an organization unless it really has been.
- The Trade Descriptions Act (1968) says much the same kind of thing.

3) The product should be of satisfactory quality.

- This means that the product should be well made — it shouldn't fall apart after a couple of uses.
- It also means that it shouldn't cause other problems for the buyer — e.g. a fridge should keep food cold, but it shouldn't make a noise like a jet plane at the same time.

For example, a pair of size ten leather shoes should be:
- the right shape for human feet to fit into (fit for purpose),
- size ten and made from leather (that's what the description says),
- of a satisfactory quality — they shouldn't fall to bits after a half-mile walk.

Consumer Protection Laws Have an Impact on Businesses

1) Businesses have to be very careful when selling products and services to their customers.
2) If products don't meet the legal requirements, customers can ask for their money back, a repair or a replacement. This ends up costing the business money.
3) It can also harm the business's reputation — in the long run, this might be much more serious.

Products need to meet a basic standard of quality...

Businesses also have to describe their products accurately. If they don't, customers have the legal right to complain to the seller. Unhappy customers won't buy from a business again, so firms need to get this stuff right.

Warm-Up and Worked Exam Questions

Warm-up Questions

1) What do the letters GDP stand for?
2) How is economic growth defined?
3) Give two problems of high unemployment levels for businesses.
4) Why does government spending go up during a recession?
5) Why do high interest rates lead to reduced spending?
6) What does it mean to say a product is 'fit for purpose'?

Worked Exam Questions

There's some tricky economics to get to grips with in this section, and the best way to master it is to practise. So make sure you work through the questions below, then have a go at the ones on the next page.

1 Dave Burns has recently started a business selling antique furniture. Part of his business involves exporting antique furniture to the United States. He borrowed a large amount of money from his bank to help him set up the business.

a) Explain the effect of an increase in interest rates on Dave's loan repayments.

The amount of interest Dave has to pay on his loan would increase. ✔[1 mark]

(1 mark)

b) Explain how high interest rates would affect Dave's income from exports.

High interest rates would cause the value of the pound to rise against the dollar. ✔[1 mark] *This would make Dave's products more expensive for his American customers to buy.* ✔[1 mark] *So Dave may lose sales and revenue.* ✔[1 mark]

(3 marks)

2 Shazia bought a jacket from a leading high street store. The first time Shazia washed it, the jacket shrank, despite her following the washing instructions.

a) Explain how consumer protection laws might help Shazia to get her money back.

The jacket shrank when Shazia washed it, so it is not fit for purpose. ✔[1 mark] *Also, the jacket was falsely described as being washable.* ✔[1 mark] *Consumer protection laws mean that Shazia is entitled to a refund or replacement.* ✔[1 mark]

(3 marks)

b) Explain how a firm can suffer financially if its products do not meet legal requirements.

The firm is obliged by law to offer a refund or replacement or to repair the product free of charge, ✔[1 mark] *which will cost the firm money.* ✔[1 mark] *Also, the firm may get a poor reputation for quality,* ✔[1 mark] *which may cause the firm to lose sales and revenue.* ✔[1 mark]

(4 marks)

Exam Questions

1 Jodie Stevens set up her hairdressing salon when GDP was increasing and consumer demand was strong. However, recently there has been negative growth in GDP and the national levels of unemployment have been rising.

a) What is the name given to times of negative growth in GDP?

....

(1 mark)

b) Explain how government revenue and expenditure may be affected by widespread unemployment.

....

....

....

(2 marks)

c) Suggest how Jodie's business might be affected by negative growth in the economy.

....

....

....

....

(4 marks)

2 Steve owns a travel agency specialising in adventure activity holidays for young people. Discuss **one** way in which each of the following might affect demand for the holidays that Steve offers.

a) An increase in the average age of the population.

....

....

....

....

(3 marks)

b) A cut in taxes.

....

....

....

....

(3 marks)

Social Influences

Businesses play a huge role in all our lives, and they can have positive and negative effects on society. Many customers now prefer to buy from firms that have responsible and ethical policies.

Ethical Issues Have Become Important for Businesses

Ethics are the moral principles of right and wrong. Some firms now have their own ethical policies.

1) Unfair exploitation of cheap labour in LEDCs (Less Economically Developed Countries) is an ethical issue. In response, some firms now import their raw materials from fair trade sources — this means they pay producers in LEDCs higher prices so they can earn decent wages.
2) Firms might also change their marketing to emphasise this social responsibility. For example, the Co-op advertises all its chocolate as fair trade produced.
3) When promoting products, firms are expected to follow codes of practice — being dishonest or slating other brands in adverts isn't allowed (although competing products can now be compared in a fair way). Certain products can't be advertised at all — e.g. cigarette adverts are now banned on health grounds.
4) Firms are also under pressure to carry out product development in an ethical way — this means using non-toxic materials, paying close attention to safety, and not using animal testing.

Ethical Issues Can Affect a Business's Competitiveness

1) If a business uses cheap labour from a LEDC, it will be able to sell its products for lower prices. These lower prices might give the business a competitive advantage over a more ethical firm.
2) If the business uses fair trade workers, the higher wages would increase the company's costs. This would lead to higher prices for the business's products — they might lose sales.
3) But a more ethical business might also gain customers and increase its profits — there are plenty of people who think that treating workers fairly is more important than price.

Business Has Social Costs...

1) Businesses can create environmental costs for society, such as pollution and traffic congestion (see next page).
2) Some businesses make products that can be harmful to people's health (e.g. tobacco and alcohol), meaning the government has to spend money on hospital treatment for people with illnesses caused by these products. You could argue that this money could be spent on other services, or used to fund tax cuts.

In the UK, rates of obesity are rising fast — some people think junk food is partly to blame.

These people want food manufacturers to market their products in a responsible way.

Due to government and social pressure, many food companies now clearly label the fat, salt and sugar levels of their products.

There's a business opportunity here, too — many firms now promote a healthy lifestyle as part of their marketing. Clever stuff.

...and Social Benefits

Business activity can have benefits that go beyond the buyer and seller. For example:

1) If you buy a toaster, you'll pay VAT on the price (see page 107). The business will also have paid other taxes in the process of making and selling the toaster. The government can use these taxes to pay for hospitals, which benefit many other people.
2) And a company that, say, makes health-related products will benefit financially from sales. But these products may also increase awareness of health issues — maybe leading to benefits for society as a whole.

Businesses are now under pressure to operate in an ethical...

Whether a business decides to adopt an ethical policy will often depend on how much it thinks it will improve the image of the business. Ethical policies can reduce profits, but there's also plenty of demand for ethical goods.

Environmental Influences

Environmental issues affect everybody — they could have a huge effect on the way we live.
There's pressure on businesses to become more environmentally friendly, but it's not always cheap and easy.

Businesses Can Affect the **Local** Environment...

Some of the effects that businesses have on the environment are fairly easy to spot.

1) **WASTE MATERIALS** Businesses use raw materials to make and package products, which are then sold to consumers. Some of these materials end up as waste. And when a product's no longer needed, it usually gets thrown away. A lot of waste ends up in landfill sites, and some becomes litter.
2) **TRAFFIC CONGESTION** Staff drive their cars to work. Lorries transport goods for delivery. These vehicles fill up roads, which can cause traffic delays and accidents.
3) **POLLUTION** Factories, cars and lorries cause air, noise and water pollution. This pollution can be an eyesore, harm plant and animal life, and is difficult and expensive to clean up.

...And This Can Lead to Major **Global** Effects

The combined environmental impact of businesses around the world could have some long-term effects.

1) **RESOURCE DEPLETION** Most resources used by businesses are non-renewable (e.g. coal and iron). If these resources run out, there's no way we can replace them.
2) **CLIMATE CHANGE** Many industries release CO_2 (and other chemicals) into the atmosphere, which are contributing to the earth's climate becoming warmer. No one knows for sure what the consequences will be, but they could include icecaps melting, sea levels rising, increased flooding... which could have knock-on effects for plant and animal life (including us).

Users of electricity generated by power stations contribute indirectly to this — including nearly all offices, shops and factories.

Environmental Issues can Affect Business **Decisions**

1) As people become more aware of environmental issues, consumers are changing their buying decisions — people are now buying more "environmentally friendly" products.
2) In response, many firms are changing their products and packaging to be more environmentally friendly. Products like electrical goods and cars are becoming much more energy efficient. Many businesses are reducing their carbon footprints by using less energy in their factories and offices.
3) Many businesses are working towards sustainability. They're using more renewable energy resources (such as wind and solar power), and recycling more of their materials.

4) Taking environmental issues seriously can give firms a competitive advantage — a "green image" can attract new customers and increase sales. The main disadvantage is cost. Green production is usually more expensive and the costs of cleaning up pollution can be high.
5) Pressure groups such as Greenpeace and Friends of the Earth campaign to raise awareness of these issues. They target the businesses they believe are causing most damage to the environment. The reputation and brand image of a business can be harmed by pressure groups — this may lead to lower profits.

...and environmentally friendly way...

Businesses can't afford to ignore environmental issues — they have to think about their impact on nature.
Many people want firms to have green policies — firms that don't may find themselves losing customers.

International Trade

International trade is trade between suppliers and customers who are located in different countries.
Imports are goods bought from abroad. Exports are goods sold to countries abroad.

*International Trade Happens for **Three Main Reasons***

1) Some products can only be produced in particular places — scotch whisky can only come from Scotland, and guano, a natural fertiliser, only comes from a few places in South America. If people in other countries want these products they have to import them.
2) Some products are far cheaper to produce in some countries than others. The UK could grow its own bananas — but only by building enormous and expensive greenhouses. So it imports them from abroad — they're much cheaper this way.
3) It may be that a foreign firm produces higher quality products at more competitive prices than a UK producer, so customers choose to buy from abroad.

*International Trade has **Benefits and Problems***

International trade increases the size of the firm's market — it has more customers but also more competitors. This increases choice for consumers, and makes firms more efficient.

BENEFITS OF INTERNATIONAL TRADE

- Consumers benefit through increased choice and lower prices. This raises living standards.
- Efficient firms benefit as they will increase sales and profits by exporting their products — they also gain economies of scale.
- The economy can specialise in what it's best at. E.g. Saudi Arabia exports a lot of crude oil — because the country has huge oil reserves.

PROBLEMS OF INTERNATIONAL TRADE

- It can be difficult for firms in one country to develop a particular industry when other countries with more experience of that industry are producing cheap exports.
- Overspecialisation can make the economy too dependent on imports and vulnerable if demand for its specialised exports falls.

Subsidies** Can Give Exporters an **Advantage

1) Some governments provide export subsidies — they give money to domestic firms to help them sell their products abroad.
2) Other countries argue this gives the exporters an unfair advantage — their own domestic producers can't compete effectively, and may go out of business.

"Domestic" means "located in the same country".

*International Trade Leads to **Extremes of Income***

1) International trade has increased the income gap between the world's richest and poorest countries.
2) Some countries are becoming richer from the income they earn from exports to the rest of the world. China is a good example — it has a large population and wages are lower than in European countries. It can produce goods at lower costs than western countries — a lot of everyday goods sold in the UK are made in China. China's economy is growing thanks to its strong export markets.
3) But countries who struggle to find export markets for their products will become poorer in comparison. LEDCs (see page 112) that don't have many natural resources can have this problem.

You'll need abroad understanding of this...

International markets can mean big money for businesses, but international trade has problems as well as benefits. Cover the page and write a list of the main points. Check your list against the page to make sure you got them all.

Exchange Rates

An exchange rate is the price at which one currency can be traded for another.
You need to know why exchange rates change and the effects of this on importers and exporters.

There are **Four Reasons** for Buying a **Foreign Currency**

A British person or firm might buy another currency, say US dollars, for four main reasons.

1) They're going to the USA for a holiday.
2) They want to invest in a US bank — possibly because US interest rates are higher.
3) They want to import a product made in the USA and need to pay the US firm in dollars.
4) They think that the value of the dollar will increase in the future and they want to make money by buying the dollar whilst it's cheap and selling it again when it's expensive.

Exchange Rates are Determined by **Demand and Supply**

1) If you want to buy dollars, you have to sell your pounds in exchange.
2) The effect of selling pounds and buying dollars is to make the pound cheaper compared to dollars. In other words, the value of the pound has fallen — it has depreciated in value.
3) If people from the USA want to buy pounds (for example to buy a British export), the value of the pound will increase — it will appreciate in value.

See page 27 for more on demand and supply

A **Weak Pound** is **Good** for **Exporters**, **Bad** for **Importers**

1) You can work out prices in different currencies by multiplying or dividing by the exchange rate. In the example on the right the value of the pound is decreasing — it can now buy fewer dollars.
2) British exports now become less expensive abroad — resulting in more sales and higher profits for British firms that export products to America.
3) The weak pound also makes it more expensive for American firms to sell their products in the UK. That's good news for UK firms that compete with goods imported from the US — they won't have to reduce their prices so much to stay competitive.
4) But it's bad news for UK firms that use imported raw materials — these are now more expensive so the production costs of these firms are higher.
5) The result is that Britain will have more exports and fewer imports, meaning the balance of payments increases.

Balance of payments = value of exports – value of imports

THE MATHS

- If £1 = \$2, a British cricket ball that costs £5 will sell in the USA for 5 × 2 = **\$10**.
  And a baseball that cost \$6 in the USA can be sold for 6 ÷ 2 = **£3** in the UK.
- If the value of the pound falls so that £1 = \$1.50 the £5 cricket ball would sell in the USA for 5 × 1.50 = **\$7.50**.
  The \$6 baseball can now be sold in the UK for 6 ÷ 1.50 = **£4**.

A **Strong Pound** is **Bad** for **Exporters**, **Good** for **Importers**

1) An appreciation of the pound makes exports more expensive and imports cheaper. It's just the opposite effect to the example above.
2) This will probably have a negative effect on the balance of payments — Britain will spend more on imports than it earns from exports.

Exchange rates describe the price of different currencies...

Exchange rates can be confusing — it's easy to multiply when you meant to divide, so check your answers carefully. The rates affect the prices of imports and exports, so they're a big factor in international trade.

International Trade Restrictions

Governments sometimes take steps to restrict imports of products — especially if this helps to protect domestic producers. This kind of support is becoming rarer, since the European Union and World Trade Organisation both push for freer trade between countries.

There are Five Main Methods of Restricting Imports

1) QUOTAS → are physical limits on the quantity of a product that can be imported — like saying a country will import 10,000 cars and no more.

2) TARIFFS → are a tax placed on products when they're imported — the revenue is collected by the government. Tariffs increase the price of imports, making them less competitive.

3) SUBSIDIES → might be given to domestic producers by the government — producers can use them to reduce their prices and so make imports less competitive .

4) PRODUCT SAFETY STANDARDS → can be used — the government sets standards that are hard for foreign firms to comply with.

5) GOVERNMENT FAVOURITISM → the government is a major buyer of things like computers, cars and paperclips. They can buy these from domestic producers — improving their economies of scale.

Governments Restrict Imports for Four Main Reasons

1) Import tariffs (see above) are a way of raising revenue for the government.
2) The government may want to protect an infant industry — a new domestic industry which doesn't yet have the economies of scale of foreign competitors.
3) The government may want to protect uncompetitive industries because they're important to the country — perhaps a lot of jobs would be lost if the domestic firms closed down.
4) The government may want to protect its domestic producers from unfair foreign competition. For example some producers may dump unsold products abroad — selling them at prices low enough to drive domestic producers out of business.

Import Restrictions have Good and Bad Effects

1) In theory, reducing foreign competition helps increase profits for domestic producers and protect domestic jobs. Reducing imports also helps to improve the balance of payments.
2) But this doesn't usually work in practice — other countries respond by imposing their own restrictions. This causes problems for a country's exporting firms — these cancel out the benefits for importing firms.
3) A genuine benefit is that safety standards can be maintained — like if a country decides it doesn't want to accept imports of GM food, or potentially BSE-infected beef.
4) A big problem is that by restricting efficient foreign competitors, governments protect inefficient domestic producers. Those domestic firms have less incentive to become more efficient. And consumers have to pay higher prices — resulting in lower living standards.

Make sure you learn these import(ant) restrictions...

Governments like to protect their domestic businesses from being swamped by overseas competition. Import restrictions are a way of doing this, but they have drawbacks as well as benefits. The usual story.

The European Union

Membership of the European Union is one of the most important external influences on British business. You need to know some of the main features of the EU, and how these features affect businesses.

The EU is a Group of Cooperative European Countries

1) The EU was formed in 1958. Its main aim was to bring the governments and economies of Europe closer together so that no EU country would gain anything by going to war with another member.
2) At the moment there are 27 member countries in the EU, including the UK, France, Germany, Spain, Denmark and Italy. The most recent members are Bulgaria and Romania, who both joined the EU in 2007.
3) Each member country has its own legal system, but some EU laws apply to every country.
4) Many EU laws are designed to make trade between member countries easier and fairer. This has benefits for businesses, but some of the laws also increase paperwork and costs.
5) For example, there are laws on product descriptions — e.g. jam can only be called jam if it has sugar in it.
6) The EU also has a competition policy — this is designed to stop some businesses that trade within the EU gaining an unfair advantage over others.

The European Social Chapter is a set of rules designed to protect the rights of employees in the EU. It requires:

- Equal rights for part-time and full-time employees.
- Improved health and safety rules
- A compulsory maximum 48-hour working week for most workers.

It Operates a Single Market

1) One of the EU's big achievements was to create a single market — it came into existence in 1992.
2) The single market has free trade between member countries. There are no barriers to trade such as different safety and product-labelling standards — they've all been replaced by an EU-wide set of rules.
3) Some EU countries also use a single currency, the Euro — 16 EU countries use Euros so far.
4) Taxation in EU member countries has also been coordinated. A common tax system stops businesses from avoiding taxes, or paying them twice. It also reduces compliance costs for businesses — they don't have to pay the costs of following different laws for different countries.

This Benefits Consumers and Efficient Producers

1) Increased competition means lower prices and increased choice for consumers. Consumers also benefit from innovation as producers compete by bringing out new products.
2) Producers have access to a bigger market. This can lead to economies of scale and lower costs. This often means increased sales and even more economies of scale — so the business becomes even more competitive.
3) More competition is bad news for inefficient producers — they'll lose market share and may close.

The EU is Very Important to UK Businesses

1) About 40% of the UK's international trade is done with EU countries, so the EU is important. But whether it's good or bad for UK business... well, it depends who you ask. Here are a couple of views...
2) At the moment, the UK imports more goods from EU countries than it exports to them. Some people say that some of these imports could be produced domestically, which would create more jobs in the UK.
3) Others say that the EU is a huge potential market for UK companies, meaning fantastic opportunities to sell goods. Plus, using cheap imports from the EU can help the UK compete in other markets.

Eee, you better make sure know all about the EU...

Make sure you know what the EU is and what it has done to create a single market. You need to know how the single market affects business who export to EU countries — remember, it has positive and negative effects.

Warm-Up and Worked Exam Questions

Warm-up Questions

1) What is shown by a "fair trade" label?
2) Why are many firms changing their products and packaging to be more environmentally friendly?
3) What problems can arise from overspecialisation of an economy?
4) What is an exchange rate?
5) List the five main methods of restricting imports.
6) How has the EU promoted free trade between member countries?

Worked Exam Questions

You should now be sufficiently warmed up to have a look at these worked exam questions.

1 GrowAcePlants plc produces organic garden fertiliser which is sold in plastic bags.

a) How could GrowAcePlants become more environmentally friendly?

Use environmentally friendly bags (bio-degradable). ✔ [1 mark]

Always try to use the information given to you in the question.

(1 mark)

b) The firm is setting itself targets to reduce pollution.
Suggest three ways the company might achieve this.

The firm could reduce pollution by using more energy-efficient machinery, ✔ [1 mark] *increasing recycling* ✔ [1 mark] *at the factory and reducing packaging,* ✔ [1 mark] *perhaps by selling larger bags of fertilizer.*

(3 marks)

2 AceBoxCo Ltd, a UK company, makes plastic containers which it sells to other companies.
The directors are planning to start exporting to the rest of the European Union.

a) Identify and explain **two** problems AceBoxCo Ltd might encounter when it starts trading in different EU countries.

There may be much greater competition in certain EU countries. ✔ [1 mark] *If the firm is inefficient it will not be able to compete on price* ✔ [1 mark] *with other firms. Sales may also suffer if the pound is strong against the euro,* ✔ [1 mark] *as this will make AceBoxCo's products more expensive overseas than domestic products.* ✔ [1 mark]

(4 marks)

b) How would selling to EU members differ from exporting to non-EU states?

Non-EU governments may be able to restrict imports, ✔ [1 mark] *especially if they want to protect domestic producers, whereas the EU is a single market, with no barriers to trade.* ✔ [1 mark]

(2 marks)

Exam Questions

1 Gems2You plc imports fine jewellery from Asia to the UK which it sells through its high street stores.

a) How would a rise in gold prices affect the business?

....

....

(2 marks)

b) Explain the effect a strong pound may have on the company, and on the UK economy at large.

....

....

....

....

(4 marks)

2 FM Hut is a UK company which exports radio equipment worldwide. Some countries that FM Hut exports to use quotas and tariffs to restrict imports.

a) One of the products FM Hut sells in the USA costs the equivalent of £68. Calculate the price paid by the customer in US dollars if £1 = $1.50.

....

....

(2 marks)

b) Explain how quotas and tariffs can be used by governments to restrict imports.

....

....

....

....

(4 marks)

c) Discuss how imposing import restrictions can have both positive and negative effects for a country.

....

....

....

....

(Continue your answer on a separate piece of paper) *(10 marks)*

Revision Summary for Section Seven

Some of this section is fairly straightforward, but there's some pretty hard stuff in there as well. So it's time to get down to the serious business of answering questions. Make sure you can do all these — if one trips you up, go back and learn the stuff again. It's the only way.

1) What is GDP and how is it calculated?
2) Give one possible benefit of economic growth, and one possible drawback.
3) Sketch and label a diagram of the business cycle. How are businesses affected at each stage?
4) Explain why businesses might benefit from an increase in their country's population.
5) Give a possible reason for an increase in average age.
How might this affect a firm that sells baby food?
6) Describe the main problems of unemployment for individuals.
7) How might some firms benefit from an increase in unemployment?
8) How are firms affected by government spending?
9) Explain how firms might be affected by a decision to reduce income tax.
10) How might cutting taxes help get the economy out of recession?
11) What effect do low interest rates have on businesses that have borrowed money?
What's the effect on savers?
12) What problems are caused by high interest rates?
13) Explain the main purpose of the Trade Descriptions Act.
14) Explain the three criteria in the Sale of Goods Legislation.
15) Describe three ethical issues that might affect a business.
16) Explain one cost and one benefit that businesses can have for society.
17) Describe some of the local effects that businesses can have on the environment.
18) Describe some costs and benefits to businesses of a "green image".
19) How can environmental pressure groups affect businesses?
20) Give three reasons why the UK would buy goods from other countries.
21) Explain two benefits and two problems of international trade.
22) How might an export subsidy give a business an unfair advantage in a foreign market?
23) How can international trade lead to extremes of income in different countries?
24) Give two reasons why a British business might want to exchange UK pounds for USA dollars.
25) Who benefits from a weak pound? And who loses out?
26) Britain wishes to protect its pineapple farmers from foreign competition — explain two methods apart from tariffs and quotas it could use.
27) What is the European Union (EU)? What does membership of the EU mean for a country?
28) What benefits does the EU's single market bring to businesses?

Flexible Working

Until recently the typical job has been full-time on a permanent contract. People would find a job after school or university and stay with the same company for years, or even for life. This doesn't happen so much now — changes in society and the law have meant that flexible working is becoming more common.

There's Been a Rise in **Part-Time Employment**...

1) Working full-time usually means around 40 hours a week.
   Part time is very hard to define — but it usually means between 10-30 hours per week.
2) Some people choose to work part-time so they can spend more time with family or on other interests. Many businesses are now more flexible about letting staff work around their family lives.
3) Other people prefer to have a full-time job, or need to work full-time for financial reasons.
4) In 1997, the UK signed up to the European Union's Social Chapter (see page 117), which gives equal employment rights to both part-time and full-time workers. As a result, employees are now more willing to take on part-time positions. (Before 1997, part-time workers weren't entitled to the same fringe benefits as full-time staff.)

...An Increase in **Temporary Contracts**...

1) A permanent contract of employment has no end date — the only ways the firm can stop employing the person is by dismissing them or making their job redundant.
2) A temporary contract is for a fixed period — for example one year. At the end of the period the firm can decide if it wants to renew the contract.
3) Temporary contracts make it easier for the firm to adjust the number of staff employed without having to pay redundancy money — though the law does now give more protection to temporary workers.
4) Temporary staff are often paid more than full-time staff. This makes temporary contracts attractive to some employees.
5) The main problem for temporary workers is that they have less job security. This might make it more difficult to get loans or a mortgage.

See page 51 for more on temporary contracts and self-employed staff.

...And Greater Numbers of **Self-Employed People**

Someone is self-employed if they run their own business, taking their income out of the profits of the firm. The number of self-employed people is still small, but it's increasing — for three main reasons...

1) Since the 1980s there's been more of an enterprise culture — people are more willing to take risks and set up on their own.
2) The recessions of the early 1980s and 1990s led to many people being made redundant. Some of these people used their redundancy money to set up their own businesses. In 2009, the UK entered another period of recession — it's likely that more people who have been made redundant will become self-employed.
3) Some firms have made staff redundant only to re-hire them later as self-employed freelancers (see page 51).

Flexible working — bend over backwards to learn this page...

Three main types of flexible working — part-time, temporary contracts and self-employment. Make sure you learn what each one is and the benefits and problems they can cause for both employers and employees. Learn, cover up the page and scribble down three mini-essays. Check your essays against the page.

New Technology — In the Workplace

Developments in technology have had a major impact on the way businesses are organised — both in making and selling products and in communicating information. You need to know how.

Computer Software Improves Productivity

1) In offices, word processing and desktop publishing software has made it easy to produce professional and attractive documents. Customers can be contacted almost instantly via e-mail and the internet.
2) Spreadsheet software can be used to calculate costs, produce invoices, and keep accounting records.

1) In manufacturing, Computer Aided Design (CAD) software can be used to create a three-dimensional computer model of the product and make instant changes to the design.
2) CAM is short for Computer Aided Manufacture — it's much more accurate than traditional methods. Both CAD and CAM can improve quality and productivity, and reduce human error.

1) In shops, electronic bar codes have made adding up customers' bills a breeze — the products just need to be scanned in. Some supermarkets now let customers do this for themselves.
2) Payment is quicker, too. Debit and credit cards now use Chip and PIN (Personal Identification Number) technology — customers can instantly authorize card payments using their PIN.

Computers Reduce Costs and Increase Efficiency

1) It's important for a business to operate efficiently — i.e. do the maximum amount of work with the minimum input of people and raw materials.
2) An efficient business will have lower operating costs — this is because fewer workers and other resources are needed to perform the same amount of work. Lower costs result in higher profits.
3) Most businesses have a network of linked computers. This means information can be stored on a central server and accessed by any member of staff quickly and easily — good for efficiency.
4) Computers are also accurate. Human brains make mistakes — cold, hard computer logic doesn't. Unfortunately, it's still possible for people to give computers the wrong information. And PCs can still crash.

5) Computer technology is improving all the time — it can be hard for businesses to keep up. Firms need to choose the technology that will benefit them most, or risk being left behind.

Computer Use has Benefits and Drawbacks for Employees

1) Computers have had a huge effect on the way employees work. Computers can now do many jobs that used to be done by humans, so many people have had to retrain and start new careers.
2) Mobile technology such as laptops and smartphones enable employees to work away from the office — e.g. at home or on the train. This can put pressure on employees to work more during their spare time.
3) Some workers have suffered from the effects of using computers for long periods. Health problems such as back pain, repetitive strain injury (RSI) in the hands and wrists, and eye-strain have all increased in recent years.

Modern technology helps firms improve their productivity...

Computers are generally great for business, but they can't yet work without human input. Learn the ways in which technology can benefit a business and the benefits and drawbacks it can have for employees.

Businesses On the Web

It's easy to take the internet for granted, but since the mid 1990s it's led to massive changes in the way businesses promote and sell their products. Customers now expect companies to have websites where they can buy products and find information at any time. The High Street is becoming less important to shoppers.

The Internet is Used to **Communicate Information**

Internet use is split into two main elements.

1) The world wide web (www) is a huge collection of websites. Anyone can put information on a website, and it can then be accessed by other computers elsewhere in the world using internet browser software.
2) Electronic mail (e-mail) lets you send messages and attachments (photos, files etc.) quickly across the world. As long as you have an internet connection, you can send and receive e-mail without a browser — it's slightly separate from the web.

Websites Can Say a Lot About a Firm...

1) Company websites give customers information about what the firm does and how it does it. The potential audience for a website is huge, so it's crucial to get the message right.
2) Websites can be updated many times a day — they can be used to give customers up-to-date information around the clock.

...And They Can Provide **Customer Services**

1) Firms design their websites to be attractive and provide easily accessible information.
2) Many sites provide answers to frequently-asked questions (FAQs) and provide online forms that customers can use to make enquiries or complain.
3) Many firms include 24-hour online ordering on their websites. This makes it easier for the customer to buy, and so should increase sales.
4) Websites can also be used for technical support — many computer companies make updates for software and hardware available on the internet.
5) Some companies also let customers set up an online customer account. This allows customers to access services on the web (for example, bank websites let their customers pay bills online, mobile phone companies let customers top up their calling credit, and so on).

Gaining Trust is Important On the Internet

1) There are thousands of firms with websites — and not all of them are trustworthy. People prefer to buy products from businesses they trust to provide a good level of service.
2) As a result, some e-commerce firms feel that providing quality of service is more important than making a short-term profit — they're building up a good brand image and customer loyalty.
3) Over time, the firm will become better-known and trusted. With a solid customer base, they can start changing their marketing and pricing to help them make more profit.

The internet has changed the way companies do business...

The internet has become absolutely essential to businesses. Every major company you can think of will have its own website, and will probably be promoting its products on other people's sites. More people around the world are getting connected to the internet every day, and it's often the first place they'll look for information.

Warm-Up and Worked Exam Questions

Warm-up Questions

1) What difference did the introduction of the European Union's Social Chapter make to the employment rights of part-time staff?
2) Give two disadvantages of being a temporary worker.
3) What does it mean to say that somebody is self-employed?
4) What do the initials CAD stand for?
5) What is email? *I know you know what it is... but how would you describe it in an exam?*

Worked Exam Questions

Exam questions love to ask you about how advances in technology have changed how businesses are run. Have a look at these worked exam questions and then have a crack at the questions on the next page.

1 Jennifer is the owner of a small florist's. She is considering whether to buy a computer for the shop. Identify and explain **one** way using a computer could benefit the business.

Jennifer could use spreadsheet software to quickly and accurately calculate her costs ✔[1 mark] *as they change, which may help prevent cash-flow problems.* ✔[1 mark]

Another way would be to make letters and flyers using word-processing or desktop publishing software, which would promote the business and should increase sales.

(2 marks)

2 A chain of travel agents has recently given each member of sales staff a new computer on which to make bookings for customers. Previously, staff made the bookings using shared computers. It is hoped that the new computers will help the firm run more efficiently.

a) What does it mean to say that a business runs "efficiently"?

It means that the business does the maximum amount of work ✔[1 mark] *using the fewest resources possible.* ✔[1 mark]

(2 marks)

b) Explain one way in which the new computers should help improve efficiency at the travel agency.

It should be much quicker for staff to make bookings ✔[1 mark] *as they will not have to wait to use the shared computer.* ✔[1 mark] *This means that the same number of staff should be able to make many more bookings.* ✔[1 mark]

(3 marks)

c) Suggest **two** concerns the employees of the travel agency may have about the new computers.

There may be redundancies as fewer staff may now be required to take bookings. ✔[1 mark] *Also, using computers for long periods can cause health problems such as eye strain.* ✔[1 mark]

(2 marks)

Exam Questions

1 Alan is the owner of a popular second-hand bookshop.
He has recently created a website to help promote his shop.

a) State one piece of information about his business Alan might include on the website.

....

(1 mark)

b) Suggest two customer services Alan could provide on his website.
Explain one possible benefit to Alan's business of offering each service online.

....

....

....

....

....

(4 marks)

2 A retailer puts this advertisement for staff in his shop window:
"Vacancy for a shop assistant, Saturdays only."

a) Is this an example of a full-time or part-time vacancy?

....

(1 mark)

b) Explain the difference between a temporary and a permanent contract of employment.

....

....

(2 marks)

c) The retailer wants to employ some extra staff in November and December.
Do you think he should give the staff a permanent or a temporary contract?
Explain your answer.

....

....

....

....

....

(Continue your answer on a separate piece of paper) *(8 marks)*

New Technology — E-Commerce

The internet has massively changed the ways businesses promote and sell their products. For example...

The Internet Can be Used to **Promote** Businesses

1) The internet can be used to get marketing messages across to millions of potential customers.
2) For example, a business can use its website to talk about how much it cares for the environment. Or it can just focus on how ridiculously brilliant its products are.
3) Businesses can also buy advertising space on other websites such as social networking sites and blogs. Internet adverts can be animated and interactive — they can attract attention to a brand on a webpage.
4) With internet use increasing, many businesses are starting to prefer online advertising to adverts in newspapers and on TV.

Buying and Selling Online is Called **E-Commerce**

E-commerce allows products and services to be bought on the internet — and it's growing fast.

1) Firms put details of their products on their website — customers can browse through the product range, or search through the firm's database using keywords to track down the products they want.
2) Products are ordered online using a credit or debit card. Encryption software converts the credit card details into a code that's difficult for hackers to steal. The products are then delivered to the customer.

E-Commerce Can be Used to Reach **International Markets**

The internet provides more places for a business to sell its products.

1) The internet can be accessed all over the world. As part of its marketing strategy, a business may want to target markets in foreign countries with online promotions.
2) Even small companies can do this, since it's much cheaper than buying advertising space in foreign media.
3) For all businesses, selling to international markets may lead to higher profits.

Buying Online Has **Benefits** and **Problems** for **Consumers**

E-COMMERCE — BENEFITS TO CONSUMERS

1) You can shop from home at any time of the day or night, and choose from a huge range of stock.
2) It's easy to look at several sites to compare products and prices offered by different firms.
3) Prices are often lower online than they are in the shops. (This is due to lower costs — see next page.)
4) It's often possible to track the progress of an order so that you know when it's likely to be delivered.

E-COMMERCE — PROBLEMS FOR CONSUMERS

1) It's often impossible to tell whether a website belongs to a trustworthy firm.
2) There's a chance that credit or debit card details could be used by others illegally.
3) Products can't be seen before buying, and it takes time for them to be delivered.
4) If goods are unsuitable, it can be difficult to exchange them, or get your money back.
5) Once you've bought from a company online, you often receive a lot of annoying direct e-mail — advertising new products, sales, and so on.

Customers always click with internet shopping...

Thanks to e-commerce, customers don't have to wait for the shops to open to buy the products they want. Businesses are happy, too — their costs are coming down. Internet shopping is booming.

New Technology — E-Commerce

Businesses that don't use e-commerce may be missing out on big potential markets. Selling on the internet may bring extra revenue into a business, but setting up online services isn't always cheap.

Businesses are **Under Pressure** to Adopt E-Commerce...

There are three main pressures on businesses to adopt e-commerce:

1. COMPETITION — if a firm's going to survive in business, it has to keep up with the competition. If one firm in the market starts to sell their goods online, then consumers will expect the same service from its competitors. There are some very successful internet companies that offer low prices and wide choice — traditional businesses have had to offer online services to compete.

2. PROFITABILITY — businesses are always looking for ways to increase their profits. E-commerce allows firms to save money by employing fewer staff, and by reducing fixed costs. It might also be possible for firms to locate in more remote areas where wages tend to be lower.

3. POLITICAL PRESSURE — the Government is keen for UK companies to create jobs — especially skilled, high-tech jobs... and especially in areas with high levels of unemployment. Online ordering can lead to firms opening remote offices or regional distribution centres, meaning lots of new jobs.

...And E-Commerce is **Reducing Business Costs**...

E-commerce can reduce a firm's costs in all kinds of ways. Here are some examples:

1) The cost of downloading information is paid by the internet user, not the provider. Things like sales brochures and product information no longer need to be printed and posted by the firm.

2) Some firms employ lots of staff to give out information over the telephone — e.g. airlines and bus companies. These companies may decide to save money by making some of those people redundant and putting the information online instead.

3) Businesses that sell online don't need to have High Street shops —they can sell direct from a warehouse. This saves the business money on rent.

...But Using E-Commerce **Isn't Always as Easy** as it Sounds

There are plenty of benefits to a firm of selling over the internet, but it's not completely straightforward. Setting up the facilities needed for e-commerce can be expensive and time-consuming.

1) Special equipment may need to be bought and installed, especially for large businesses with many customers. (A sole trader may be able to launch a website from their home computer with no problems.)

2) Firms may need to employ specialist website designers, who'll have to be paid. Other staff might need to be trained in using the equipment and in providing good customer service.

3) Some consumers are reluctant to buy online — they might not have internet access, or they might prefer to visit a shop where they can see what they're getting. As a result, firms might have to spend more on marketing to try to persuade more people to use their online services.

E-commerce has benefits and drawbacks for businesses...

When it comes to marketing, e-commerce has given firms access to places that would previously have been out of their reach. The costs of setting up e-commerce may be high, but if a business wants to stay competitive in modern markets, they don't have much choice about paying them.

Globalisation

A lot of what's been covered in this book so far helps explain why the trend in business is towards a small number of very large firms competing in a single global market.

Economies of Scale Lead to Integration

1) Industries such as car manufacturing and telecommunications have enormous fixed costs — for instance, it can cost millions of pounds to research and develop a new car.
2) Very few firms can afford this — so the trend is for mergers and alliances to create a small number of mega-firms that have the resources to compete worldwide.

More International Trade is Creating a **Global Market**

1) There are fewer and fewer barriers to international trade. As a result the world is increasingly being seen as one big market place.
2) Only the largest firms can afford the costs of marketing on this scale — so again the trend is for fewer, larger firms.

Technology is Making **Global Communication** Possible

1) New information technologies such as satellite TV and the internet mean that it's possible for a single advertising campaign to reach a global audience.
2) As a result, consumers are starting to buy the same things all around the world — like fashion goods and soft drinks.
3) Some brand names are changing — firms are increasingly using a single brand name that can be remembered and understood all over the world.

UK Businesses Face Major **International Competition**

1) In the last twenty years, many countries have increased their trade in international markets. This includes India, Russia, China and parts of Eastern Europe.
2) This has created new markets for UK firms to sell to — but also means more competition.
3) A large country like China has a huge workforce and low wage bills. It also has more natural resources than the UK.
4) To stay competitive, UK businesses need to be creative and innovative. And they can keep their costs low by using materials and workers from other countries — for example, many UK call centres are now based in India.

GLOBALISATION — GOOD OR BAD?

1) Whether globalisation is a good or bad thing is hotly debated.
2) The arguments are mostly the same as the ones about monopolies and multinationals.
3) Globalisation leads to big global firms which may produce more efficiently and at a lower cost.
4) These firms become tremendously powerful — in some ways as powerful as governments. Unlike most governments, though, they aren't democratically accountable.
5) Some say that the economic growth that globalisation brings will benefit everyone.
6) Others contend it will benefit the rich at the expense of the poor and the environment.

The trend in business is toward a small number of large firms...

Globalisation has given a few businesses a lot of power — I'm sure you can think of a McXample. I mean example. The entire world is now a potential market for businesses — as long as they can compete.

Warm-Up and Worked Exam Questions

Warm-up Questions

1) Give one reason why a firm might choose to advertise a new product on the internet rather than in a newspaper.
2) What is meant by e-commerce?
3) Why might a company in the UK want to sell to international markets as well?
4) How can e-commerce reduce a firm's costs?
5) Why is there a trend in the car manufacturing business towards a small number of large firms?

Worked Exam Question

Remember that exam questions require you to apply all this knowledge of technology to specific businesses.

1 Read **Item A** and then answer the questions that follow.

Item A

Prin-T is small chain of shops which sell custom printed t-shirts and other accessories. They currently have a website which contains information on what the business does and their contact details. They have recently decided to also offer e-commerce facilities on their website.

a) State two ways in which e-commerce might increase the costs of Prin-T.

They may need to buy specialist equipment or software to set up the website. ✔[1 mark] *Also, they will probably have to employ somebody to maintain the website once it's set up.* ✔[1 mark]

(2 marks)

b) Identify and explain two factors which may put pressure on Prin-T to adopt e-commerce.

Prin-T's competitors may already allow customers to order products online, ✔[1 mark] *so Prin-T may need to offer e-commerce to avoid losing sales to these firms.* ✔[1 mark] *All businesses are under pressure to be profitable,* ✔[1 mark] *and by offering e-commerce, Prin-T may be able to increase its sales,* ✔[1 mark] *and therefore profits.*

(4 marks)

c) Explain one reason why firms offering products like Prin-T's should keep their high-street shops as well as selling online.

Firms like Prin-T offer a specialised service, ✔[1 mark] *and sell customised products. People may want to visit the shops* ✔[1 mark] *to get advice* ✔[1 mark] *about the product they are buying and see examples* ✔[1 mark] *of similar products.*

(4 marks)

Exam Questions

1 Ramish wants to buy a new monitor for his computer. He sees one in a shop on his local high street for £90, and he sees exactly the same type of monitor on the internet for £82. He decides to buy the monitor from the high street, and says that it is worth paying the extra £8 for peace of mind.

a) What concerns might Ramish have had about buying over the internet?

....

....

....

....

(4 marks)

b) What can a business that sells online do to ensure that customers' credit card details are safe?

....

....

(2 marks)

2 a) What do you understand by the term "globalisation"?

....

....

....

(3 marks)

b) Explain how global communication technology has influenced the marketing strategies of multinational firms.

....

....

....

(3 marks)

c) Do you think that, in general, globalisation is a good thing? Explain your answer.

....

....

....

....

(Continue your answer on a separate piece of paper) *(9 marks)*

Revision Summary for Section Eight

Things change fast in the world of business. People's working patterns have moved away from full-time, permanent jobs towards more flexible contracts. Computer technology has made businesses faster and more efficient, and the internet has given them access to new markets all over the world. A small number of businesses have become recognised globally, and they've become seriously powerful in the process.

Luckily, some things are still predictable — you've got to the end of a section, so there are some questions for you to answer.

1) What is the difference between full-time and part-time employment?
2) Why might some workers like to work part-time?
3) Explain why part-time work became more attractive after Britain signed up to the EU's Social Chapter in 1997.
4) Give one advantage to employers of hiring staff on temporary contracts.
5) Give one disadvantage to workers of being hired on a temporary contract.
6) What does being 'self-employed' mean?
7) Give three reasons why the number of self-employed people is increasing.
8) List three things that a business can do with spreadsheets.
9) What are CAD and CAM, and how have they improved productivity in manufacturing?
10) Explain three ways that businesses have benefited from computerisation.
11) Why might some people be concerned about more computerisation in the workplace?
12) Give three ways that a business can provide customer service through its website.
13) Explain why providing a good quality of service is important to businesses that sell products online.
14) How might a business use its own website to promote itself?
15) Explain the pros and cons of internet advertising for a small business.
16) Give three benefits to a consumer of buying products online.
    When you've done that, give three problems that buying online might cause a consumer.
17) Why are businesses under pressure to adopt e-commerce?
18) How has e-commerce helped reduce business costs?
19) Explain what globalisation is, and give the main reasons for it.
20) Discuss the UK's place in the global market.
    What do UK businesses need to do to compete internationally?

Controlled Assessment

Controlled assessment — you'll have a lot of things to do, and only a certain amount of time to do them in.

Know What *Your* Controlled Assessment Will Involve...

For all boards, the controlled assessment is an important part of your GCSE — it'll be worth about a quarter of your total mark. Here's some basic info...

AQA: Unit 3 — Investigating Businesses

- You'll be given a business scenario. You'll then need to produce some kind of report.
- The task will probably be quite open (e.g. "think of a great idea for a local business").

Edexcel: Unit 2 — Investigating Small Business

- You'll have to choose one of five possible tasks.
  The tasks will look like normal essay-style questions about Business Studies, but you'll have to show how your Business Studies knowledge relates to a real business.
- You will need to research a real business (your teacher can help you choose one).

OCR: Unit A291 — Marketing and Enterprise

- You'll need to choose one of two possible tasks, and then produce a report.
  Both possible tasks contain three investigations.
- There are 60 marks available — 10 marks for the first investigation, and 25 marks each for the second and third investigations.
- Each task comes with a whole stack of data. For the first investigation, you'll need to analyse just this data. For the second and third investigations, you'll need to collect other information too.

Controlled Assessment Tasks are Quite "*Open*"

1) All controlled assessment tasks are quite specific. For example, you might have to:
   - Produce a business plan for a new business.
   - Recommend the best course of action for an existing business.
   - Research the methods a business uses to compete in its market, and decide which is the most important.
2) But there will always be loads of ways to approach the tasks.
   The important thing is to weigh up the evidence and come to your own conclusions.

Ten people could answer the same question in ten completely different ways, but all get full marks.

First You'll *Do Research*, Then You'll *Produce a Report*

All the boards give you time to do some research.

For AQA you get 5-8 hours. Edexcel give you up to 6. For OCR you get up to 10 hours. Your teacher will be able to tell you more.

- You can ask your teacher for help during research time. (But your teacher can't help you with some things — like analysing your research.)
- You can work in a group while you're doing research.
  But... make sure you get the information you need.

You'll then be given more time to produce your actual written-up piece of work.

AQA and Edexcel allow 3 hours, while OCR allows 6.

- You'll be supervised by your teacher, but you can't ask for help with this.
- And you can't work with friends. You're not even allowed to use other people's research.

Research task #1: find out which exam board you're doing...

Controlled assessment tasks can look daunting — the key is to keep your head and not panic.
It helps if you know what to expect. If you don't know already, find out which exam board you're studying.

Controlled Assessment — Some Advice

So you know what you've got to do. But what's the best way to go about it...

Use Your Research Time *Wisely*

1) All the exam boards expect you to do research. (For OCR, your teacher will hand you a load of data and information as well as the task itself, but you will need to find out some stuff for yourself as well.)
2) Use your research time efficiently. Don't go mad — quality is more important than quantity.
3) Organise yourself... work out what information you need, then go and find that out. Don't just browse the web and see what you come across.
4) Use varied sources of information (you'll get marks for doing this). Use books, newspapers, catalogues, price lists, the internet... whatever. But keep your research focused — don't end up with a pile of notes that you can't use in your report.
5) Don't just copy and paste stuff from the internet and pretend you wrote it — that's naughty. But you can use small bits of other people's work as long as you say where you found it.

Always keep a record of where your information came from. Write the name of the book or website where you found the information on a printout or photocopy — that'll make things easier later.

Analysis Means **Understanding** What Your Data's Saying

1) Analysis is all about organising and explaining a load of separate bits of information so that they make some kind of overall sense — so that you can describe everything as though it's a kind of 'story'.
2) This makes judging what you (or a business) should do easier.
3) Always relate your research data to your Business Studies knowledge (this'll be good revision too).
4) Stick to the point of the task. Keep re-reading the question.
5) And back up your conclusions using evidence (i.e. your data and Business Studies knowledge).

Your **Report** Needs to Be as **Clear** and **Precise** as Possible

1) Once you've found your information, you'll need to find an appropriate way to present it.
2) Partly, this is a case of organising your data — picking out the parts that are most relevant to your task and putting them into some kind of logical order.
3) But it's also to do with presenting the info in the clearest way — for example as text, in tables, as graphs... You need to choose the best method for your data.

Sales of turnip juice in 2009

Jan	10,000	May	11,090	Sep	13,150
Feb	9,200	Jun	10,291	Oct	14,360
Mar	10,000	Jul	12,180	Nov	15,600
Apr	10,184	Aug	11,520	Dec	17,200

Not very clear — hard to see what's going on...

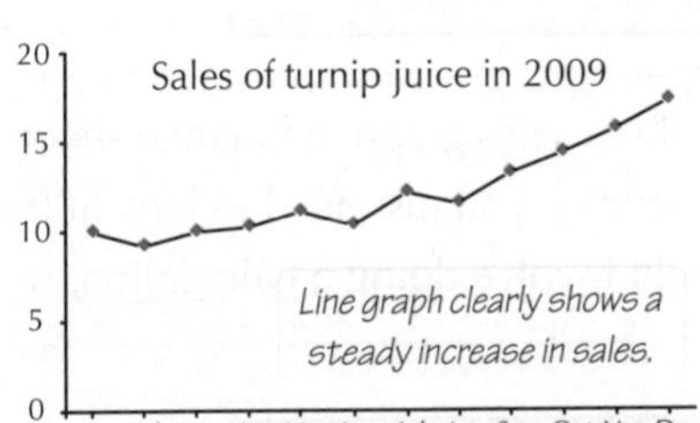

4) Before you start writing, decide what your conclusion is going to be. Then make sure that everything builds up to this in a logical way. And link bits of information together to make it as easy to follow as possible.
5) Examiners love attention to detail. If there are bits of information that don't fit in with an overall pattern — pick these out. If you can explain why they don't fit, then that's great. But even making a note of them without an explanation shows you're thinking.
6) Use plenty of appropriate technical terms. And watch out for spelling, punctuation and grammar, too.

Research task #2: use your data to write a story...

Don't just describe evidence... you need to work out what events must have happened to cause the evidence. This means trying to understand why your data is as it is. It's not easy, but it's the key to analysis.

What Your Exam Will Involve

So... your brain is packed with Business Studies knowledge. But the exams are still a mystery. This section gives you a few tips on what to expect, and how to maximise your marks.

Know What **Your** Exam Will Involve

Most AQA and OCR questions will describe a scenario — the questions will then be based around that scenario.

AQA:

- A 1-hour paper on Unit 1 — Setting Up a Business. Worth 60 marks.
- A 1-hour paper on Unit 2 — Growing as a Business. Worth 60 marks.

  Both these papers are a mix of short- and long-answer questions.

OCR:

- A 1-hour paper on Unit A292 — Business and People. Worth 60 marks.

  Contains two compulsory multi-part questions, based around business scenarios.
- A 1½-hour paper on Unit A293 — Production, Finance and the External Business Environment. Worth 90 marks.

  Contains three compulsory multi-part questions on the case study you'll be given before your exam (but you'll be given a clean copy of this on the day too).

Edexcel:

- A 45-minute paper on Unit 1 — Introduction to Small Business. Worth 40 marks.

  Mainly multiple-choice questions — you won't need to write long answers. There will be a question on balance sheets.
- A 1½-hour paper on Unit 3 — Building a Business. Worth 90 marks.

  The paper is pretty varied — a mix of multiple-choice, written-answer, data response and scenario-based questions.

You won't be given a formula sheet — so learn all those equations.

There Are **Different Types** of Question to Look Out For

WRITTEN-ANSWER QUESTIONS

1) These are the types of question you'll spend most of your time answering (except in Edexcel Unit 1).
2) For these questions, always look at the marks available and the amount of space you've been given. If a question's worth 10 marks, say, you'll have plenty of space for your answer — use it wisely.
3) Some short-answer questions will just ask you to remember and state a fact about Business Studies.
4) Other questions will give you a business scenario and ask you to apply your knowledge to that situation — but you won't be asked about anything you haven't been taught.

DATA RESPONSE QUESTIONS

1) These questions give you information (or data) about a particular business — it might be a sales graph, a balance sheet, or even a newspaper article.
2) Don't panic — you just need to look at the information and apply your knowledge to the data.
3) This might involve doing a calculation, or making a recommendation based on the material.

MULTIPLE CHOICE QUESTIONS

(if you're doing AQA, you won't see any of these)

1) Often you'll be asked to choose more than one answer — always tick the right number of boxes.
2) Sometimes you'll need to choose the most likely reasons for something (or effects of something). All the reasons in the list might be okay, but you need to choose — you guessed it — the most likely.
3) If you don't know the answer to a multiple choice question, it's worth guessing. Before you guess, try to rule out any options you know are wrong — that'll improve your chances of hitting the right ones.

All your questions about questions answered...

Each exam board sets its exams in a different way, but they're basically all testing you on the same skills. But different questions require different types of answers — there's more on this over the next couple of pages.

Command Words

All exam questions have a key "command" word that tells you what the examiner wants you to do.
If you don't do what the command word says, you're not answering the question — so you'll lose marks.

These Words Test Your **Knowledge...**

Questions that include these command words tend to be worth just a few marks — they test what you know.

Define or **What is Meant By** — E.g. "What is meant by the term E-Commerce?" These questions are easy marks if you've learned all the definitions. You just have to know what the term means.

Describe — These usually need a bit more than "Define..." questions — e.g. "Describe the role of branding in a business." You'll have to make several points to answer this.

State or **Identify** — These words ask for a statement — you don't need to back it up with evidence.

Give an Example — Pretty obvious — use your knowledge to give an example of something. You might also be asked to find an example from a diagram or a set of figures.

...These Words Test Your Knowledge and **Understanding...**

These questions test that you understand the concepts you've learned. This means they're usually worth more marks, so spending more time on your answers would be a good move.

Explain — These questions are about giving reasons for things. You need to show that you understand the connection between things that happen in the world and the effects they have on businesses.

Analyse — This means "Examine in detail." Make sure you talk about the main features of the thing you're analysing. Then explain how or why these features work together to lead to the end result.

Calculate — Some questions ask for a bit of maths. Remember to show your working if you're asked to.

...And These Ones Also Test Your **Judgement**

Examiners also like to test your ability to make judgements. To get top marks, you'll need to structure your answer — your ideas should flow in a logical way, and every point should lead towards your conclusion.

Give Reasons for Your Answer

If you see this phrase in a question, make sure you include plenty of Business Studies points and explain why they're relevant to your answer. Link your ideas together to build a balanced argument.

Recommend **Discuss** **Assess** **Which is Most Likely/Appropriate** **Evaluate**

These types of questions are all pretty similar. You'll be given some information about a particular business — you need to use this information and your knowledge of Business Studies in your answer.

- In business situations, there are usually advantages and disadvantages to think about — to get all the marks, you'll need to give both sides of the argument before coming to a conclusion.
- Before you get started on your answer, make sure you've read the whole question carefully and you've understood what you're being asked to do. You'll lose marks if you take the wrong approach.

Do you think

When examiners ask you what you think, they're not just asking for an opinion off the top of your head. As usual, make sure you back up your point of view with evidence and a structured argument.

Sick of revision yet? Give reasons for your answer...

Command words aren't set in stone — the same word might be used in slightly different ways in different questions. But if you read the whole question, it should be clear what you need to do to get the marks.

What Examiners Look For

Mark schemes explain exactly what examiners can give marks for, and what they can't.
If your answer's not on the mark scheme, you won't get marks for it. So don't waffle.

Mark Schemes Tell the Examiner How to Mark Answers

Here's a sample question about an entrepreneur who's planning to set up a small café business.

> Alice is planning to open a new vegetarian café in Manchester. Assess the importance of good customer service in increasing the competitive advantage of Alice's café. *(8 marks)*

1) The command word here is "Assess". Your answer needs to talk about both the advantages and disadvantages of customer service to Alice's business.
2) There's no "right" answer — you'll get marks depending on the quality of your assessment.

Here's the mark scheme for this question — it's split into three levels:

Level	Description of Answer	Marks
0	The answer contains no relevant material.	0
1	The answer contains some relevant points about customer service, but no clear judgement is made. Written communication contains frequent spelling, punctuation and grammar errors.	1-2
2	A judgement is made, but the supporting argument lacks detail and structure. The answer uses appropriate technical terms and shows a clear understanding of the effect of customer service on competitive advantage. There are some errors in spelling, punctuation and grammar.	3-5
3	Several effects of customer service are referred to in the answer, and there is a clear explanation of how these effects relate to each other. The judgement made is well supported, and there is a high standard of written communication.	6-8

1) A LEVEL 1 answer shows that you know about some features of customer service. To get more marks, you'll need to assess those features.
2) You're also marked on the quality of your writing.

1) To get to LEVEL 2, you'll need to use some technical terms and show that you understand the effects of customer service on a business.
2) Show you understand by explaining the points you make — describe how each feature you mention affects the business.

1) A LEVEL 3 answer will explain several effects of customer service. You'll also need to structure your ideas to show how they relate to each other. The examiner will be impressed if you can judge which features of customer service are most likely to affect the café's competitive advantage.
2) Your writing will need to be clear and accurate — take care with spelling, punctuation and grammar. Here's an example of the sort of thing you could write for part of your answer:

> Training staff to provide good service can be expensive, and these costs may lead to higher prices. However, people are often prepared to pay slightly higher prices for good service (and are often put off by poor service). As long as prices do not become too high, Alice may be able to increase customer loyalty by offering a better customer experience than competing cafes, meaning that customers will choose to return to Alice's café.

3) You've been asked to assess the situation, so you'll need to come to a conclusion. For example:

> Overall, the benefits of customer service should outweigh the costs to the business (and the potential cost of not offering a decent level of service could be very high indeed if it puts customers off). Offering a high level of customer service could be a way for Alice to differentiate her café from competitors', and achieve a crucial competitive advantage.

4) Remember there's no right answer here — just make sure you support your judgement with evidence.

These schemes are useful — you mark my words...

The mark scheme above is just an example, but it gives you an idea of how the marking system works. Always look at the number of marks available for a question — the more marks available, the more detailed your answer will need to be. It sounds like an obvious point, but it's easy to forget in a stressful exam.

Controlled Assessment

All being well, you now know all the Business Studies facts that you'll need for your assessment.
But Business Studies is a real-world subject, and so you need to be able to use your knowledge in the real world.
That's what the Controlled Assessment is all about — applying your knowledge to real businesses.

Controlled Assessment Practice — just like the ones your Exam Board will set...

The Controlled Assessment tasks for AQA, Edexcel and OCR are all similar, but all slightly different too (see page 132).
Over the next few pages, we've provided three sets of tasks that are just like the real thing.

Controlled Assessment: Set A — these are just like the AQA tasks
— we've provided three tasks, but you only need to do **one**

Controlled Assessment: Set B — these are just like the Edexcel tasks
— we've provided three tasks, but you only need to do **one**

We've provided some spares — in case you want some extra practice.

Controlled Assessment: Set C — these are just like the OCR tasks
— you need to do **all three** investigations

How you should use these Practice Controlled Assessment tasks

- In the real Controlled Assessment, you'll have to go and visit real businesses to collect your data. But we realise that while you're revising, you might not have time to do that, so we've tried to write tasks that you can either research over the Internet, or that you might be able to find out about easily.
- That **doesn't** mean you **shouldn't** go and visit local businesses — if you can, then great. But if you can't, that shouldn't stop you doing one (or more) of the tasks for practice.
- Don't worry if you don't have time to writing a beautifully polished report. It's still worth thinking about how you'd approach the task — what data you'd try to collect, and how you'd analyse it. See p133 for more info.

And remember...

There are no right or wrong answers in a Controlled Assessment... only answers backed up by evidence, and answers that aren't. (See page 166 to see what answers we came up with for some of the tasks.)

Practice Exam Paper GCSE Business Studies **CGP**

General Certificate of Secondary Education

Business Studies

Controlled Assessment

Time allowed	Set A (per task)	Set B (per task)	Set C (for all 3 Investigations)
Research/data collection:	6 hours	8 hours	10 hours
Writing your report:	3 hours	3 hours	6 hours

- Your may either write your report by hand, or use a word processor.
- Your report should use a clear structure.
- You should include tables, graphs and images in your report.
- You may create your tables, graphs and images during your research/data collection time.

Controlled Assessment: Set A (AQA)

The Government is arranging an award for the Best Young Entrepreneur of the Year. To win the award, you need to present an idea for **one** of the following.

List of tasks

1. An idea for a new business providing a service **either** locally **or** nationally.

You should complete a business plan describing:

- what the service is
- why it would be a good business idea
- where the service would be provided
- the materials and equipment that would be needed
- estimated sales and profit figures

2. An idea for improving the service offered by a company in your local area.

You should complete a business plan describing:

- which service provider you have chosen
- how you think it could be improved
- why you think these improvements would make good business sense

3. An idea for how an existing company in your local area could attract more customers.

You should complete a business plan describing:

- which company you have chosen
- why you think there is the potential for improving customer numbers
- how you would attract these extra customers

Controlled Assessment: Set B (Edexcel)

Choose any **one** task from the list below.

You should then:

- choose a business that you will be able to research:
  either – a local business (ideally a small business),
  or – a business that you can research on the internet
- collect and analyse useful data
- evaluate your findings, and present your conclusions in the form of a report

List of tasks

1. To what extent has a business you are familiar with been affected by recent changes in economic conditions?

2. How would you explain the marketing mix of a company you have researched?

3. How does a business that you have researched compete with its rivals?

Controlled Assessment: Set C (OCR)

For the investigations below, you are acting as a consultant to **one** of these two companies:

Deluxatel — this company runs a chain of luxury hotels in Southwest England. They have twelve hotels in ten towns. Their hotels usually have a swimming pool, sauna, gym and restaurant for hotel customers, but these can also be used by the public.

Baker19 — this company runs a chain of cafés and takeaway food outlets. They sell a range of products, including pre-packed sandwiches, sausage rolls and cakes.

- For the company you have chosen, use the data provided on page 140 **and** your own research to write a report on a number of marketing issues.
- To write your report, you will need to carry out **all three** of the investigations below.
- You should explain the reasoning behind any recommendations that you make.

Investigation 1

The company would like to open a new establishment in either Wharton Sands or Frogley.
The company would like you to advise them which location is more suitable.
You should:

- study the information provided on page 140
- discuss the advantages and disadvantages of each location
- present your conclusions in the form of a report

Investigation 2

The company wants to know what services and facilities it needs to offer at its new establishment in order to maximise its turnover.
They would like you to investigate the situation and advise them.

For the location you chose in Investigation 1, you should consider:

- the market that the company would most likely wish to target
- the information provided on page 140

You may wish to carry out separate research to investigate

- the facilities or services that similar companies offer
- the facilities or services that are important to different groups of people

Investigation 3

The company plans to diversify by organising parties for special occasions.
Recommend a promotional campaign for this new venture.

You should consider

- the types of promotional strategies currently used by similar companies
- the target audience(s) and the influence of promotional material on them

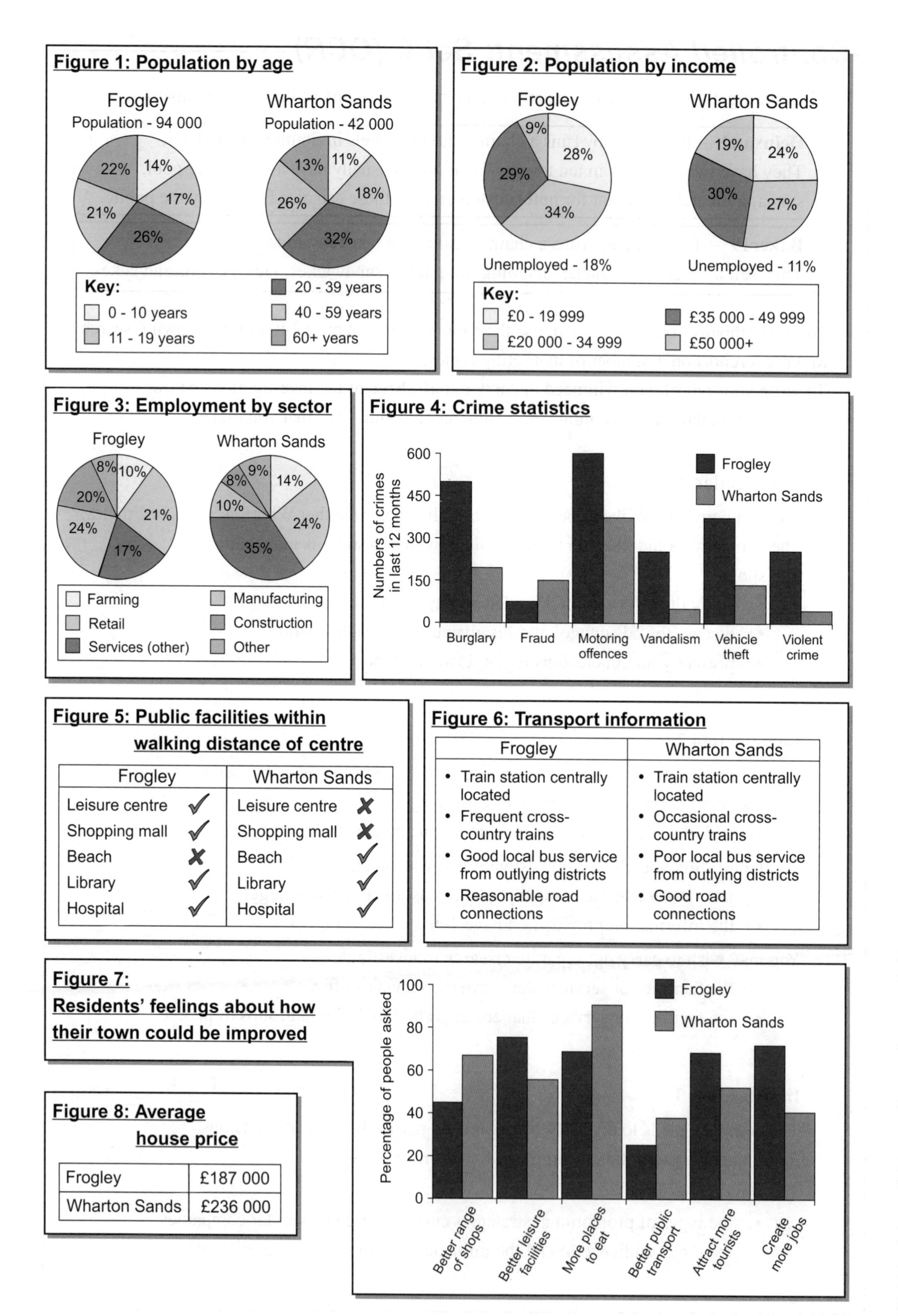

Figure 5: Public facilities within walking distance of centre

Frogley		Wharton Sands	
Leisure centre	✓	Leisure centre	✗
Shopping mall	✓	Shopping mall	✗
Beach	✗	Beach	✓
Library	✓	Library	✓
Hospital	✓	Hospital	✓

Figure 6: Transport information

Frogley	Wharton Sands
• Train station centrally located	• Train station centrally located
• Frequent cross-country trains	• Occasional cross-country trains
• Good local bus service from outlying districts	• Poor local bus service from outlying districts
• Reasonable road connections	• Good road connections

Figure 8: Average house price

Frogley	£187 000
Wharton Sands	£236 000

Practice Exam

Once you've been through all the questions in this book, you should feel pretty confident about the exam.
As final preparation, here are two **practice exam papers** to really get you set for the real thing.

(Note for students doing the Edexcel course: We didn't include multiple-choice questions, but if you can answer the questions on these papers, you'll be able to answer any multiple-choice question you might eventually be faced with.)

CGP Practice Exam Paper GCSE Business Studies

General Certificate of Secondary Education

GCSE
Business Studies

Centre name					
Centre number					
Candidate number					

Surname	
Other names	
Candidate signature	

Paper 1 time allowed: 1½ hours

Paper 2 time allowed: 1½ hours

Instructions to candidates

- Write your name and other details in the spaces provided above.
- Answer **all** questions in the spaces provided.
- Do all rough work on the paper. Cross through any work you do not want marked.
- If you need additional space, you should continue your answers at the end of the paper, indicating clearly which question you are answering.

Information for candidates

- The marks available are given in brackets at the end of each question or part-question.
- Marks will not be deducted for incorrect answers.
- In calculations show clearly how you work out your answers.
- There are 5 questions in each of these papers.
- The maximum mark for each paper is 90.

Advice to candidates

- Work steadily through the paper.
- You will be assessed on your ability to organise and present information, ideas and arguments clearly and logically, using specialist vocabulary where appropriate. Your use of spelling, punctuation and grammar will also be taken into account.
- If you have time at the end, go back and check your answers.

PAPER 1

1. Read **Source 1** and then answer the questions that follow.

Source 1

Eve wants to run her own beauty salon. She has saved up £7500 of her own money. Eve thinks she'll need another £7500 to set up her business. Eve is unsure whether to open up her own shop as a sole trader selling products she has made herself, or open a franchise of *Natural Mind & Body*, a large chain of beauty salons.

(a) What is meant by "sole trader"?

....

....

(2 marks)

(b) (i) Identify two possible sources of finance for Eve's salon.

....

....

(2 marks)

(ii) Which one of these sources do you think would be the most suitable for Eve's salon? Give reasons for your answer.

....

....

....

....

....

(5 marks)

(c) Recommend to Eve whether she should open as a sole trader or as a franchise. Give reasons for your answer.

....

....

....

(Question continues on next page)

Leave blank

....

....

....

....

....

....

....

(9 marks)

2. Read **Source 2** and then answer the questions that follow.

Source 2

Darren runs a restaurant. The restaurant has been open for two years. It broke even in its first year of trading. In its second year, it made a profit every month.

Recently, a large chain restaurant opened up nearby. The restaurant offers similar food to Darren's restaurant. Darren is worried that the new restaurant will take away some of his customers. He is planning on carrying out some market research to help him decide how to respond to the threat of the new restaurant.

(a) What is meant by "market research"?

....

....

(3 marks)

(b) Explain two suitable methods of market research that Darren could use.

....

....

....

....

....

(5 marks)

(Question continues on next page)

(c) Discuss the ways in which Darren might respond to the competition from the large chain restaurant. Give reasons for your answer.

....

....

....

....

....

....

....

....

....

....

....

(9 marks)

3. Read **Source 3** and then answer the questions that follow.

> **Source 3**
>
> Tony owns his own business customising guitars. He runs the business from a workshop at his house. He has calculated that his monthly fixed costs are £600.
>
> Tony has created 30 designs which customers can choose from. Each guitar design costs £15 to recreate. He charges customers £55. Tony has been told that it is important that he works out the break-even point for his business.

(a) Last month, Tony customised 22 guitars.

(i) Calculate the revenue earned by Tony during that month.

....

....

(2 marks)

(Question continues on next page)

Leave blank

(ii) Calculate the profit or loss made by Tony in that month.

....

....

....
(3 marks)

(b) What is meant by "break-even point"?

....

....
(2 marks)

(c) Calculate Tony's break-even point. Show your working.

....

....

....

....
(3 marks)

(d) Explain how Tony's break-even point would be affected if his fixed costs increased.

....

....

....
(2 marks)

(e) Suggest **two** ways that Tony could try to increase his profits.

....

....

....

....

....
(5 marks)

4. Read **Source 4** and then answer the questions that follow.

Source 4

Keith runs a coffee house. He imports most of his coffee from Brazil and Vietnam. He knows that currency exchange rates fluctuate, and so he checks them weekly to help him decide how large an order to place with each of his suppliers.

At the moment, Keith is thinking of switching suppliers in Brazil. He has found a new supplier which provides better working conditions and wages to its workers than his current supplier. The coffee will cost around 15% more than his current supplier.

(a) (i) What is meant by a "fluctuating exchange rate"?

....

....

(2 marks)

(ii) Explain how Keith's business would be affected if the pound became weak against the Brazilian Real (R$).

....

....

....

....

....

(5 marks)

(b) Keith is expecting interest rates in the UK to fall.

Explain two ways in which a lower interest rate might benefit Keith's business.

....

....

....

....

....

(4 marks)

(Question continues on next page)

Leave blank

(c) Do you think Keith should switch to the new supplier in Brazil?
Give reasons for your answer.

....

....

....

....

....

....

....

....

....

....

....

....

(9 marks)

5. Read **Source 5** and then answer the questions that follow.

Source 5

ParmaPharma is a pharmaceutical company. Its offices and research and development sites are based in the UK, Japan and the USA, whilst its manufacturing plants are primarily based in China and Eastern Europe. ParmaPharma has expanded from a small business to a multinational enterprise (MNE) over the past ten years.

(a) What is meant by "multinational enterprise"?

....

....

....

(2 marks)

(Question continues on next page)

(b) Explain one benefit to ParmaPharma's employees of the company's expansion.

....

....

(2 marks)

(c) Suggest **two** reasons why becoming multinational has resulted in ParmaPharma becoming much more profitable than it was when operating from a single country.

....

....

....

....

(5 marks)

(d) ParmaPharma wishes to build a new manufacturing plant in India. Discuss the potential advantages and disadvantages for the Indian people and government.

....

....

....

....

....

....

....

....

....

....

....

(9 marks)

Leave blank

PAPER 2

1. Read **Source 1** and then answer the questions that follow.

> **Source 1**
>
> *Hawke's Gardens Ltd.* is a small chain of garden centres. The company employs about 250 permanent staff. During busy times, the company recruits extra staff in temporary positions. Every new employee is given induction training before starting work.

(a) What is meant by "induction training"?

....

....

(2 marks)

(b) (i) Explain why *Hawke's Gardens Ltd.* might choose to hire temporary staff at busy times instead of taking on more employees on a permanent basis.

....

....

....

....

....

....

(5 marks)

(ii) Would you recommend advertising locally or nationally for these positions? Give reasons for your answer.

....

....

....

(3 marks)

(Question continues on next page)

(c) One of the company's stores is recruiting a senior supervisor.

Do you think this post should be advertised internally or externally? Give reasons for your answer.

....

....

....

....

....

....

....

....

....

....

....

....

(8 marks)

Leave blank

2. Read **Source 2** and then answer the questions that follow.

Source 2

Minerva's Menagerie, a small business that produces bespoke animal homes and equipment, has been trading for three years. One year ago, Minerva's Menagerie merged with Perry's Pet World, a similar-sized company that also produces pet products. The takeover resulted in economies of scale for the resulting company, Perry's Menagerie.

Perry's Menagerie made more in its first year as an integrated company than the combined profit of the two smaller companies the previous year. However, eight employees were made redundant following the merger, and others have complained that they are dissatisfied with the level and nature of communication in the company.

(a) What is meant by "economies of scale"?

....

....

....

(2 marks)

(b) Explain **three** ways in which economies of scale might have made Perry's Menagerie more profitable.

....

....

....

....

....

(6 marks)

(Question continues on next page)

(c) Discuss the problems that the merger may have created, and suggest how they might be resolved.

....

....

....

....

....

....

....

....

....

....

....

(9 marks)

Lea
bla

3. Read **Source 3** and then answer the questions that follow.

Source 3

Connor runs a chain of skateboard shops with branches in six cities. He makes a small profit each year, but is contemplating using e-commerce as an alternative to selling on the high street, as he believes it may be more profitable.

(a) What is meant by "e-commerce"?

....

....

(1 mark)

(Question continues on next page)

Leave blank

(b) Suggest **two** ways in which Connor could use the internet to promote his business.

....

....

....

(4 marks)

(c) Explain one advantage and one disadvantage for Connor's customers of a switch to an e-commerce based business.

....

....

....

....

....

(4 marks)

(d) Should Connor move from a high-street-based business to an e-commerce business? Give reasons for your answer.

....

....

....

....

....

....

....

....

....

....

....

(9 marks)

4. Read **Source 4** and then answer the questions that follow.

Source 4

Ashberry's is a small cookware shop.

Some extracts from its accounts from two consecutive years are shown below.

Trading, Profit and Loss Account Year Ending 31st August 2008	£000
Turnover	66
Cost of sales	18
Gross profit	
Other expenses	22
Net profit	

Balance Sheet 31st August 2008	£000
Fixed Assets	150
Current assets	22
Current liabilities	24
Net assets	

Trading, Profit and Loss Account Year Ending 31st August 2009	£000
Turnover	82
Cost of sales	26
Gross profit	
Other expenses	29
Net profit	

Balance Sheet 31st August 2009	£000
Fixed Assets	150
Current assets	32
Current liabilities	44
Net assets	

(a) By how much did Ashberry's turnover increase between these two years?

....

....

(2 marks)

(b) What was the percentage change in Ashberry's turnover between these two years?

....

....

....

(2 marks)

(c) Calculate the net assets of Ashberrys on 31st August 2009.

....

....

(3 marks)

(d) For the year ending 31st August 2009, calculate the:

(i) net profit

....

....

(2 marks)

(ii) net profit margin

....

....

(2 marks)

(Question continues on next page)

Leave blank

Leave blank

(e) For 31st August 2009:

(i) calculate the current ratio

....

....
(2 marks)

(ii) What does this ratio tell you about the financial health of Ashberry's?

....

....
(2 marks)

(f) Calculate the return on capital employed for 31st August 2009.
(You may use your answers from earlier questions.)

....

....

....
(3 marks)

5. Read **Source 5** and then answer the questions that follow.

Source 5

Roger runs a furniture-manufacturing business. Roger employs five members of staff to make the furniture. The furniture is made using job production.

At the moment, Roger is considering replacing the workshop's old machinery with newer, faster equipment and switching to batch production methods.

(a) What is meant by "job production"?

....

....
(2 marks)

(Question continues on next page)

(b) Discuss ways in which sales and profits might be affected by the switch to batch production.

(7 marks)

(c) Discuss the possible impacts of the shift to batch production on Roger's staff.

(9 marks)

Answers

We've tried to make these answers as useful for you as possible. This is why we haven't used the 'levelled' marking scheme described on page 136 — they take a bit of practice to use and, well, we thought you'd probably have other things on your mind — like learning loads of Business Studies facts and concepts.

We have tried to make our allocation of marks consistent with the marking schemes used by real exam boards, though. So if you score well using the mark scheme in these answers, you should be able to score well using the mark scheme in your real exam.

Note about "Judgement" Questions

In Business Studies, you're expected to show that you can "**analyse** and **evaluate evidence** to make **reasoned judgements**".
(These kinds of questions often say "What do you think...", "Recommend...", "Discuss whether you think...", and so on.)

In the answers to this type of question below, we've tried to show the kind of answer you *could* give in an exam — so we've made a judgement about a situation and tried to back up that judgement using ideas from Business Studies. But there's often no 'right' answer to judgement questions. So if you disagree with our conclusion and have written something different, then that's fine... **as long as you've explained how you arrived at your conclusion**.

(As well as sample answers to judgement questions, we've sometimes also included some extra factors that you might want to mention in your answer.)

Section One — Business Basics

Page 6 (Warm-Up Questions)

1) To make a profit in order to survive.
2) It is easy to set up as a sole trader.
Sole traders have the freedom to decide for themselves how to run the business and spend the profit.
3) A business that is owned and controlled by its workforce (producer cooperative) or customers (retail cooperative).
4) Private limited company; public limited company
5) A person/firm who has bought the right to sell another firm's products or trade under the name of another firm.

Page 7 (Exam Questions)

1 a) A business or other institution ***(1 mark)*** owned by the government ***(1 mark)***.

b) A business that has bought the right to sell another firm's products ***(1 mark)*** and trade under that firm's name ***(1 mark)***.

c) Anna is selling established products that have already shown themselves to be popular ***(1 mark)***, using a proven business model ***(1 mark)***. She may also receive help from the franchisor in running the business (e.g. with training and marketing) ***(1 mark)***. However, she will probably not have complete freedom to run the business as she wishes ***(1 mark)***.

2 a) For example:
1. initiative ***(1 mark)*** — to seek out opportunities and be willing to take advantage of them ***(1 mark)***
2. networking skills ***(1 mark)*** — these allow an entrepreneur to identify people who will be willing and able to help in the enterprise activity ***(1 mark)***

b) A calculated risk is one where the probability and benefits of success ***(1 mark)*** have been weighed up against the probability and consequences of failure ***(1 mark)***, and the risk is believed to be worth taking ***(1 mark)***. Planning is important to make sure that the venture has the greatest possible chance of success ***(1 mark)*** and that the consequences of failure are minimised ***(1 mark)***.

Page 14 (Warm-Up Questions)

1) Internal: owners (shareholders), employees (including directors).
External: customers, suppliers, local community, government
2) Sole trader
3) The people who are most affected by or have the most knowledge about those decisions, often relatively junior employees
4) By function; by product; by region. ('With a centralised structure' and 'with a decentralised structure' are also possible answers.)
5) At first, a firm might be mostly concerned with survival. As it grows, its objectives might change to reflect the priorities of the wider stakeholders (e.g. it might seek to maximise its market share, or minimise the environmental damage it causes).

Page 15 (Exam Questions)

1 a) A hierarchy is a structure containing different levels ***(1 mark)*** where people on a particular level are responsible for and have authority over the people on lower levels ***(1 mark)***.

b) An organisation where decisions are made by a senior manager, or a small group of senior managers, ***(1 mark)*** at the top of the hierarchy ***(1 mark)***.

c) For example:
1. There may be redundancies ***(1 mark)*** if certain roles are no longer necessary — middle management jobs might be affected if the company decides to 'delayer' the hierarchy, for example ***(1 mark)***. (You could also mention wage cuts.)
2. If there are redundancies, some of the employees who remain might be asked to take on more responsibility ***(1 mark)*** — this could even lead to wage increases ***(1 mark)***.

d) <u>For example</u>: (But see the notes on p157 about 'Judgement' questions)
I think the directors should try to cut costs in this way ***(1 mark)***. If the firm is not being as efficient as possible ***(1 mark)***, then its prices may well be higher than the competition's ***(1 mark)***, which could lead to loss of market share ***(1 mark)*** and bigger problems for the firm in the long run ***(1 mark)***. This does not mean that the firm cannot also try to increase profits using other methods ***(1 mark)*** (e.g. by increasing prices).

Section Two — Marketing

Page 25 (Warm-Up Questions)

1) Product, place, price, promotion.
2) A market where small groups of consumers buy specialist products.
3) Strengths, weaknesses, opportunities, threats.
4) Field/primary research, desk/secondary research.
5) Information about people's feelings and opinions that can't be expressed as numbers.
6) Development, launch, growth, maturity, decline.

Page 26 (Exam Questions)

1 a) Collecting and analysing information that does not already exist ***(1 mark)*** using techniques such as questionnaires and phone surveys ***(1 mark)***.

b) It's expensive to collect the information ***(1 mark)*** and needs a large sample size to get meaningful results ***(1 mark)***.

c) To find out if there is enough demand for a sports bar ***(1 mark)*** without which, Bob's bar wouldn't make enough money to survive ***(1 mark)***. Bob could also find out how much similar businesses in the area charge for certain products ***(1 mark)***. He could then price his products to make sure he is competitive ***(1 mark)***.

d) <u>For example</u>: (But see the notes on p157 about 'Judgement' questions)
No, based on the information in the table, I don't think Bob should open his bar ***(1 mark)***. From his questionnaire, only about a third of the people he asked said they would go to his bar at least once a week ***(1 mark)***. This indicates that there isn't much demand for the bar ***(1 mark)***. However, Bob's results might not accurately reflect the population ***(1 mark)***, so the decision would depend on the total market size ***(1 mark)***, and other factors such as the location of the bar or other similar businesses in the area ***(1 mark)***.
(2 marks also available for a well written and well structured answer.)

Page 34 (Warm-Up Questions)

1) The law of supply is that as the price of a product increases, the quantity supplied increases and vice versa.
2) Penetration pricing is where a firm charges a low price when the product is new to get people interested in it. The price is increased once the product becomes established. Skimming is the opposite — firms charge a high price to begin with, so that the product is desirable to people with large incomes. The price may be decreased later to help it become a mass-market product.

3) To make consumers aware of new products, to remind consumers about existing products, to persuade consumers to switch from rival products, to promote the business' brand image.
4) Any five from: Buy one, get one free; Discounts; Competitions; Free gifts; Product trials; Point-of-sale advertising; Generous credit terms (e.g. buy now, pay later)
5) Marketing which is sent directly to potential customers.
6) Manufacturer — wholesaler — retailer — consumer

Page 35 (Exam Questions)

1 a) They could send flyers offering a sales promotion ***(1 mark)*** (e.g. 10% off) to people living in the town ***(1 mark)***.

b) People may not like receiving junk mail ***(1 mark)*** so it may put them off visiting The Bakehouse ***(1 mark)***.

c) Offering higher levels of customer service than its competitors will lead to increased sales for the restaurant ***(1 mark)***, as satisfied customers are more likely to make return visits ***(1 mark)*** to the restaurant or recommend the restaurant to family and friends ***(1 mark)***. People who usually eat at other restaurants may now visit The Bakehouse instead ***(1 mark)***, so the competitors will lose sales ***(1 mark)***, increasing The Bakehouse's market share ***(1 mark)***.

d) "Cost-plus" pricing means setting the price of a product either by adding a percentage mark-up to the cost of the product ***(1 mark)***, or by setting a required profit margin ***(1 mark)***.

e) For example: (But see the notes on p157 about 'Judgement' questions) Penetration pricing could allow the restaurant to win market share quickly ***(1 mark)***. This would enable sales to grow rapidly and help the restaurant to survive ***(1 mark)***. However, as they are a newly established business, they may not be totally sure of their costs and run the risk of making an unaffordable loss ***(1 mark)***.

I think Matt and Nida should use cost-plus pricing ***(1 mark)***. This would be a safer approach since it means the business can definitely cover its costs ***(1 mark)***. They should try to use their excellent customer service to win market share, rather than artificially low prices ***(1 mark)***. Using cost-plus pricing also means that the restaurant won't have to increase its prices at a later date, which could force customers to go elsewhere. ***(1 mark)***.
(2 marks also available for a well written and well structured answer.)

Section Three — Production

Page 40 (Warm-Up Questions)

1) Tertiary
2) Primary
3) Secondary
4) To make their production more efficient.
5) Interdependence
6) Economies of concentration

Page 41 (Exam Questions)

1 a) Production chains enable firms to specialise in what they do best ***(1 mark)***. Concentrating on one area of the production process is a more efficient way to produce goods than if one firms tries to do everything ***(1 mark)***.

b) (i) The term interdependent describes the way businesses in the same production chain rely on each other ***(1 mark)***.

(ii) As the suppliers didn't produce as much wool, Karen may receive less ***(1 mark)*** and therefore be able to make fewer clothes ***(1 mark)***. Karen may then struggle to supply her customers ***(1 mark)***, which could result in her customers looking elsewhere for suppliers ***(1 mark)***, which could be bad for Karen in the longer term ***(1 mark)***.

c) For example: (But see the notes on p157 about 'Judgement' questions) I don't think Karen should relocate to the city. Although there would be advantages, such as a good supply of labour ***(1 mark)***, which Karen will need for expansion ***(1 mark)***, and better communication and transport links ***(1 mark)***, I think these are outweighed by the disadvantages. For example, the cost of new premises in the city will probably be much higher ***(1 mark)***, and Karen will be further away from her source of raw materials and the retailers she currently sells to ***(1 mark)***. Personal factors may also be important to Karen, since she would have to leave behind family and friends and a way of life that she enjoys in the country ***(1 mark)***.
(2 marks also available for a well written and well structured answer.)

Page 45 (Warm-Up Questions)

1) Job production
2) Job production and flow production
3) An approach to making products using as few resources as practicable.
4) To reduce the costs of having to hold stocks of raw materials until they are needed.
5) Reorganising a company to increase efficiency.
6) Total Quality Management

Page 46 (Exam Questions)

1 a) Quality control aims to ensure that no faulty products ***(1 mark)*** reach customers ***(1 mark)***.

b) If any faulty products reach customers ***(1 mark)***, the firm may get a reputation for low quality ***(1 mark)***, which may result in fewer customers in the future ***(1 mark)***.

c) (i) TQM means encouraging a culture of quality throughout the business ***(1 mark)***, so that every employee feels quality is their concern ***(1 mark)***.

(ii) Quality circles are where groups of workers from different departments meet ***(1 mark)*** to identify problems and suggest solutions ***(1 mark)***.

d) Outsourcing means paying another company to perform a task ***(1 mark)***. A different firm could have less rigid quality control standards, so outsourcing could result in a fall in quality ***(1 mark)***.

e) For example: (But see the notes on p157 about 'Judgement' questions) I think the company should eventually move to a culture of total quality management. However, this could take a long time to implement ***(1 mark)***, so in the short term, I think they should increase the number of quality checks ***(1 mark)***. This could be expensive ***(1 mark)***, but low quality could be the basic problem behind the falling customer demand ***(1 mark)***, and so should be addressed urgently. If the firm's quality and reputation improve, increased sales may mean that this is money well spent ***(1 mark)***.
(Plus 2 marks for a well written and well structured answer.)

Section Four — People

Page 53 (Warm-Up Questions)

1) 48 hours
2) Both employers and employees.
3) If the job they are doing no longer exists.
4) Performance-related pay.
5) Any reward that is not part of a worker's main income.
6) Authoritarian

Page 54 (Exam Questions)

1 a) It is the minimum hourly rate ***(1 mark)*** that can be legally paid to a worker ***(1 mark)***.

b) Workers who are poorly motivated are likely to work slowly ***(1 mark)***, as they will not feel inclined to push themselves ***(1 mark)***. They may also produce work that is of a lower quality ***(1 mark)***, meaning work may have to be re-done ***(1 mark)***.

c) For example:
Authoritarian managers make decisions on their own, without consulting any other workers ***(1 mark)***. This may be demotivating ***(1 mark)*** for some staff, who may feel that their views aren't considered important ***(1 mark)***. These workers may feel more motivated ***(1 mark)*** by laissez-faire managers, who allow workers to make their own decisions ***(1 mark)***. However, some workers may feel demotivated by the lack of support provided by their manager ***(1 mark)***.

d) For example: (But see the notes on p157 about 'Judgement' questions)
I think the firm should introduce a bonus scheme *(1 mark)*. If workers knew that they could receive a bonus for meeting certain targets *(1 mark)*, they would be more motivated to work harder to meet those targets *(1 mark)* — increasing productivity. Increasing wages could cost the company a lot of money, with no guarantee that productivity would increase *(1 mark)*. It could also even lead to demotivation of the hardest working employees *(1 mark)*, who may feel that they are not being rewarded for working harder than other employees *(1 mark)*.
(Plus 2 marks for a well written and well structured answer.)

Page 59 (Warm-Up Questions)

1) To get as many suitable people to apply for the job as possible.
2) The job description gives details about the job itself, whereas the person specification describes the ideal person for it.
3) Letter of application, CV (Curriculum Vitae), application form
4) To introduce new employees to their workplace.
5) To protect the interests of their members in the workplace.
6) Strike, work-to-rule, go slow, overtime ban.

Page 60 (Exam Questions)

1 a) To assess a candidate's confidence, social and verbal skills *(1 mark)* and whether they will fit in with the other workers in the department *(1 mark)*. Candidates can all be asked the same questions and their answers compared *(1 mark)*.

b) Employers can test the actual skills needed to perform the job *(1 mark)*.

c) Fully trained employees will be able to do their jobs better *(1 mark)* so there is less chance of them making expensive mistakes *(1 mark)*. They are also more likely to be happy in their job, and less likely to leave the firm *(1 mark)*. This will reduce Riveted's recruitment costs *(1 mark)*.

d) For example: (But see the notes on p157 about 'Judgement' questions)
Unless they are required to by law, I don't think Riveted should negotiate with the union *(1 mark)*. If they do, this could make it more difficult to reward good employees with higher salaries without increasing pay for everyone *(1 mark)* — this would make it difficult to use high salaries to motivate individual employees *(1 mark)*. However, it is important that Riveted makes sure that employees feel that their opinions and concerns are being listened to *(1 mark)*. Otherwise workers may lose motivation and productivity may suffer *(1 mark)*. I would recommend that Riveted set up a works council, so that workers can discuss issues directly with the firm's management *(1 mark)*. This should make workers less likely to feel that they need to join the union in the first place *(1 mark)*.
(Plus 2 marks for a well written and well structured answer.)

Section Five — Finance

Page 68 (Warm-Up Questions)

1) E.g. managers' salaries, telephone bills, office rent.
(Other answers are possible here.)
2) Variable costs + fixed costs = total costs
3) Average cost = total cost ÷ output
4) It shows the level of output at which the firm will just cover its costs.
If its output rises above this level, the firm will make a profit.
If output is below this level, the firm will make a loss.
5) Working capital is the money (cash) required to meet the day-to-day running costs of the business.
6) The length of time the finance is needed for, the amount of finance needed, the cost of the finance, the size and type of the company.

Page 69 (Exam Questions)

1 a) Average cost = total cost ÷ output *(1 mark)*.
Therefore, average cost = £100,000 ÷ 50,000 = £2 per tray *(1 mark)*.

b) Rearrange the formula "average cost = total cost ÷ output" to get:
output = total cost ÷ average cost *(1 mark)*.
Therefore output = £110,000 ÷ £2 = 55,000 trays *(1 mark)*.

c) Joe could remortgage his garden centre *(1 mark)*. He will have to pay back the loan with interest, but these interest payments are relatively low compared to other forms of loan *(1 mark)*. However, Joe's whole business could be at risk if he fails to keep up the payments *(1 mark)*. Joe could also try to get a venture capitalist to invest in his business *(1 mark)*, though the investor may want to take a stake in the business *(1 mark)*, meaning Joe would no longer be in complete control (and could no longer be a sole trader) *(1 mark)*.

2 They need start-up capital to buy or rent assets to run the business, e.g. business premises and computers *(1 mark)*. They will need money to avoid cash-flow problems initially. For example, they may have to secure bookings with deposits before their clients have paid for their holidays *(1 mark)*. They will need enough cash to meet the day-to-day running of their agency (working capital) *(1 mark)*. They will also need finance to promote their business *(1 mark)*.

Page 75 (Warm-Up Questions)

1) False
2) Direct
3) gross profit = revenue – direct costs
4) It shows where the profit of a limited company has gone.
5) The fall in value of an asset due to wear and tear.
6) £7000

Page 76 (Exam Questions)

1 a) A = £120 000 – £50 000 = £70 000 *(1 mark)*
B = £6 000 + £40 000 + £5 000 + £8 000 = £59 000 *(1 mark)*
(or B = £70 000 – £11 000 = £59 000)

b) Gross profit is the difference between sales revenue and the direct costs of making the products *(1 mark)*. Net profit is the difference between sales revenue and the total costs of the business (the amount that a firm is actually left with once all costs have been paid) *(1 mark)* — direct costs of making the products plus indirect costs of running the business *(1 mark)*.

c) Since the bank would be risking its money in See-Saw *(1 mark)*, the bank manager will want to know that it is a sound, profitable business *(1 mark)*. Without evidence that See-Saw is a profitable business, the bank manager may not risk granting See-Saw a loan because of the risk that the bank will lose its money if the business fails *(1 mark)*. The net profit figure for the past year will give the bank manager some idea of how much is a reasonable amount to lend See-Saw *(1 mark)*, and how long it will take the company to repay the loan *(1 mark)*.

Page 82 (Warm-Up Questions)

1) A current asset
2) A creditor is someone that a business owes money to.
A debtor is someone who owes money to the business.
3) Long-term liabilities
4) Turnover
5) Gross profit margin = gross profit ÷ sales
Net profit margin = net profit ÷ sales
6) It shows how much net profit a business generates per pound of capital employed.

Page 83 (Exam Questions)

1 a) Current ratio = current assets ÷ current liabilities *(1 mark)*

b) The firm does not have enough current (or 'liquid') assets *(1 mark)* to pay its current debts *(1 mark)*, and so may face cash-flow problems in the future.

2 a) First find Net Profit = Turnover – Cost of Sales – Expenses
= £500 000 – £200 000 – £100 000 = £200 000
Net Profit Margin = (Net profit ÷ Turnover) × 100%
= (£200 000 ÷ £500 000) × 100% = 40%
(2 marks for correct answer, otherwise 1 mark for finding Net Profit)

b) ROCE = (Net Profit ÷ Capital Employed) × 100%
= (£250 000 ÷ £1 000 000) × 100% = 25%
(2 marks for correct answer, otherwise 1 mark for stating correct formula)

c) It would be better to invest in Tops and Bottoms plc *(1 mark)*. The amount of capital employed is the same, but Now plc's ROCE of 20% compared to 25% for Tops and Bottoms shows that it does not use the money as efficiently *(1 mark)*.

Section Six — Growth of Firms

Page 89 (Warm-Up Questions)

1) E.g. You have more freedom than when working for someone else's company — for example, you can choose to run the company how you think is best.
2) Thinking creatively (or 'outside the box').
3) Where the costs of running the business will be least; where the income from the business will be greatest.
4) Personal details of important personnel; Mission statement; Company objectives; Product description; Production details; Staffing requirements; Financial investment required.
5) Any three from: Business Link; the Department of Business, Enterprise and Regulatory Reform; banks; local Chambers of Commerce; charities such as the Prince's Trust.

Page 90 (Exam Questions)

1 a) (i) A business plan is a description of what a business will do ***(1 mark)***, how it will do it ***(1 mark)***, what resources will be needed (financial resources and staff) ***(1 mark)*** and the profits that can be expected ***(1 mark)***.

(ii) Even if Eve's plan is good, the business may still fail if circumstances change in unpredictable ways ***(1 mark)***. For example, there could be a recession in the economy ***(1 mark)***, or a competitor might launch a popular new product ***(1 mark)***.

b) (i) For example:
Business Link offers financial support to businesses.
It also provides guidance, and training on how to produce a business plan.
The government also underwrites some loans made to small businesses, to encourage lenders to invest in new businesses.
(1 mark each for any two correct answers.)

(ii) Banks (which often have small business advisors who can offer help).
Some charities (e.g. the Prince's Trust).
Chambers of Commerce.
(1 mark each for any two correct answers.)

c) (i) Making a product that customers are willing to pay more for ***(1 mark)*** than the firm spends in producing the product ***(1 mark)***.

(ii) Any two from:
A company can make a product more convenient to use ***(1 mark)***, so that customers are willing to pay a higher price for that extra convenience ***(1 mark)***.
A company can make their products higher quality ***(1 mark)***. Customers are willing to pay more for products that have been built to higher standards ***(1 mark)***.
A company can make a product more easily or more quickly available to customers ***(1 mark)***, so customers are willing to pay for the speed of delivery ***(1 mark)***.
A company can have a strong brand ***(1 mark)*** that customers are willing to pay more for ***(1 mark)***.
A company can have a unique selling point (USP) that differentiates it from competing products ***(1 mark)*** and which customers feel is worth paying for ***(1 mark)***.
(4 marks available in total — 1 mark for identifying and 1 mark for explaining each of two ways to add value.)

Page 97 (Warm-Up Questions)

1) Internal (organic) expansion and external expansion (takeovers and mergers)
2) Diseconomies of scale are instances when the growth of a company leads to an increase in a firm's costs.
3) horizontal; forward vertical; backward vertical; conglomerate
4) Any three of: purchasing economies (buying in bulk); marketing economies (lower cost per unit); managerial economies (employing specialist managers); financial economies (banks will be prepared to back you); technical economies (you can use more advanced machinery); risk-bearing economies (you can afford to take risks with different products).
5) In writing; verbally
6) The number of workers who report to one manager in a hierarchy.

Page 98 (Exam Questions)

1 a) (i) Forward vertical integration happens when a firm takes over a customer ***(1 mark)***.

(ii) Harry will have direct access to consumers ***(1 mark)***, and a guaranteed outlet for his products ***(1 mark)***. However, he may have difficulties managing the larger business, since retailing is a very different type of business to growing produce, and this may not be something Harry is good at or feels confident doing ***(1 mark)***.

b) (i) For example:
Messages may have to be sent using a less effective communication method because Harry will always be physically separated from some of his workers ***(1 mark)***.

(ii) For example:
Excessive communication can mean that workers spend too much time passing on messages and not working ***(1 mark)***, so the efficiency of the business suffers ***(1 mark)***. Insufficient communication can result in workers feeling that they aren't being listened to ***(1 mark)***. This can lead to demotivation of workers and a drop in productivity ***(1 mark)***.

c) Any four from:
- buying in bulk means they obtain stock more cheaply than Harry, and so can offer cheaper prices to consumers;
- widespread and relatively cheap advertising, since advertising campaigns may be run nationally;
- specialist management and administrative staff;
- easier finance from banks;
- can stock a wider variety of products, and so offer consumers more choice

(1 mark for each point — maximum of 4 marks).

Page 102 (Warm-Up Questions)

1) Multinational enterprise
2) They can: invest money into the country; create employment; generate tax revenue for the host country's government; introduce new technology and skills.
3) When there is only one supplier of a product or service.
4) If a company is a monopoly, then the company can charge higher prices than it could if it were competing against other companies. This usually leads to bigger profits for the company, and for the shareholders.
5) Overtrading is when a firm takes on too many orders, buys raw materials and hires staff to meet these orders. Something goes wrong and the firm doesn't get enough money in from sales to pay its debts.

Page 103 (Exam Questions)

1 a) (i) Competitive markets are markets where there are lots of producers selling similar products ***(1 mark)***, and no single producer is powerful enough to dictate prices ***(1 mark)***.

(ii) Competitive markets usually encourage producers to be efficient ***(1 mark)***, meaning products can be offered at lower prices ***(1 mark)***, which can improve people's standard of living ***(1 mark)***.

b) A country in the Far East could benefit from the company's presence because it creates employment in the host country ***(1 mark)***. Global may also introduce foreign technology into the country ***(1 mark)***. The host government may also benefit directly since Global will need to pay tax on it profits ***(1 mark)***, and export revenue raised by Global's sales abroad can improve the host country's balance of payments ***(1 mark)***.

c) Jobs created by Global may be unskilled and low paid ***(1 mark)***, and working conditions may be poor ***(1 mark)***. If Global is important to the host country's economy, it might demand reduced taxes and even subsidies from that country's government in order to locate there ***(1 mark)***. There is also a danger that Global might contaminate the environment ***(1 mark)***.

d) For example: (But see the notes on p157 about 'Judgement' questions)
I believe that, on balance, multinational enterprises do more good than harm ***(1 mark)***. They create employment in the countries they operate in ***(1 mark)***, and although many of those jobs are low-paid, they may be better than the alternatives available ***(1 mark)***. I also think that they can improve the living standards of people in various countries ***(1 mark)*** by being able to offer goods at lower prices ***(1 mark)***. However, multinational enterprises need to behave in an ethical way ***(1 mark)***, otherwise they could easily end up doing a lot of damage in their host country ***(1 mark)***.
(Plus 2 marks for a well written and well structured answer.)

Section Seven — External Influences

Page 110 (Warm-Up Questions)

1) Gross Domestic Product.
2) The yearly percentage change in GDP.
3) There may be a lack of demand for their products from the unemployed. Unemployed workers may lose skills, requiring businesses to spend money retraining them.
4) Because more people are unemployed, so the government has to spend more on social security payments.
5) Consumers may have less disposable income, as mortgage and loan repayments become more expensive.
6) The product does the job it was designed to do.

Page 111 (Exam Questions)

1 a) Recession ***(1 mark)***

b) The government will collect less taxation revenue as fewer people are earning ***(1 mark)***. It will also have to pay out more in welfare payments for the unemployed, e.g. Jobseeker's Allowance ***(1 mark)***.

c) In a recession consumers may lose their jobs and have less income to spend ***(1 mark)***. As consumer demand is weakened, Jodie may have fewer clients or they may want their hair cut less often ***(1 mark)***. So Jodie's sales revenue might go down ***(1 mark)***. She may be able to increase demand by reducing prices ***(1 mark)*** (but profits may still be lower than before the recession).

2 a) Steve's target market is made up of young people ***(1 mark)***. An increase in the average age of the population may mean that there are fewer people in this target market ***(1 mark)*** so demand for his holidays will fall ***(1 mark)***.

b) A cut in taxes will mean that people have more money ***(1 mark)*** and are more likely to be able to afford luxuries like holidays ***(1 mark)***. This should mean that demand for Steve's holidays should increase ***(1 mark)***.

Page 118 (Warm-Up Questions)

1) It means the producers have been paid what is thought to be a genuinely fair price for the product.
2) To respond to consumer demand — a "green" image can attract new customers and increase sales, and prevent existing customers moving to other more environmentally friendly firms.
3) The economy becomes vulnerable if demand for its specialist products falls.
4) The price at which one currency can be traded for another.
5) Quotas, tariffs, subsidies, product safety standards, government favouritism.
6) By introducing certain EU-wide laws covering import restrictions and aspects of products such as safety and labelling. This means there are fewer barriers to trade between EU countries. The introduction of the euro also means that many businesses have lower costs, since they don't have to convert currencies as often as they used to — these "exchange costs" were also a form of trade barrier.

Page 119 (Exam Questions)

1 a) A rise in gold prices would increase costs of production for jewellery producers ***(1 mark)***. These cost increases are likely to be passed on to Gems2You plc. This may mean that Gems2You has to increase its prices in its stores ***(1 mark)***.

b) The strong pound should make it cheaper to import foreign products into the UK ***(1 mark)***. Gems2You plc imports jewellery so prices in its stores should fall ***(1 mark)***, causing an increase in sales and ultimately in profits ***(1 mark)***. The UK will have fewer exports and more imports ***(1 mark)***, which will have an effect on the balance of payments ***(1 mark)***.

2 a) $68 \times 1.5 = \$102$
(2 marks for the correct answer, otherwise 1 mark for the correct method.)

b) Quotas are limits on the quantity of a certain product that can be imported ***(1 mark)***. Tariffs are a tax placed on imported products ***(1 mark)***. Both make the price of imported goods greater than domestic goods ***(1 mark)***, so reducing demand for imported goods ***(1 mark)***.

c) For example: (But see the notes on p157 about 'Judgement' questions)
Import restrictions protect domestic producers ***(1 mark)***, which means profits for these companies increase and domestic jobs are supposedly protected ***(1 mark)***. However, domestic producers who rely on exports may suffer if other countries respond by imposing their own import restrictions ***(1 mark)***, which may in facts put jobs at these companies at risk ***(1 mark)***. People in the country may benefit because tariffs raise extra revenue for the government of the country ***(1 mark)***, which can be used for public spending or to fund tax cuts. However, import restrictions can have the effect of protecting inefficient domestic producers ***(1 mark)***, so consumers have to pay higher prices for goods from these producers ***(1 mark)***. This can result in lower living standards ***(1 mark)***.
(Plus 2 marks for a well written and well structured answer.)

Section Eight — Business and Change

Page 124 (Warm-Up Questions)

1) The European Union's Social Chapter gave part-time employees the same employment rights as full-time employees.
2) They have less job security. They may also find it harder to get a loan or mortgage.
3) It means they run their own business and take their income from the profits of the business.
4) Computer Aided Design.
5) It is a way of quickly sending electronic messages and attachments to computers anywhere in the world.

Page 125 (Exam Questions)

1 a) E.g. directions to the shop, contact details, a history of the business ***(1 mark for any sensible suggestion)***.

b) Alan could use his website to provide the answers to frequently-asked questions ***(1 mark)***. This could save Alan having to employ an extra member of staff to answer telephone calls to answer these questions ***(1 mark)***. He could also allow customers to order books online ***(1 mark)***. This should increase his sales as it does not restrict his potential customers to the people who live close to his shop ***(1 mark)***.

2 a) Part-time ***(1 mark)***.

b) A temporary contract is only valid for a fixed period of time, e.g. six months ***(1 mark)***, but a permanent contract has no end date ***(1 mark)***.

c) For example: (But see the notes on p157 about 'Judgement' questions)
I think the retailer should give the extra staff temporary contracts to just cover November and December ***(1 mark)***. These months are very busy in the retail industry, because it is the run-up to Christmas ***(1 mark)*** so the retailer would want the extra staff to help him cope with the extra demand ***(1 mark)***. However, after this period, the retailer will not need the extra staff and may not be able to afford to keep paying them ***(1 mark)***. If the staff were employed on permanent contracts, it would be very difficult for the retailer to stop employing them ***(1 mark)***. There is no such problem if they are employed on temporary contracts which expire at the end of December ***(1 mark)***.
(Plus 2 marks for a well written and structured answer.)

Page 129 (Warm-Up Questions)

1) An advert on the internet can be seen globally, by many more people than a newspaper advert.
2) Buying and selling goods and services on the internet.
3) To increase the number of potential customers it can sell to.
4) By allowing them to provide product information online rather than printing and posting sales brochures and by allowing firms to sell direct from a warehouse, saving them money on renting a high-street shop.
5) Businesses in the car manufacturing industry have huge fixed costs. Only very large firms can afford these costs, so many smaller companies have joined together through mergers and alliances.

Page 130 (Exam Questions)

1 a) Ramish may have been worried that the company selling online was not trustworthy ***(1 mark)*** and that his bank details would be used illegally ***(1 mark)*** or he would be pestered by direct mail from the company after buying from them ***(1 mark)***. He may have also been concerned that the monitor would get damaged in the post (or about some aspect of customer service if there's a problem) ***(1 mark)***.

b) Companies can use encryption software ***(1 mark)*** which converts credit card details into a code which cannot be read by hackers ***(1 mark)***.

2 a) The reduction in international trade barriers ***(1 mark)*** leading to a small number of very large firms ***(1 mark)*** trading in a global market place ***(1 mark)***.

b) Satellite TV and the internet ***(1 mark)*** means that a single advertising campaign can reach audiences all over the world ***(1 mark)***. This means that global firms are changing their marketing to use a single brand name that can be understood around the world ***(1 mark)***.

c) For example: (But see the notes on p157 about 'Judgement' questions) Yes, in general, I think globalisation is a good thing because it benefits consumers worldwide ***(1 mark)***. Economies of scale mean that global firms can produce goods at a lower cost ***(1 mark)***. This means that products are cheaper to buy for consumers ***(1 mark)***. World trade also results in greater choice for consumers ***(1 mark)*** as goods and services from many different countries and cultures are more readily available ***(1 mark)***. However, globalisation can mean that some firms become very powerful without being democratically accountable ***(1 mark)***. So I think it is important that the activities of global firms are carefully monitored ***(1 mark)***. ***(Plus 2 marks for a well written and well structured answer.)***

Exam Paper 1

Question 1 — page 142

a) A sole trader is a business owned and run by one person ***(1 mark)***. The owner is not legally separate from the business ***(1 mark)***.

b) (i) Suggested answers include:
Bank loan
Family and friends
Business Link
(1 mark each for any two sensible suggestions)

(ii) For example:
(But see the notes on p157 about 'Judgement' questions)
I think Eve should use a bank loan as a source of finance for her salon ***(1 mark)***. Although Eve will have to pay back a bank loan with interest ***(1 mark)***, the bank may provide extra support and information for Eve's business ***(1 mark)***. Eve might also be able to apply to have her bank loan underwritten by the government ***(1 mark)***, meaning the government would pay back the loan if her company failed ***(1 mark)***.

c) For example: (But see the notes on p157 about 'Judgement' questions) I think Eve should set-up as a franchise, so that her salon uses an established brand ***(1 mark)***. This is less risky than selling her own products, as people will already be aware of the brand ***(1 mark)***. For this reason, Eve may also find it easier to get a loan from the bank ***(1 mark)***. The franchisor will also probably offer advice, e.g. on how to run the business, as well as help with marketing and promotion ***(1 mark)***, which will increase Eve's chance of success ***(1 mark)***. Although Eve would have less independence than as a sole trader ***(1 mark)***, she would still have a separate business and would still be able to run most aspects of her business in the way that she wants to ***(1 mark)***.
(Plus 2 marks for a well written and well structured answer.)

Question 2 — page 143

a) Market research means gathering information on the needs and wants of customers ***(1 mark)*** and finding out about existing businesses ***(1 mark)*** to help a business understand the market and spot any gaps for potential products and services ***(1 mark)***.

b) Darren's business is small so his research methods will need to be low-budget and not take up too much time ***(1 mark)***. He could ask his customers to fill in a questionnaire after their meal ***(1 mark)***. He could also run a focus group of relevant people to discuss the topics he is interested in ***(1 mark)***. He might get more useful information from a discussion and it would be cheap to organise ***(1 mark)***.
(Plus 1 mark for a well written and well structured answer.)

Other potential answers include:
- Conducting surveys over the telephone or internet.
- Desk research, e.g. looking at articles in magazines or on the internet, which might show Darren how other businesses had reacted in similar circumstances.

c) For example: (But see the notes on p157 about 'Judgement' questions) Darren would need to look carefully at the results of his market research, to work out what his customers want ***(1 mark)***. He may find it hard to compete on price ***(1 mark)***, but he could make eating in his restaurant attractive in other ways, for example, by providing excellent customer service ***(1 mark)***. This would help him build up a good reputation and loyal customer base ***(1 mark)***. Repeat business will help him remain competitive ***(1 mark)***. Since the new restaurant offers similar food to Darren's restaurant, Darren could introduce a new menu with different types of cuisine to attract new customers ***(1 mark)***. This would mean that his restaurant was sufficiently different from the large chain restaurant that it would not be in direct competition ***(1 mark)***.
(Plus 2 marks for a well written and well structured answer.)

Question 3 — page 144

a) (i) Revenue = quantity sold × price = 22 × £55 = £1210
(2 marks for the correct answer, otherwise 1 mark for the formula 'revenue = quantity × price'.)

(ii) Profit = revenue – costs
Costs = £600 + (22 × £15) = £930
Profit = £1210 – £930 = £280
(3 marks for the correct answer, otherwise 1 mark for the formula 'profit = revenue – costs', and 1 mark for correctly calculating last month's costs.)

b) The point at which a company's sales cover their costs ***(1 mark)*** without making any profit or loss ***(1 mark)***.

c) Contribution per unit = £55 – £15 = £40
Fixed costs = £600
Break-even quantity = fixed costs ÷ contribution per unit
= 600 ÷ 40 = 15 guitars
(3 marks for the correct answer, otherwise 1 mark for finding the contribution per unit, and 1 mark for dividing the fixed costs by the contribution per unit.)

d) If Tony's fixed costs increased the break-even point of his business would also increase ***(1 mark)***, meaning he would have to customise more guitars to break even ***(1 mark)***.

e) For example:
Tony could increase the number of guitars he sells ***(1 mark)***. To achieve this he could perhaps advertise more widely or make his product appeal to a wider market, e.g. by creating more designs ***(1 mark)***.

He could also increase the price he charges customers ***(1 mark)*** to increase his contribution per unit. However, this might mean he loses some business if customers aren't prepared to pay his new prices ***(1 mark)***.
(Plus 1 mark for a well written and well structured answer.)

Question 4 — page 146

a) (i) An exchange rate is the price at which one currency can be traded for another ***(1 mark)***. The rates change (fluctuate) depending on the demand and supply of the different currencies ***(1 mark)***.

(ii) A weak pound would mean that importing goods from Brazil would become more expensive ***(1 mark)***. Keith will either have to pay more for Brazilian coffee or he may decide not to import as much coffee from Brazil ***(1 mark)*** until the pound becomes stronger. This will mean that he either has to charge a higher price for Brazilian coffee (or make less profit from it) ***(1 mark)***, or that he has a smaller selection of coffee to sell ***(1 mark)***. As a result he may lose business ***(1 mark)***.

b) On the whole, customers will have more disposable income ***(1 mark)*** so Keith's sales might increase ***(1 mark)***. Also, Keith would have to pay less interest on any loans he has ***(1 mark)***. This will save Keith money, which he could use to invest in his business ***(1 mark)***.

c) For example: (But see the notes on p157 about 'Judgement' questions) I think Keith should switch to the new supplier in Brazil, as long as he believes that his current supplier's pay and working conditions are unfair on its workers ***(1 mark)***. Buying coffee from the new supplier could show that Keith's business has sound ethical policies ***(1 mark)***. Consumers are becoming more concerned about ethical issues ***(1 mark)***, so although Keith will probably have to charge a higher price ***(1 mark)***, he may find that his sales do not fall ***(1 mark)***, as long as he promotes the fact that his coffee comes from ethical sources ***(1 mark)***. In fact, he may even gain custom if people previously had worries about buying coffee that might have come from an unethical supplier ***(1 mark)***.
(Plus 2 marks for a well written and well structured answer.)

Question 5 — page 147

a) Multinational enterprises are businesses ***(1 mark)*** that have operations in more than one country ***(1 mark)***.

b) ParmaPharma employees will benefit from greater job security ***(1 mark)***, because larger businesses are less likely to fail than smaller businesses ***(1 mark)***.

c) For example:
By moving their production facilities to countries where land and labour are relatively cheap, e.g. China and Eastern Europe ***(1 mark)***, ParmaPharma will be reducing their costs ***(1 mark)***.
By having branches in many regions, ParmaPharma ensure that they have an up-to-date knowledge of local markets around the world ***(1 mark)***, allowing the company to maximise its revenues from different countries ***(1 mark)***.
(Plus 1 mark for a well written and well structured answer.)

d) For example: (But see the notes on p157 about 'Judgement' questions)
A ParmaPharma manufacturing plant would mean increased investment in the country ***(1 mark)*** and would create jobs for locals ***(1 mark)***. However, any jobs created are likely to be unskilled and poorly paid ***(1 mark)***. It may still be the case, though, that ParmaPharma jobs are better than the alternative forms of employment available to the locals ***(1 mark)***. If there are similar existing businesses in the country, the new PharmaPharma plant might have a negative effect on them ***(1 mark)***.
Also, if the new plant becomes important to the local economy, PharmaPharma may ask for reduced tax rates and improved infrastructure ***(1 mark)***. The manufacturing plant may also cause a lot of environmental damage ***(1 mark)***.
(Plus 2 marks for a well written and well structured answer.)

Exam Paper 2

Question 1 — page 149

a) Induction training is given to staff as an introduction to their job ***(1 mark)***. New staff are introduced to their co-workers and to the company's rules, e.g. health and safety procedures ***(1 mark)***.

b) (i) Extra workers are needed to help out when there is too much work for current staff ***(1 mark)***. However, the garden centre probably has quiet periods ***(1 mark)***, so there may not be enough work to sustain extra staff all year round ***(1 mark)***. Employing temporary staff offers an easy way for Hawke's Gardens to adjust the size of its workforce ***(1 mark)***, without the commitment of having to pay redundancy money ***(1 mark)***.

(ii) I would recommend advertising locally. This is because local advertising will be cheaper ***(1 mark)***. Also, because the positions are likely to be at quite a low level and are only temporary ***(1 mark)***, candidates will probably not be willing to travel far to take one of these jobs ***(1 mark)***, so national advertising would be wasteful.

c) For example: (But see the notes on p157 about 'Judgement' questions)
I think Hawke's Gardens should advertise the job internally, at least initially. This is a much cheaper method of advertising ***(1 mark)*** than external advertising. The advert could be posted on a staff notice board ***(1 mark)*** and seen by all staff ***(1 mark)***. Advertising internally also means that whoever gets the job will already have a good understanding of the company and how it works ***(1 mark)***, and the post can also be filled more quickly ***(1 mark)***. If no suitable candidates emerge, the company can always advertise externally at that point ***(1 mark)***.
(Plus 2 marks for a well written and well structured answer.)

Question 2 — page 151

a) Economies of scale are reductions in the average cost ***(1 mark)*** that come from producing on a large scale ***(1 mark)***.

b) For example:
Perry's Menagerie could buy in bulk ***(1 mark)***, and therefore get stock at a cheaper price than either single company ***(1 mark)***.

Advertising campaigns would be run for one large company, rather than two small ones ***(1 mark)***, which would cut overall advertising costs ***(1 mark)***.

Perry's Menagerie could employ specialist managers with expert knowledge, e.g. accountants ***(1 mark)***, who could come up with ways to cut costs and increase profits ***(1 mark)***.

c) There were redundancies within the larger company ***(1 mark)***, which may have caused worry and resentment within the workforce ***(1 mark)***. However, if the company can become even more profitable and expand, it may be able to take on more staff — the workforce should be given this reassurance ***(1 mark)***. Another problem caused by the merger seems to be concerned with communication ***(1 mark)***. As the company increased in size, chains of communication may have become longer ***(1 mark)***. This may have resulted in employees not receiving relevant messages and feeling demoralised ***(1 mark)***. This could be addressed by removing some of the layers of management within Perry's Menagerie ***(1 mark)***.
(Plus 2 marks for a well written and well structured answer.)

Question 3 — page 152

a) E-commerce is the buying and selling of goods and services on the internet ***(1 mark)***.

b) For example:
Connor could create his own website ***(1 mark)*** to advertise his products ***(1 mark)***.
He could advertise his skateboards on other websites ***(1 mark)*** that he thought his target market might use e.g. social networking sites, skateboarding forums ***(1 mark)***.

c) *Advantages include:*
Customers could shop from home at any time of the day or night ***(1 mark)***, which means they don't have to travel anywhere in order to shop and they're not tied to store opening hours ***(1 mark)***.

Prices might be lower online than in the shops because of the lower business overheads (e.g. there would be no need to rent and maintain a high-street shop) ***(1 mark)***, so customers can save money or afford a better skateboard ***(1 mark)***.

Disadvantages include:
Customers can't examine the products before buying them ***(1 mark)***, so it may be harder to judge from a website whether the product is precisely what they want ***(1 mark)***.

By paying online, customers run the risk that their credit or debit card details may be used illegally ***(1 mark)*** if Connor's website is hacked into ***(1 mark)***.

(Maximum of 4 marks available: 2 marks for explaining one advantage and 2 marks for explaining one disadvantage.)

d) For example: (But see the notes on p157 about 'Judgement' questions)
I think that Connor should move from the high street to an e-commerce business. He wouldn't have to rent shops or employ as many staff ***(1 mark)***, so he would save money and therefore increase his profits ***(1 mark)***. Or, since his costs will be lower, Connor will be able to reduce the price of his goods ***(1 mark)***, meaning that his business can become more competitive ***(1 mark)***. Although Connor may lose some sales if his shops are no longer on the high street ***(1 mark)***, overall he should gain customers since selling online would mean that people all over the world would be able to buy Connor's skateboards ***(1 mark)***. However, Connor should be aware of the costs of setting up an e-commerce business, such as having to buy specialist equipment and perhaps employing a web designer ***(1 mark)***.
(Plus 2 marks for a well written and well structured answer.)

Question 4 — page 154

a) Increase in turnover = turnover in 2009 – turnover in 2008
= £82 000 – £66 000 = £16 000
(2 marks for the correct answer, otherwise 1 mark for subtracting the earlier turnover from the later one.)

b) % change in turnover
= increase in turnover ÷ original turnover × 100%
= £16 000 ÷ £66 000 × 100%
= 24.2424... = 24%
(2 marks for the correct answer, otherwise 1 mark for dividing the change in turnover by the original turnover.)

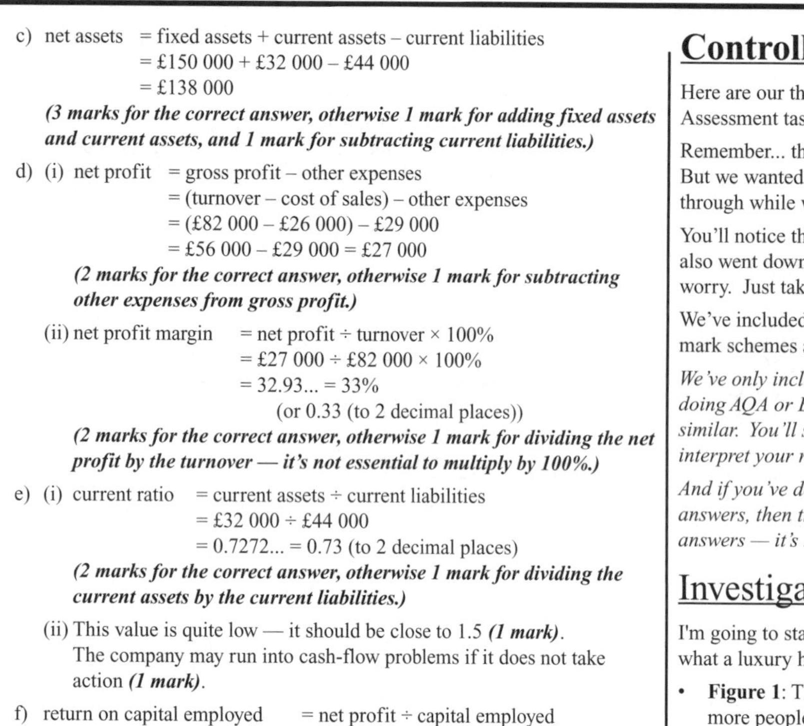

c) net assets = fixed assets + current assets – current liabilities
= £150 000 + £32 000 – £44 000
= £138 000
(3 marks for the correct answer, otherwise 1 mark for adding fixed assets and current assets, and 1 mark for subtracting current liabilities.)

d) (i) net profit = gross profit – other expenses
= (turnover – cost of sales) – other expenses
= (£82 000 – £26 000) – £29 000
= £56 000 – £29 000 = £27 000
(2 marks for the correct answer, otherwise 1 mark for subtracting other expenses from gross profit.)

(ii) net profit margin = net profit ÷ turnover × 100%
= £27 000 ÷ £82 000 × 100%
= 32.93... = 33%
(or 0.33 (to 2 decimal places))
(2 marks for the correct answer, otherwise 1 mark for dividing the net profit by the turnover — it's not essential to multiply by 100%.)

e) (i) current ratio = current assets ÷ current liabilities
= £32 000 ÷ £44 000
= 0.7272... = 0.73 (to 2 decimal places)
(2 marks for the correct answer, otherwise 1 mark for dividing the current assets by the current liabilities.)

(ii) This value is quite low — it should be close to 1.5 ***(1 mark)***.
The company may run into cash-flow problems if it does not take action ***(1 mark)***.

f) return on capital employed = net profit ÷ capital employed
= £27 000 ÷ £138 000
(since capital employed = net assets)
= 0.1956...
= 0.20 (to 2 decimal places)
(3 marks for the correct answer, otherwise 1 mark for dividing net profit by the capital employed, and 1 mark for using the correct figure for capital employed.)

Question 5 — page 155

a) Job production means making one-off goods ***(1 mark)***, often according to a customer's specification ***(1 mark)***.

b) The switch to batch production should make the company more efficient ***(1 mark)***. The quantity of furniture produced should increase ***(1 mark)*** and the price can decrease ***(1 mark)***, meaning sales should increase ***(1 mark)***. However, this also means that each piece made will no longer be unique ***(1 mark)***, so the company may lose some customers who would prefer something more individual and who are prepared to pay for hand-crafted furniture ***(1 mark)***. It's difficult to know what the overall effect on profit will be ***(1 mark)***.

c) For example:
By switching to batch production and using more efficient machinery, fewer workers may be needed to actually make furniture ***(1 mark)***, so some workers may lose their jobs ***(1 mark)***. Also, the workers who remain may no longer be required to produce furniture by hand ***(1 mark)***, so they would no longer be using the same technical skills ***(1 mark)***, which could be demotivating ***(1 mark)***. However, operating the new machinery would create opportunities to learn different skills ***(1 mark)***. This would make them more versatile and therefore more employable elsewhere if they wanted to change jobs in the future ***(1 mark)***.
(Plus 2 marks for a well written and well structured answer.)

Controlled Assessment

Here are our thoughts on how we went about tackling one of the Controlled Assessment tasks (*we tackled the Set C (OCR) Investigations*).

Remember... there's no single correct way to do a Controlled Assessment task. But we wanted to give you a feel for some of the thought processes *we* went through while we were trying to put together our report.

You'll notice that there were times where we weren't sure what to do next, and we also went down a couple of dead ends. You'll probably do that too — don't worry. Just take stock, and remember what it is you're trying to achieve.

We've included our final written-up report and some details from the relevant mark schemes as well.

We've only included our sample answer for the OCR investigation — but if you're doing AQA or Edexcel, the approach for your Controlled Assessment will be very similar. You'll still need to come up with ideas, make a plan, do your research, interpret your results, and write a report.

And if you've done the OCR investigations and come up with completely different answers, then that doesn't mean you should worry. There are loads of possible answers — it's how you use your evidence that counts.

Investigation 1

I'm going to start by looking at the information on page 140 while thinking about what a luxury hotel might need, and what it might be able to offer.

- **Figure 1**: There's a higher proportion of older people (> 60) in Frogley, and more people of working age (say 20-59) in Wharton Sands. And the population of Frogley is more than double that of Wharton Sands. This might be important, but I'm not quite sure how.
- **Figure 2**: Frogley has a higher proportion of people earning £0-34 999, and Wharton Sands has a higher proportion of people earning £35 000 and over, so Wharton Sands looks more affluent. There's also a lower percentage of unemployed people there. Average house prices (see **Figure 8**) are also significantly higher in Wharton Sands, which backs up this idea of Wharton Sands' greater affluence.
  That feels like it's going to be important for a luxury hotel.
  Hmmm... but if I multiply these percentages by the total populations of the towns, then I can work out how many people fall into these wage brackets, and that's quite interesting:

Earnings (£)	Frogley	Wharton Sands	Frogley	Wharton Sands
	%	%	Number	Number
0-19999	28	24	26320	10080
20000-34999	34	27	31960	11340
35000-49999	29	30	27260	12600
50000+	9	19	8460	7980

  So there are actually more 'well-off' people in Frogley than in Wharton Sands. I hadn't expected that. But it's still true that for every 100 people in Wharton Sands or Frogley, more of them will be well-off in Wharton Sands than in Frogley. So Wharton Sands is still more affluent if you look at it in the right way. (*It's good to question data in this way — to see if your initial thoughts stand up to a bit of scrutiny.*)
- **Figure 3**: The main difference is that Frogley has a higher percentage of people working in manufacturing and construction, whereas Wharton Sands has a much higher percentage of people employed in services. Maybe construction companies could help build a hotel? And lots of people working in service industries might mean people with the right skills to work in a hotel would be available?
- **Figure 4**: Wharton Sands seems to have less crime. But Wharton Sands has about half the population of Frogley, so maybe I'd expect less crime there anyway — might need to think about this a bit.
  Okay... the figures for violent crime, vandalism and burglary in Wharton Sands are <u>much</u> less than half of those in Frogley, so I think there probably <u>is</u> less crime in Wharton Sands. This is probably important — violent crime especially could put customers off coming to an area to stay in a luxury hotel.
- **Figure 5**: Frogley has more local facilities, but not necessarily things that would attract tourists. Wharton Sands has a beach, though, which could attract people to the area. Maybe Wharton Sands' lack of local facilities could be good for Deluxatel? Deluxatel hotels have a swimming pool, gym and sauna, so perhaps people in Wharton Sands might be willing to pay to use them, even if they're not staying in the hotel? Might be worth thinking about.

- **Figure 6**: Both towns have a central train station, but Frogley looks more accessible by train from a long way off. Frogley also has good local bus services, so people from outside town could maybe get into town to use the hotel facilities if they wanted. Wharton Sands is less accessible by public transport, but road connections are good. Not sure what to make of this. Maybe Deluxatel guests might use cars more than public transport — maybe it doesn't really matter?
- **Figure 7**: In Frogley, people's priorities seem to be better leisure facilities, more places to eat, more visitors and more jobs. People in Wharton Sands would like a better range of shops, better leisure facilities and more places to eat. On the plus side, if the hotel's facilities *were* open to non-guests, it sounds like they might be popular in both towns. But people from Wharton Sands might be able to pay a bit more to use them perhaps?

Okay... I need to summarise my thoughts before I start writing my report. Deluxatel run luxury hotels, so I reckon their customers (who will be fairly well off) are more likely to want to stay in a town that's fairly affluent, safe, and attractive. So I'm going to go for the seaside town of Wharton Sands — this probably fits the bill better than Frogley. And I need to mention the possibilities for allowing the local population to use the hotel's facilities.

Investigation 2

This question's asking for some extra research about hotels. But before launching into that, I guess I should think first about what my key research areas might be. The question asks for the likely target market, so I reckon my first question should be:

Who do I want the hotel to appeal to?
I looked at some other hotels' websites and found they were mostly trying to attract these three main groups of customers:

- Business travellers
- Couples on romantic breaks
- Families

So I need to work out which of these groups is likely to be the most profitable market for Deluxatel. A bit more internet research on 'family holiday' websites shows that price is a high priority for families — maybe an average family might not be prepared to pay for a luxury hotel. Cost seems to be less of a priority for the other two groups (lots of other luxury hotels seemed to aim their marketing at these groups, anyway), so they're both possible target markets for Deluxatel.

I'm not sure how to choose between these two groups.
I think I really need some more information about Wharton Sands...

- If there are lots of big companies in the area then appealing to the business market might be sensible (lots of international business people might be coming to town).
- But if there are lots of tourist attractions, then aiming for the romantic market might be better.

Obviously, I can't go and visit the towns to check things out, so my options are:

- See if there are any clues in the information on page 140,
- Make it clear in my report that my conclusions are quite 'tentative' (i.e. say that I can't be 100% sure about them, and explain why).

The data on page 140 shows me that there's a beach, which might attract some romantic couples. Importantly, there are also lots of people working in the service industry. I wonder if they might be businesses that get a lot of business people visiting... this doesn't seem *un*likely — lots of businesses usually mean lots of business meetings, I reckon.

I noticed that other luxury hotels also often cater for business *conferences*. That sounds interesting — I reckon Deluxatel should bear this potential market in mind as well.

Right then... I think I'm going to assume there *will* be business visitors (but I'll make clear in my report that I need more information here really). That's good, because business trips and conferences happen all year round (whereas holidaymakers might be more of a summer thing).

Okay... I guess my next question should be:

What services or facilities appeal most to business travellers?
I reckon the best way to research this is to look at some other hotels that are trying to attract business travellers, and see what they offer. I looked at some more hotel websites... first off, my research shows that these are the things that business people would need in order to stay at the hotel or hold a conference there:

- Large meeting room(s), seating at least 50 people
- Internet access and computing facilities, e.g. projectors
- High quality catering for large groups of people
- Easy access (public transport in Wharton Sands doesn't seem very good, so I'll have to think about this — maybe some kind of taxi service from local towns would be useful?)

And then there are the other facilities that guests would expect or want. Most hotels set up for business travel offer:

- A gym, swimming pool and spa
- A bar
- Comfortable, attractive rooms
- Team-building activities

Actually... there seems to be a fair bit of overlap between what business travellers want and what couples on romantic breaks want — so maybe I don't have to choose between business travellers and romantics — maybe Deluxatel can appeal to both markets.

Next question... how can I decide which of these facilities are essential, or whether Deluxatel should just provide them all?
I asked a couple of people I know who travel on business, and they said that when planning a trip they look at the range and quality of facilities on offer, convenience of location, and cost.

So ideally, the hotel should be easy to get to and offer at least as many facilities as its competitors. Hmmm... competitors. That makes me think I should think about another question...

What will bring people to this hotel rather than any other?
The business people I talked to told me that business travellers often use the same hotel repeatedly — this is good, as long as Deluxatel can tempt customers away from the hotel where they usually stay in the first place. Deluxatel could offer better facilities or lower prices than their competitors. I can't really recommend what facilities they might go for without some more information about what other hotels in the area have to offer, but Deluxatel could use an introductory offer — maybe a special low price for the first few months.

Okay... I think I'm probably ready to write up this bit of the report.

Investigation 3

This question also calls for some extra research, but before I get too bogged down in detail I'll have a think about what the question is actually asking. I need to come up with a promotional campaign — so I guess I need to break that down into manageable chunks. I guess I need to think about:

- what the campaign is trying to achieve,
- who it's aimed at,
- the best way of persuading them that they really want to use this service.

I also need to know how much I can spend. And maybe I should also include something about working out how successful the campaign has been.

Campaign objectives —what the campaign is trying to achieve
Well, that's easy enough. I want to make people aware that Deluxatel are organising special events, and try to make the new service look as tempting as possible.

Target market — who the campaign is aimed at
I need to think about different age groups, geographical locations, how much disposable income people have and what kind of events might prove most popular. Hopefully this will help me work out how and where to promote the service.
A bit more research on other luxury hotel websites suggests that weddings, birthday parties and anniversaries are the most common events held somewhere like Deluxatel. Deluxatel will be offering a premium service, so it's going to be fairly pricey — maybe I should target people in the higher economic brackets. Older people are going to have more disposable income and be more likely to shell out on a big party than, say, teenagers, so I think I need to aim the campaign at them. The data provided shows that about 50% of people in Wharton Sands earn more than £35 000 and around 75% are aged over 20, so there should be plenty of people in the target market locally.
I can't find much online about what makes for a good location for this kind of service, but I asked a few of my friends who've been to weddings or birthday parties in hotels, and it seems like most people want to organise events locally — I guess it's more convenient for the guests. So I should make the campaign fairly local to avoid spending too much for no good reason. But there may be some cheap ways of promoting it more widely, so I'll have a think about those too.

Budget
This will have been worked out by Deluxatel. They're a fairly big company, so they must have a bit of money, but they might not be able to stretch to anything like a month-long advertising campaign on prime-time TV.

The message — what to say and how to say it
I guess this is the most important thing — working out what will appeal to my target audience. I also need to think about how to structure the promotion, and what's the best medium for presenting it.

I reckon this is where a bit of research might be useful. I had a look at how luxury hotels promote their 'party' service, and there are a few ways that stood out:

- Special offers, discounts, etc.
- Posting a link to the hotel website on other relevant websites.
- Producing mugs, chocolates or whatever with the company name and web address on. These are handed out to guests as they leave, as a memento of their party.
- I've heard/read similar adverts for this kind of thing on the radio or in the paper.

I've also remembered some cool promotional campaigns that I've heard about for other products — some of them generate loads of publicity without costing the company much. Maybe one of these could work for Deluxatel:

- Charging customers only what they (i.e. the customers) think something is worth.
- Auctioning off something online, so the lowest unique bid wins — might generate a bit of publicity.
- Loads of companies seem to have loyalty cards, or a membership club for existing customers, offering them discounts etc.
- Lots of companies sponsor an event or a sports team or something, and that helps to raise their profile.

Most of these could work, but I guess I need to decide on one or two that are likely to be most effective. Maybe talking to people in the target audience would help me work out what sort of campaign to go for. To do this properly I'd have to talk to people in Wharton Sands, which I can't do. So instead I talked to my parents, a few of my friends, plus I also found some 'random' people (there's a nice hotel not too far from here — so I went and talked to the hotel manager, plus he didn't mind me very politely asking a few of the guests a couple of questions) who I think would be in the target market. The main points that they agreed on were:

- They all found radio and TV adverts annoying.
- They dislike junk mail and spam (though some people have taken notice and bought things after getting a leaflet through the door).
- Saving money is a big priority, but so is quality.
- Most people thinking of organising a big event would look online (younger people more likely to do this than older people) or in the local paper (older people more likely to do this) for potential venues.

Assess the success of the campaign
This isn't really part of the campaign, so I'm not certain whether to include it. But it's pretty important for working out whether the campaign worked and whether it's worth repeating, so I guess I could mention it. I suppose it could involve asking people within the target audience whether they remember the promotion, whether they liked it and whether it influenced them to use the service. It could be quite easy — maybe just asking people who book an event at Deluxatel a few questions about why they chose Deluxatel and whether they were influenced by the campaign.

So I've got a structure and lots of ideas about a campaign. I reckon it's time to write the final report for this section.

Final report — Investigation 1

Deluxatel is a luxury hotel chain. Such a company should locate their new establishment in a town that is affluent and safe, with local attractions to bring people to the town. I will argue that Deluxatel should open their new hotel in Wharton Sands, since I believe that this town fulfils these criteria better than Frogley.

I have also tried here to assess the potential demand for the hotel's facilities from the local population.

What Kind of Town Best Suits a Luxury Hotel?

I believe that the most important factor in Deluxatel's decision is the town's ability to attract customers willing to pay luxury prices. The nature of the town is important here.

Town Character: Income

Wharton Sands seems to be slightly more affluent than Frogley, since there is a greater percentage of people in higher income brackets.

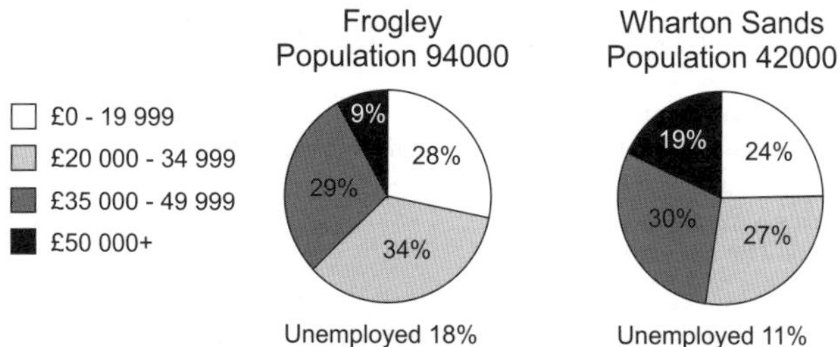

However, there are actually more people with high incomes in Frogley than in Wharton Sands. On balance I think that it is the percentage figure that is more important, because it is this that might create a general atmosphere of affluence in the town.

Also, Wharton Sands also has lower unemployment and higher average house prices. Again, I believe this means Wharton Sands will have a more affluent character overall than Frogley.

Town Character: Attractions

I think that Wharton Sands' beach is a very important factor for Deluxatel. I think this means that customers are more likely to be visiting and staying in Wharton Sands than in Frogley.

Town Character: Crime

Although Frogley is more than twice the size of Wharton Sands, crime figures (especially for more serious crimes, such as violent crimes, vehicle theft, and burglary) are generally *more* than double those in Frogley. This should be an important factor for Deluxatel.

Access to Town

Wharton Sands is not easily accessible by public transport. However, I think that many of Deluxatel's customers may be likely to arrive by car, and so the better road connections of Wharton Sands may be more relevant.

Potential Use of Hotel Facilities by Local Residents

The new Deluxatel hotel would incorporate a swimming pool, gym and sauna. Since Wharton Sands does not currently have a leisure centre, it could expect a lot of locals to use these facilities if they were open to non-guests.

Although 75% of people in Frogley would like better leisure

facilities, the high percentage of people with lower incomes may mean that many people will be unwilling to pay Deluxatel's prices.

Around 90% of people surveyed in Wharton Sands said that the town needs more places to eat. This, together with the fact that Wharton Sands has a greater percentage of high-earners, means that the hotel restaurant could prove popular. The swimming pool and other leisure facilities may prove popular for similar reasons.

Summary

Both towns have advantages and disadvantages, but on the basis of the available data I would recommend locating the hotel in Wharton Sands. I think a luxury hotel is probably better sited in a more affluent town with lower crime rates. I also think that Wharton Sands' beach is a key attraction that could potentially bring visitors to Wharton Sands.

Final report — Investigation 2

Finding the Best Target Market

In deciding what facilities and services would be most important in their new hotel, the key decision that Deluxatel face is deciding which market they should cater for. There are three main groups that use hotels:

- business travellers,
- couples on romantic breaks
- families

However, families are often quite concerned about their budget, and are therefore less likely to be prepared to pay to stay in a luxury hotel.

The business market has several advantages over the romance market:

- Conferences happen throughout the year, so this could be a constant source of business, whereas holidaymakers are more likely to visit in the summer
- Business conferences will mean large numbers of people wanting to stay in the hotel
- Repeat custom is likely

I would therefore recommend that Deluxatel Wharton Sands focuses on appealing to business travellers, as long as:

- there is sufficient demand in the Wharton Sands area for luxury business accommodation, <u>or</u>
- it seems likely that there would be demand for a conference venue in the area

This would require further local research to be sure.

However, if the hotel can also cater for couples on romantic breaks, then this would provide a good second source of income. I think a good quality business hotel could also be attractive for a romantic couple, since many of the facilities required are identical, as I shall explain below.

What Services and Facilities to Offer?

The facilities and services that appeal to business travellers and conference organisers can be divided into necessary requirements and desired extras (see table).

Necessary requirements	Desired extras
• Large meeting room(s) for 50+ people • Computing facilities, e.g. projectors • Internet access • High quality catering for large groups • Easy access	• Gym, swimming pool and spa • Bar • Comfortable, attractive rooms • Team-building activities

Apart from team-building activities, all of the 'desired extras' are usually offered by hotels catering for romantic breaks, suggesting that the hotel could easily cater to both markets. The additional services/facilities generally offered by hotels aimed at the "romance market" are:

- Unique rooms (i.e. quirky or individual)
- 'Englishness' — open fires, cream teas etc.
- Activities such as guided nature walks, punting and wine tasting

All of these could be offered without putting off business travellers. I would therefore recommend that Deluxatel Wharton Sands offers the following facilities and services:

- At least one large (50+ seats) meeting room with up-to-date computing facilities
- A separate bar and restaurant
- A very good chef and catering team
- Free wireless internet in all rooms
- A swimming pool and gym
- A spa with hot tubs, saunas, steam rooms etc.
- Free pick-ups and drop-offs at local stations/airports etc., given the relatively poor public transport in Wharton Sands
- Plentiful parking
- A variety of activities, e.g. punting, assault courses, golf, clay pigeon shooting, guided walks etc., and open space where other activities could be organised
- All rooms/suites individually designed and decorated
- Traditional feel, e.g. open fires, afternoon tea available etc.

To Ensure Regular Repeat Custom

Given the importance of repeat custom, I would recommend that Deluxatel set up a system to keep in touch with guests after their stay, e.g. by sending emails advising them of special offers, sending brochures to businesses etc.

To Ensure People Try the New Deluxatel Hotel

The remaining challenge is to ensure that people choose Deluxatel Wharton Sands over competitors in the area.

A good strategy would be to offer a service or facility that no other hotel in the area offers — a USP (unique selling point).
Further competitor research would be required in order to work out what this service or facility might be.

Deluxatel could also use an introductory offer to try and tempt customers to use Deluxatel instead of their usual hotel, in the hope that they will prefer Deluxatel for their future visits. This offer could be, for example, cut price rooms, extra activities included at no extra cost, or a block booking discount (e.g. three nights for the price of two).

Summary

These recommendations should ensure that Deluxatel appeals to a range of potential customers, is able to attract business initially and is likely to attract repeat custom.

Final report — Investigation 3

Deluxatel is an established company, so the main objective of a promotional campaign is to inform the target market of the new service offered by Deluxatel, rather than inform people of the Deluxatel brand more generally.

Finding a Suitable Target Market

The first step is to work out exactly who the service is most likely to appeal to, since this group will form the target market. Most hotels that offer a 'party service' seem to cater for weddings, birthday parties and anniversaries. Some informal research suggests that people are more likely to want to hold their party somewhere near where they live (although some will come from further afield).

I would therefore suggest that the Deluxatel promotional campaign should be focused on the Wharton Sands region, but that a larger-scale campaign may also be worthwhile, provided it can be achieved relatively inexpensively.

Because of the nature and cost of the service, the campaign should be aimed primarily at people aged 30+ with a relatively high income. Wharton Sands has a large number of people who fulfil these criteria.

Choosing a Promotional Campaign

There are various possible approaches Deluxatel could use to publicise their party service. For example, they could advertise in local newspapers, on the Internet or on local radio. I carried out a survey to find peoples' responses to various advertising media. My results are illustrated by the graph below.

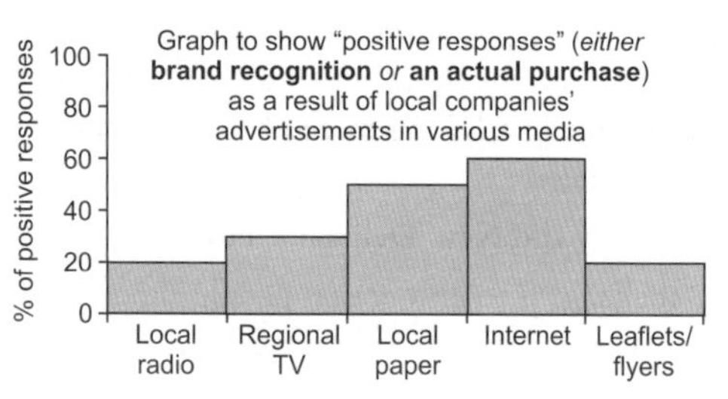

My findings were that:

- No one likes junk mail or spam. However, some people did admit that they had bought insurance after receiving information through the post that they had not asked for.
- TV and radio adverts are generally annoying. However, most people did recognise the names of companies who advertise on the radio, while companies that didn't advertise on the radio seemed to be less well known.
- Older people generally looked first in local newspapers and local telephone directories when trying to find a local service. Younger people generally looked on the Internet first.
- The cost of the service is important, but only if quality is not affected. No one would want to save a small amount of money on a party if that would make it a less special occasion.

I would therefore recommend that Deluxatel places adverts in the local newspaper, and on relevant websites (e.g. popular search engines, plus websites offering wedding goods or birthday cards). Presumably, the Deluxatel chain also have their own website, which should carry an advertisement for the new service.

I would also recommend a special introductory offer. This could be, for example, an offer where the first ten people to book an event get the event half price, or perhaps free accommodation in the hotel for a certain number of people on the night of the event.

Alternatively, Deluxatel could organise a competition where the prize is a free party at the new hotel. The local newspaper could be invited to attend as well to photograph and write about the lucky winner, and ensure some good publicity for the hotel.

Repeat Business and Good "Word of Mouth"

All of the above measures are intended to attract new customers. Deluxatel will also need to do whatever they can to ensure that people who have used its party service want to use it again for other special occasions. I would recommend handing out free mementos of the event (e.g. chocolates and photo albums), which may seem a 'nice touch' and make customers recommend the service to their friends and family. I would also recommend handing out small gifts such as key rings, mugs and pens with the hotel name and website on to other guests in order to encourage other people to use the service.

Emails or brochures could also be sent to former customers (unless they opt not to receive them) in order to collect feedback about what could be improved about the Deluxatel party service.

Assessing the Promotional Campaign

Deluxatel will want to be able to assess how effective these promotional methods are. I would therefore also recommend that Deluxatel ask customers to fill in a questionnaire when they book their event, to find out how they found out about the service, and whether the promotional campaign influenced them.

This would be relatively cheap, and could provide useful information about whether it would be worth repeating features of this campaign in the future.

Summary

In summary, I believe that Deluxatel should aim their promotional campaign primarily at the local/regional market, by advertising in local papers and online. Running a competition or offering a discount would raise the profile of the service. This should then be followed up by a survey in order to assess how successful the campaign had been, and how the service could be improved.

Details from Mark Scheme for Investigation 1

You should:

- **recall, select and communicate your knowledge and understanding of marketing concepts, issues and terminology in the context of the investigation.**
- **apply your knowledge and understanding of concepts, issues and terminology in planning and carrying out the task in the context of the investigation.**
- **analyse and evaluate evidence, making detailed and evidence-based judgements**
- **present appropriate conclusions in the context of the investigation**

Details from Mark Scheme for Investigations 2 and 3

You should:

- **recall, select and communicate your knowledge and understanding of marketing concepts, issues and terminology in the context of the investigation.**
- **consistently apply your knowledge and understanding of concepts, issues and terminology in planning and carrying out the task in the context of the investigation.**
- **analyse and evaluate evidence, making detailed and evidence-based judgements in the context of the investigation**
- **make recommendations and conclusions that arise logically from a critical analysis of the gathered evidence**
- **present appropriate conclusions in the context of the investigation**
- **express yourself clearly**

Index

Index

Index